Michael C. Thomsett

Style Guide for Business Writing

Michael C. Thomsett

Style Guide for Business Writing

Second Edition

ISBN 978-1-5474-1618-9
e-ISBN (PDF) 978-1-5474-0021-8
e-ISBN (EPUB) 978-1-5474-0023-2

Library of Congress Cataloging-in-Publication Data
A CIP catalog record for this book has been applied for at the Library of Congress.

Bibliographic information published by the Deutsche Nationalbibliothek
The Deutsche Nationalbibliothek lists this publication in the Deutsche Nationalbibliografie; detailed bibliographic data are available on the Internet at http://dnb.dnb.de.

Published by Walter de Gruyter Inc., Boston/Berlin
Cover image: ExperienceInteriors / E+ / getty images
Printing and binding: CPI book GmbH, Leck
♾ Printed on acid-free paper
Printed in Germany

www.degruyter.com

Acknowledgments

A project of this scope cannot possibly be compiled in isolation. The language is rich and varied, not to mention complex. I appreciate the lifelong efforts of so many people to ensure that my grammar and style were always "proper." My late mother's reminders were relentless, even to the point of indiscretion, as no one enjoys being corrected in front of others. She liked to chide me by asking, "Don't you know the Queen's English?"—to which I once replied, "Is she?"

This response, described by my mother as "cheeky," further reveals the complexity of the language. Her question takes on entirely different meaning by mentally shifting the apostrophe by only one letter—Queen's versus Queens'.

In school, many teachers tried to further describe and explain grammar, punctuation, and more. I am grateful to all of them as well, most notably to Daniel Caldwell, English and Drama teacher at Tamalpais High School in Mill Valley, California, who taught me so much about language and writing, and equally important, about self-confidence.

Finally, I applaud the energy and effort put forth by the editorial team at De Gruyter, Jeffrey Pepper, Jaya Dalal and Mary Sudul, whose eye for detail and precision transformed my manuscript into a finished, updated, and exact description of the many aspects involved in the idea of *style* when writing, whether a book, article, report, or e-mail.

Michael C. Thomsett
February, 2018

DOI 10.1515/9781547400218-201

Contents

Introduction

This book is designed for business managers, employees, editors, authors, and reporters. The art of self-expression is challenging and, as schools have emphasized this less and less, the need for guidance is more critical than ever.

Modern language changes continually. Here are some examples of how the complexities of language change over time. The distinction between singular and plural forms of words is not absolute—common usage ultimately defines the proper form. For example, the word "data" is a plural word (the singular form is "datum"). However, "data" is used broadly as both singular and plural, and "datum" has become archaic. As a result, usage has redefined the word away from strict application. The same is true for the word "media" (the plural of "medium"). Common usage allows "media" to be used as both singular and plural. The word "whom" is used less and less, and "who" has become both subjective and objective. Many writers at every level can tend to use words that are not truly words (such as "irregardless"), resort to cliché expressions rather than effective communication, and switch voice between first, second, and third person. Everyone develops writing habits that take away from effective communication, and no one standard can solve all of those problems.

The purpose of this book is to offer some basic standards for not just the essentials of punctuation, grammar, and style, but also for how more advanced expressions can be made uniformly more effective. This ideal (effectiveness rather than absolute conformity to original rules) applies in every form of writing. For example, in describing a statistical report, great care ensures that statistical inference is supported by the facts and not just assumed to be applicable. Even worse than lack of proper inference is inference in error. Many of the errors that occur in writing—including statistical narratives and financial reports—can lead to the wrong conclusion. For example, a budget variance report may blame overruns on lack on control when, in fact, they were caused by the addition of unanticipated new product lines during the year. In this case, the inference was in error, so that the narrative is misleading.

The importance of clear and precise writing makes a difference in how a communication is received. Documentation supporting conclusions is of critical importance in proposals, reports, and articles of every kind; so developing and applying basic skills is at the beginning of the process of becoming effective. For the experienced business writer, revisiting the basics ensures that gradually deteriorating habits are kept in check and prevented from negatively impacting communication style and accuracy.

DOI 10.1515/9781547400218-203

The book is arranged alphabetically by major topic and appropriate cross reference is provided at the conclusion of each entry. The index provides an additional cross reference to quickly and easily find the section needed. The goal of each entry is to address the very basic elements of expression known as *style* and to provide a series of "rules" for how particular ideas should be communicated. For example, when communicating a date, what at first would seem a basic and simple task involves many variables and a need for agreement about consistency and usage—there are many varieties of expression for the year, month and year combined, day, approximate date, and season.

With that in mind, this style guide is intended as a reference that may be of value in many different situations. Over time, the "rules" change. For example, guidelines for email and online messages did not even exist a few decades ago. In the future, new modes of communication are likely to present similar challenges. As language grows and expands, the perpetual challenge is both exciting and demanding. This style guide—aimed at business communication specifically—is a worthwhile starting point in mastering the art of self-expression.

A

A or an

As a general rule, use “A” when the following word starts with a consonant, and “an” when it starts with a vowel.

Examples:

A man
A woman
A bus
An elephant
An octopus

There are exceptions. Some consonants have a vowel sound and are preceded by ‘an’:

Examples:

An hour
An honor
An herb
An MBA

Some vowel-starting words have a “y” or “w’ sound and are preceded by ‘a’:

A Utopian ideal
A one-time event

In summary, it is the *sound* of the word following the article that determines which to use, rather than the actual letter.

Abbreviation

An abbreviation is a form of shorthand, enabling readers to understand the meaning of a word or phrase without needing to see it written out in full. Abbreviations may take the form of letters to represent a longer organization or agency name (see also Acronym) or a few letters used to represent a longer word. Use consistent and universally accepted forms of abbreviations for common words.

DOI 10.1515/9781547400218-001

1. Know when to use abbreviations.

In most formal business writing, do not abbreviate mathematical symbols, numbers, days of the week, or months when used in sentences. However, these may be abbreviated in technical writing, financial reports, and graphic presentations.

Incorrect:

The deadline is the 3rd Wed. in Oct.

Correct:

The deadline is the third Wednesday in October.

Informal writing, including brief memos and notes, may include abbreviations of many terms, with few rules except one: The meaning should always be clear.

Unacceptable due to lack of clarity:

D.L.3rd W/10

Acceptable in informal writing:

The deadline is the 3rd Wed. in Oct.

Abbreviations for units of measure should never be used unless combined with a numeric value, and never if the number is spelled out.

Incorrect:

The current budget covers a three mo. period.
A budget is broken down by mo. and yr.
The $ amount of the budget has been approved.
How many in. long is your desk?

Correct:

The current budget covers a three month period.
A budget is broken down by month and year.
Our $6,000 expense budget has been approved.
There is room for a 60-inch desk.

2. Know when to use periods with abbreviations.

When abbreviating the names of organizations or agencies, do not use periods.

Incorrect:

I.R.S.
A.B.C.
A.M.A.
M.M.M.
N.Y.C.
T.S.E.

Correct:

IRS
ABC
AMA
MMM
NYC
TSE

In technical writing, omit periods after most abbreviations of units of measurement, except *no.* and *in.* (because they have entirely different meanings as short words).

Incorrect:	*Correct*:
in [inch or inches]	in.
no [number]	no.
lb. [pound]	lb
ft. [foot or feet]	ft
yd. [yard or yards]	yd
doz. [dozen]	doz

Abbreviations of phrases usually include a period after each letter.

Incorrect:

am. or am
pm.
eg. or eg

Correct:

a.m.
p.m.
e.g.

Abbreviations of single words include one period only. Do not use two periods when an abbreviation comes at the end of a sentence.

Incorrect:

I work as a receptionist for SampleCo, Inc..

Correct:

I work as a receptionist for Sample Company, Inc.

3. **Use the same abbreviation for singular and plural units of measurement.**

When abbreviating a unit of measurement, use the same abbreviation for singular and plural.

1 cm
1 ft
1 gal
1 yd
3 cm
6 ft
9 gal
4 yd

4. **For other plural abbreviations, add the letter** s **and place the period at the end.**

Singular	*Plural*
mgr.	mgrs.
dept.	depts.
acct.	accts.

5. **Spell out unfamiliar abbreviations the first time you use them.**

When using an abbreviation not readily identified by your reader, clarify by using the full term at the first usage only. Use parentheses around the full wording.

Example:

From now on, the BRC (budget review committee) will meet every other Wednesday. Members of the BRC should notify their supervisors of this commitment at least one day prior to scheduled BRC meeting dates.

Some abbreviated names that contain more than one word can be expressed by using capital letters in place of periods.

Acceptable formats:

RevCom
Revcom.

Such alternative usage is normal within an organization, where such abbreviations become commonly recognized. When communicating to the outside, spelling out the name of an internal group is a preferable practice. Some organizations will name their products or their company using internal caps. If so, the wishes of the organization should be followed unless there is inconsistency in their own usage.

Example:

The Budget Review Committee of Greatco, Inc., meets every other Wednesday. The committee is responsible for ensuring that new policies and procedures meet management's objectives.

6. Abbreviate titles only when they precede a name.

Titles should be abbreviated only when they precede an individual's name.

Incorrect:

Our technical division is headed by a Dr.
The speaker at today's luncheon is a prof. from the university.

Correct:

Dr. Adams is vice president of our technical division.
Prof. Johnson will speak at noon today.

Most abbreviations are not to be used as the first word in a sentence. Titles are an exception; when titles are not spelled out in common usage, such as *Mr.* and *Ms.*, they can be used to start a sentence.

Incorrect:

Dept. supervisors will meet this morning.
Mister Hansen reports to Ms. Green.

Correct:

Department supervisors will meet this morning.
Ms. Green is vice president of the finance division.

7. Observe punctuation rules.

When abbreviating a word before a comma or semicolon, precede the punctuation mark with a period.

Incorrect:

At GreatCo, Inc, employees receive good benefits.
He was hired by GreatCo, Inc; it was the job he had long been waiting for.

Correct:

At GreatCo, Inc., employees receive good benefits.
He was hired by GreatCo, Inc.; it was the job he had long been waiting for.

An interrogatory sentence ending with an abbreviation should include a period followed by the question mark.

Incorrect:

Is this GreatCo, Inc?

Correct:

Is this GreatCo, Inc.?

Abridgement

A condensed, summarized, or reduction of a work is called an *abridgement*. This may be of a book, article, manual, or other source. The style goal in abridging a work is to retain its core message and character while providing a brief overview.

The abridged version will represent the opinion of the individual performing the work, and the purpose should be to represent the larger version fairly and accurately. This practice is of value in a business setting, notably for textbooks, technical manuals, and books or articles based on theories of interest to the business audience. Those unable or unwilling to read a full version may gain from the abridged summary, assuming it truly represents the original in every respect.

Abstracts

An *abstract* is a summary of a work, normally appearing at the beginning of a journal article or in a book review, for example. Its purpose is to explain what the reader may expect to find in reading the entire piece.

Example, abstract of a published paper:

This paper examines the risk tendencies among IT personnel to discover whether vulnerabilities unique to this area of operations can be addressed in a unique manner. Observations have included a tendency to apply exceptions to accepted risk-preventive practices based on an assumption of exceptional risk awareness. This appears from several studies to increase in severity as actual risk levels rise. We base our research on several recent studies as well as on interviews conducted in three organizations over a six-month period.

Example, abstract of a book:

The *Motivated Manager* studies several management styles and contrasts them to one another. Among conclusions drawn and documented are (a) a direct correlation between self-motivation and an ability to motivate others; (b) relationships between inspirational leadership and employee responsiveness; and (c) popularity as a test of respon-

> siveness and motivation. The book contains 14 chapters and is well-documented. It includes interviews with 30 managers and 63 employees, with conclusions based on common themes observed among those interviewed. The primary value in the book is its strong guidelines for development of successful management skills and the ability of managers to motivate others.

The abstract should define the scope and benefits of the work, but be as brief as possible. Style should be narrowly focused on the purpose, benefit, and quality of the larger work.

Accessibility

The concept of *accessibility* refers to the design of devices or services for disabled persons. The purpose is to facilitate both direct access (without assistance) and indirect access (via assistive technology). Business writers requiring accessibility due to special needs (for example, hearing or vision impairment) may face special challenges in acquiring devices or services. The accessibility standard most often is applied to employees and students, for example. A consulting business writer might be assumed to not need the same level of assistance. As a consequence, accessibility for many business writers presents special and often difficult adjustments, both for the writer and for the organization.

Accessibility is related to *universal design*, creation of devices or services aimed for the widest range of utility and situations. Universal design aids access for everyone, whether disabled or not.

Assistive technology is used to create accessibility, and includes the use of devices for learning or task completion that would not be possible otherwise. Examples for the disabled include screen readers or listening devices. *Adaptive* technology is modification to existing devices to enable a disabled person to participate in activities. Examples include remote control and specialized adjustment to word processing programs.

These accessibility technologies may be applied in cases of communication, hearing, visual, and mobility disabilities; and further to assist those with physical, mental, or learning disabilities. Web-based accessibility was initiated as party of the World Wide Web Consortium and identified as the Web Accessibility Initiative (WAI), intended to ensure web accessibility to everyone, including the disabled. The Web Content Accessibility Guidelines (WCAG) 2.0 are the standard for accessibility. Four principles within WCAG 2.0 are that technology and information should be (1) perceivable, (2) operable, (3) understandable, and (4) robust.

Acknowledgments

Some forms of business writing include *acknowledgments* for help received from others. This is appropriate in books, articles, and journal papers, but not normally seen in internal reports.

The typical acknowledgment is written in the first person. However, avoid passive voice when writing acknowledgments.

Examples, passive voice acknowledgments:

I would like to express my thanks to ...

I want to also thank my mentor and friend ...

Examples, active voice acknowledgments:

My thanks to ...

Many thanks to my mentor and friend ...

An acknowledgment should be reserved for those who actually assisted in preparation, research, or editing of the work. Some acknowledgments also include past acquaintances, family members or teachers—these are less relevant to the current project, but are also appropriate for inclusion if the influence was directly associated with the work.

Acronyms

Acronyms are abbreviated names of longer multiword organizations or technologies. They are usually formed by taking the first letter from each word of a multiword combination in such a way that the abbreviation can be pronounced as a word.

1. Follow the rules of capitalization.

The letters of an acronym are usually capitalized when the first letters of the corresponding words are capitalized when spelled out. But some acronyms that describe technologies eventually come into such common use that they are lowercased.

Examples:

NASDAQ (National Association of Securities Dealers Automated Quotations)

SPEND (System Plan Expenditure Numerical Database)

radar (*ra*dio *d*etecting *a*nd *r*anging)

Some acronyms are constructed from syllables rather than from the letters of corresponding words or from a combination of syllables and letters.

Examples:

BUZOFF (Business Office Functions)

AUTOCAP (Automatic Consumer Action Program)

Some acronyms are capitalized even though their corresponding words are not, and some commonly used acronyms are never capitalized. The rule to follow is that of convention; common usage dictates proper form, even though the result is inconsistent. Consult a dictionary for specific acronyms.

Examples:

CAD (computer-aided design)

cal (computer-aided learning)

2. Introduce unfamiliar acronyms to your reader.

When using an acronym in text for the first time, spell it out in full for the reader's benefit.

Examples:

We intend to incorporate the System Tabulation and Evaluation Accounting Ledger (STEAL) as our primary financial control mechanism.

In order to introduce a new acronym, the full name can be spelled out, followed by the acronym, the first time it is used. The acronym can be placed within text, in quotation marks, or in parentheses.

Examples:

Our project leader is a member of the Professional Association of Consulting Engineers, also known as PACE.

The system is called the Automatic Tabulating, Listing, and Sorting System, or "ATLAS."

Complaints should be directed to the Business Efficiency and Expediting Function (BEEF) office.

Active and passive voice

Use of the active voice is preferable in most writing because it instantly identifies the action with the person who is performing that action. It creates strong, lively writing. In comparison, a passive voice form may be less clear because it does not identify the doer of the action until much later in the sentence, and it sometimes avoids identifying the doer at all. Nevertheless, passive voice is sometimes useful to create variety within a paragraph, when you deliberately want to draw attention to the action rather than to who did it, or for emphasis.

1. Learn the differences between active and passive.

The following examples demonstrate the differences in clarity between active and passive voice.

Active voice:

My department prepared the report.
I recommend that we perform a study.
The division earned a profit last year.
I will start working on that task next week.

Passive voice:

The report was prepared by my department.
The report was prepared.
It is my recommendation that a study be performed.
A profit was earned last year by the division.
Next week is when I will start working on that task.

2. Be aware of your writing habits and traps.

Be aware of writing habits to avoid the trap of using passive voice when active voice is a more effective way of expressing yourself. Remember these rules of thumb:

- Avoid beginning sentences with the object rather than with the subject, or actor. “My department” is the actor that prepared “the report,” the object. Place the actor before the verb and the object after the verb.
- Avoid indirect nouns, often represented at the beginning of a sentence with the words "it is." Your writing will vastly improve by simply avoiding this phrase (see also *False subjects*). You may use indirect pronouns (*I*, *we*, or *me*, for example) in business writing and avoid the awkward sentence structure common to excessive passive voice sentences. In a document of any kind, decide on the use of I, you, and so on and stick with it, “you” being more friendly than the use of the word “one” which should be avoided. People are less likely to buy a book if the word “one” is used in this manner. The use of “you” eliminates the problem and is well liked by readers. “I” gets authors into binds sometimes. First person is rarely appropriate in business writing other than e-mail.
- Edit your writing by replacing passive voice sentences with the active voice. This change will clarify your statements by eliminating unnecessary and awkward construction.

3. Use passive voice when called for.

Passive voice is preferred in three instances:

1. When you do not know the identity of the subject.

   Examples:

   The report was not prepared because essential information was not provided in time.

   Our company picnic was delayed because of unexpected changes in the weather.

2. When you want to place greater emphasis on the receiver than on the subject. By arranging sentences according to active or passive voice, you determine where to place emphasis.

   Examples:

   Complete documentation of procedures is required by our internal auditing department.

   Deborah was hired by a major law firm.

3. To affect a better transition between thoughts.

   Passive voice:

   The upcoming management seminar was planned to include a forum for discussion of unnecessary committees in business. A panel presentation for that purpose is scheduled.

   Without expressing the first sentence in the passive voice, the transition would not have been as smooth.

   Active voice:

   Managers can discuss excessive use of committees in the forum of the upcoming management seminar. A panel presentation for that purpose is scheduled.

4. Change verbs to eliminate passive voice.

Replacing one verb with another or eliminating entire phrases can clarify your writing while removing both passive voice and unclear expression of ideas.

Before editing:

Accounting processes may be thought of as a means for achieving balance control.

After editing:

Accounting processes achieve balance control.

Adnouns

When an adjective is used as a noun in a sentence, it is termed an *adnoun*. This is common in English usage, notably in business writing. However, excessive use of adnouns may cross into the realm of cliché and should be used with caution.

Examples:

Tax cuts for the rich. (Adnoun "rich" is a reference to rich people.)

The passive will not be promoted. (Adnoun "passive" refers to passive employees.)

Afterword

Any concluding section of an article, paper or book is a form of *afterword* (not to be confused with "afterward" or "afterwards"). It is intended to summarize, wrap up, and conclude what the primary work presented. In some cases, a topical publication may be appended with an afterword if the original conditions evolved beyond the body of the work.

An afterword may be written with several names, including epilogue (or epilog), postscript, or conclusion. It is usually written by the author of the larger work, but may also be penned by someone else—this is seen in cases when the original author is deceased and a new edition of a book or reprint of an original article is published. The afterword in this instance may be a commentary on the continued applicability of arguments presented in the original document.

Agreement

Agreement, a rule of English grammar, states that singular subject nouns are to be accompanied by singular verbs and plural subject nouns must be accompanied by plural verbs.

1. **Connect singular subject nouns to singular verbs and plural subject nouns to plural verbs.**
   Singular subject nouns are always connected to verbs that are also singular.
   Examples:
   The office is located downtown.
   The manager arrives today.

Plural subject nouns are always connected to verbs that are also plural.

Examples:

The buildings are located downtown.
The managers arrive today.

Avoid the mistake of having the verb agree with its complement, not its subject.

Correct:

The topic of concern to managers was expenditures during the last quarter.

In this example, the subject *(topic)* and the verb *(was)* are in agreement. The verb should not agree with the complement *(expenditures)*.

Incorrect:

The topic of concern to managers were expenditures during the last quarter.

2. Connect compound subject nouns to compound verbs.

When a sentence contains more than one subject, the verb should be plural as well.

Incorrect:

Supervisor and employee is required to follow this rule.

Correct:

Supervisor and employee are required to follow this rule.

Subject nouns connected by joiners, as in the examples above, are usually accompanied by plural verbs. There is an exception: when the two subjects are in fact a single noun (as in a company name) or when a single entity is made up of many parts.

Examples:

Smith and Jones is our accounting firm.
Our best friend and worst enemy is the vocal customer.
Baker and Brown is responsible for its image.

Certain modifiers demand plural nouns. These include the words *both, few, several,* and *many.*

Examples:

Few employees are working overtime.
Many suppliers were planning price increases.

Some modifiers can confuse the selection of singular or plural verbs. The subject, however, dictates agreement.

Examples:

All of the work is complete.

All of the employees are in the office.

In the first example, *work* is a singular subject, so the verb, *is*, is singular as well. In the second example, *employees* is a plural subject, so the verb, *are*, is plural as well. The same rules apply to modifiers such as *any, more, most, none,* and *some.*

3. Use singular or plural verbs for collective nouns based on context.

Some nouns identify groups of individuals but are treated as singular subjects, such as *committee, group, public, government,* and *audience.* The verb used with these subjects depends on the context:

a. **A singular verb is used when the subject refers to the group singularly.**

Example:

The committee is meeting in room 305.

b. **A plural verb is substituted when reference is clearly to the individual members of the group.**

Example:

The committee are working through their agenda.

c. **Subjects representing measurement or value are expressed in singular form when presented as one unit.**

Examples:

Four thousand dollars is too high a variance.

Three months is enough time to complete a report.

d. **Special treatment is allowed in conventional use for certain words.** These include data and number. Data is a plural word whose singular form, datum, is rarely used. Using data exclusively has become common use and practice. In fact, readers of books and reports tend to reject the use of "data" as a plural ("the data are conclusive," for example). It is distracting and in spite of the proper usage, the language is evolving and "data" is transforming into a singular reference. Common usage (data as both singular and plural) replaces strictly correct usage. The same applies to media as singular and plural with rare use of "medium" as the singular form.

Correct:

The data [plural] are compiled and available.

The media [plural] are reporting on this matter.

Incorrect but in common usage:

The data [plural subject] is [singular verb] in my office.

The media [plural subject] is [singular verb] reporting on this matter.

The word *number* may be used in either singular or plural form, depending on the intent of the writer. Generally, if *number* is preceded by *the*, it is singular, and if preceded by *a*, it is plural.

Examples:

The number of employees [singular] is growing.

A number of employees [plural] are attending.

e. **Words ending in ics are singular if referring to a science or body of information and plural if referring to action or a quality.**

Examples:

Economics [singular] is the study of money.

The market tactics [plural] depend on the market environment.

4. **Avoid awkward phrases.**

When subjects are connected with phrases such as *together with, as well as,* and *in addition to,* the subjects are treated as singular and should be coupled with singular verbs. This construction is often awkward and should be avoided in the interest of clarity of expression.

Examples:

Top management, together with each department, wants to work to improve profitability.

The western division, as well as the central division, has effectively controlled costs.

Proper procedure, in addition to controls, ensures lower budget variances.

Use of the phrase *one of those who* requires a plural verb. However, this is an awkward form of expression and should be replaced with a clearer, more concise alternative.

Examples:

I am one of those who believe [plural] managers should become involved only if a problem emerges.

I believe managers should become involved only if a problem emerges. [clearer alternative]

Some qualifying words require singular verbs when they are used in front of plural subjects. For example, *part, portion, series,* and *type*. Avoid using these phrases to eliminate awkward sentences.

Correct but awkward:

Part of the activities in our department is [singular] the control of costs and expenses.

Clearer:

Control of costs and expenses is one of the activities in our department.

5. **Do not be confused when a phrase intervenes between subject and verb.**

When a phrase with a plural noun is inserted between a singular subject and the verb, the verb is singular.

Example:

A marketing plan [singular], including advertising budget or promotional efforts [plural], has [singular] been our most profitable way of moving products to market.

6. **Use "they" or "their" as a singular reference is some cases.**

The word "they" is a plural; however, there are instances in which agreement can be suspended.

Examples:

Remind the new employee that they must attend orientation.

An employee is expected to respond to their supervisor.

Who prepared their evaluation in a timely manner?

Although these mixed agreements have become normal, they can also be avoided with a revision to the form of a statement.

Examples:

Remind new employees that they must attend orientation.

Employees are expected to respond to their supervisors.

Who prepared evaluations in a timely manner?

Alphabetizing

Two primary methods for alphabetizing may be used: letter-by-letter and word-by-word. Use either one but only one—that is, make a decision and apply it consistently to avoid problems of inconsistency in a filing system or index.

Under the letter-by-letter method, strict alphabetizing is applied regardless of where word breaks occur and regardless of spaces, commas, or periods. In the word-by-word method, a break occurs at the end of each word in a title or multiword name. Each unique word is completed before proceeding to the next. Word-by-word is the more commonly used method.

Letter-by-Letter Method	*Word-by-Word Method*
Mace, Barbara	Mace, Barbara
Mane, J.	Man, M.J.
Manis, R.	Man, Steven
Man, M.J.	Mane, J.
Man, Steven	Manis, R.

1. **Arrange names of people by last, first, and middle.**

   a. **For proper names of individuals, alphabetize in the order of last name, first name, and middle initial.**

   Arrange all identical last names, followed by alphabetized first names, and third by middle initial.

   Examples:

   Adams, Andrew A.
   Adams, Andrew B.
   Adams, Betty R.
   Adams, Charles L.
   Adams, Charles M.

   b. **Initials precede full names.**

   Examples:

   Adams, A.
   Adams, Andrew

   Names beginning with **Mc** and **Mac** should be filed in strictly alphabetical order, regardless of capitalization or spacing within the name.

   Examples:

   Mabley
   Mackinley

MacTavish
Mason
McDonald

c. **Prefixes should be treated as part of the name, regardless of capitalization or spacing.**

Examples:

de la Guardia
Des Norte
van der Hope
von Schmidt

d. **Alphabetize *St.* as though spelled out *Saint.***

e. **File by name even when professional designations are included.** Use designations only as a last default for filing otherwise identical names.

Name	*File as:*
Dr. Hal Adams	Adams, Hal, Dr.

f. **Alphabetize abbreviated names as though spelled out in full.**

Name	*File as:*
Jones, Wm.	Jones, William
Smith, Chas.	Smith, Charles
Thomas, Bill	Thomas, William

g. **File nicknames in strict alphabetical order when the individual is known by that name. Cross-reference to legal names when known.**

Name	*File as:*
Big Willy	Big Willy
	Jones, William, *see* Big Willy
Illinois A	lIllinois Al
	Jones, Al, *see* Illinois Al

2. **Name locations by unique name rather than designation.**

a. **Alphabetize place names by the unique name, not by the type of place.** However, when the full name is the name of a city, file by the first word.

Name	*File as:*
Lake Tahoe [lake]	Tahoe, Lake
Lake Tahoe [city]	Lake Tahoe
Mount Adams [mountain]	Adams, Mount
Mount Adams [city]	Mount Adams

b. **File non-English article names (*de, el, la,* etc.) by article, as part of the full name.**

Name	*File as:*
El Dorado	El Dorado
Los Angele	sLos Angeles

3. **Name organizations by first name, but exclude articles (the, a, an).**
   a. **File organization names by the first word of the organization's name.**

Name	*File as:*
Union Carbide	Union Carbide
Standard Oil	Standard Oil
The Smith Co.	Smith Co.

b. **When the organization name is also a personal name, follow rule *a*.** Cross-reference the individual name.

Name	*File as:*
William Jones Corp.	William Jones Corp. Jones, William, Corp., *see* William Jones Corp.

c. **Treat corporate names according to rules 3*a* and 3*b*, even when titles are used as part of the name.**

Name	*File under:*
Sly Guy Pizza	S
Captain Bob Parker	C
Miss Fashion	M
Happy Time	H

d. **Disregard articles, conjunctions, prepositions, and punctuation in organizational names unless they are integral parts of the name.**

Name	*File under:*
The Anderson Co.	A
In the Know, Inc.	I
Oh Vermont	O

e. **File abbreviated organizational names at the beginning of the letter category when companies are commonly known by those names.** Cross-reference the full name.

Name	*File as:*
IBM	IBM
	International Business Machines, *see* IBM
MMM	3M
	Minnesota Mining and Manufacturing, *see* 3M

f. **Some organizational names are derived from acronyms or purposely misspelled words.**

Alphabetize exactly as spelled, ignoring spacing, capitalization, and punctuation.

Examples:

BusConsult
Buy-Chek
Buy-N-Sav
Buz Net

4. **Alphabetize numbers as though they were spelled out.**

Numbers should be alphabetized as though spelled out, whether expressed in alpha or numeric form.

Number	*File as:*
81	eighty-one
800	eight hundred
50	1five hundred and one
1,000	one thousand
700	seven hundred
22	twenty-two
2	two

5. **Cross-reference when placement is uncertain.**

Provide file cross-references in the following circumstances:

1. You are uncertain of the correct file placement.
2. More than one version of the same name exists as an acronym, nickname, or alternative spelling.
3. The organizational name is the same as the name of an individual.

4. An exceptionally large file section is placed outside the normal filing sequence. For example, an insurance company may have a large section filed as "Claims." Under the "C" section in the main file, cross-reference to the location of "Claims" files.

6. Alphabetize consistently.

Be consistent with alphabetizing methods. Select your method for filing based on the volume, scope, and purpose of the files. Most business files will be arranged in the word-by-word method. The organization's filing policies should be described and summarized as a brief written procedure that all employees with access to the files can refer to. Periodic file audits can check for consistency of method.

In an automated filing system, alphabetizing is normally assigned automatically. However, some of the rules (such as filing for cases beginning with numbers) might not conform to a generally understood set of rules.

Annotations

Annotations are notes to expand on an introduced subject, and are organized in several different formats. In books and articles, annotations may be listed as footnotes, chapter endnotes, or a section of endnotes at the end of the book.

Annotations may include citations of sources, definitions, or sidebar information related to the referenced topic. A sidebar, often found as a footnote, may be listed in the following manner:

> The calculated price/earnings ratio describes whether or not the current reported price of stock is a bargain price or an inflated price. This conclusion is based on the calculated multiple. As a general observation, a reasonably priced stock is expected to report price/earnings at multiples between 10 and 25.*

*The ratio, also called P/E, is calculated by dividing current price per share by the most recently reported earnings per share. The result, the multiple, represents the number of years' earnings reflected in the current price.

Another form of annotation is the sidebar or callout. This is a brief explanation of something in the text, and often is set apart by a box or different font in the text.

> **Sidebar:** a highlighted annotation placed within narrative to define or expand on the topic.

The sidebar may also be used to add explanation or highlights to a chart or graph, in which case it may be accompanied by arrows from the explanatory sidebar to the section of the referenced graphic.

A variation on the sidebar is the margin note which consists of notation, often in long-hand within a book, written by a student to draw attention to a passage or to elaborate on it.

An annotated bibliography provides a summary of cited works within a book or article. The section normally is placed at the back of the document between endnotes and the index. See sections for "Bibliography" and "Citations" to compare style (APA, Chicago or MLA) in formatting an annotated bibliography.

Examples:

Levey, M. (1996). Florence: A Portrait. Cambridge MA: Harvard University Press.

Mumford, L. (1999). The City in History. New York: Harcourt.

Parsons, N. T. (2008). Vienna: A Cultural and Literary History. Oxford UK: Signal Books.

Robinson, A. (2011). Genius: A Very Short Introduction. New York: Oxford University Press.

Annualization

In reporting financial information (dollar values, percentages, returns), side-by-side comparisons are made valid by *annualization* so that all outcomes are expressed on the same timeframe, even when the actual time being compared is not the same.

For example, two investments are opened and closed in a corporate portfolio during the year. One yielded 4% over a seven-month holding period and the other yielded 3% over a four-month timeframe. An unannualized conclusion would be that the 4% return was superior to the 3% return, but this would be inaccurate.

Based on the number of months, each return is annualized with the following calculations:

*4% ÷ 7 months * 12 months = 6.86%*

*3% ÷ 4 months * 12 months = 9.00%*

Through annualization, the two outcomes are expressed with a like-kind basis. This may be done using months, weeks, or days. The daily method may be the most accurate. For example, if the actual number of days was rounded up to seven months and four months, it is less accurate than using actual days:

*4% ÷ 213 days * 365 days = 6.85%*

*3% ÷ 116 days * 365 days = 9.44%*

This procedure should be applied whenever dissimilar periods of time are involved in creating outcomes. For example, a new division is added but is in operation only seven months. Comparing this to other divisions in operation for the full year would distort outcomes.

Anonymous publication

Publication credits are common for academic papers, magazine articles, and books. Authorship is commonly excluded from internal reports, however. The source department may be listed on a cover page of a report, but the name of the employee preparing the report is not included in most instances.

Many works of literature and art have been produced anonymously, either because the names have been lost with repeated editions, or because the author purposely declined credit (due to threat from authorities in power at the time, for example).

Online blogs or websites often are published without an author's name or with a fictitious name. The use of a pen name (*non de plume*) is a form of anonymous publishing. For example, the well-known website *The Motley Fool* is the title of an organization but does not directly name its owners or authors. Many blogs are published anonymously, including hacker blogs or those blogs so controversial that the author does not want direct association. Some authors choose to write under a pseudonym to avoid controversy or for personal safety reasons.

A question arises when an employee writes critically about the company itself. Criticism often is not welcomed by organizations, and freedom of speech ensured by the government does not extend to members of organizations (although many people believe that it does, or that it should). Fear of retaliation, including the possibility of losing a job, is a reason to publish anonymously.

Anthology

An *anthology* is a collection of works compiled with a common theme. This is associated with many literary forms. For business application, an anthology is useful for describing a range of sources for relevant materials applicable within a specific industry or for a particular form of research.

Examples include *Business in Ethical Focus: An Anthology*, *Bioethics: An Anthology*, and *Anthology of Business Strategy*.

Antonyms

Words with definitions opposite that of other words are *antonyms*. In many cases, antonyms are unintentionally used when the opposite is intended. For example, the word "inflammable" has the same definition as "flammable."

1. Graded antonyms.

Some versions of antonyms deal with degrees or grades of difference. For example, "low" is an antonym of "high," but it may be further distinguished as lower or lowest. These gradings apply to many other words as well.

2. Relational antonyms.

Some antonyms involve *converse words*, in which the relationship between the two sides is opposite.

Examples:

Win and lose
Inside and outside
Above and below
Parent and child (also father and son, or mother and daughter)
Buy and sell

3. Complementary antonyms.

Some antonyms are absolute, with no grading or relational adjustments.

Examples:

Alive and dead
Mortal and immortal
Solvent and insolvent
Worker and employee

4. Creating antonyms with a prefix.

Some antonym forms are created with a prefix, such as "non," "un," "in," or "anti."

Examples:

Existent and nonexistent
Profitable and unprofitable
Tolerant and intolerant
Consistent and inconsistent
Expansion and contraction

Appendices

Appendices (preferred plural of "appendix" over alternative of "appendixes") are materials incidental to the main text in reports and other documents. By including appendices, business writers can keep reports short and clear, with major points easily found in the main body of the report. Supplying the supporting data statistics, lists, studies, tables, and so forth, in one or more appendices can help the reader verify information of interest, without cluttering the report.

1. Use appendices to keep the main report brief.

Short, easy-to-read reports get more attention from busy executives than longer, less-organized ones. Emphasize the most important information in a one-page report summary, and break down the rest of the report in major sections. When additional but incidental information is referred to, create an appendix for it. Do not include unnecessary information in an appendix.

2. Cross-reference materials accurately and thoroughly.

When a report or section of a book refers to information supported by an appendix, include a cross-reference to the appendix, citing its number or title. Number appendix information as continuation of the book's paging. For example, if the body of the book ends on page 315, begin the first appendix with page 316. The same guideline applies for generation of paging for reports, articles and papers.

Appositives

An *appositive* is a noun or noun phrase that renames or clarifies a preceding noun. It may consist of a single word or a phrase of several words. An appositive should be used in business writing only when absolutely necessary. Concise form prefers avoiding unnecessary appositive expression.

Examples, excessive appositive use:

Robert Smith, <u>who is my manager and friend</u>, wrote the report.

We initiated Six Sigma, <u>a project management system</u> to improve efficiency.

Mr. Brown, <u>who formulated the widely used management program</u>, has retired.

Examples, necessary appositive use:

Smith, <u>author of the widely published report</u>, was my manager and a friend.

> Six Sigma, a project management system, is designed to improve efficiency.
> The management program, a widely used system, was designed by Mr. Brown.

In each of these examples, the initial form of expression is distracting and awkward. By turning the sentences around, the appositive adds value and clarification. For example, in the second sentence, many readers might be unfamiliar with Six Sigma, so the appositive explains what it is.

Apps

For business writers needing to improve skills, many writing *apps* can be downloaded and used to check style and tone, and to modify the method of expression to strengthen the message. Some of these apps are free and others charge a fee. Many are available only through limited outlets (such as the App Store) and can be down loaded only for certain devices (such as iOS, for example).

Apps worth reviewing for possible download include Danger Text, Flowstate, Refly Editor, Writefull, Ulysses, Paragraphs, Rough Draft, iA Writer and Scrivener. One editing tool is Expresso, an online text editor that does not require download. A sample of any size is uploaded to the page and it is analyzed for style, usage, and voice.

For example, the following sentence was uploaded to Expresso:

> The purpose in drafting this report is to initiate a dialogue among supervisors, and to improve our internal control systems.

An analysis reported 33.3% weak verbs, 125 characters in 20 words, 20 words per sentence, average 1.9 syllables per word, breakdown by parts of speech (nouns 35%; pronouns 5%; verbs 15%; adjectives 5%; other parts of speech 40%). It further identified the sentence as declarative with 45% stopwords (words not necessary or containing significance).

Archive

The term *archive* refers to a collection of records, documents, and other material that contains valuable information, either as primary source documents, records required to be retained, or collections of historical value.

In writing procedures for retention of records, retrieval methods, and limitation of what must be included in an archive, determining factors should be defined in advance and enforced internally. For organizations, an archive may be described as two primary types.

First are those records required for legal, tax, or verification purposes. These should be stored with identification of retention time. For example, a series of records that must be kept for the current year plus three additional years should be labeled "C+3."

The second broad classification includes permanent archives containing items of historical or cultural value. Examples of well-known historical archives include the World of Coca-Cola museum (Atlanta, GA), and Levi Strauss Museum Archives (San Francisco, CA).

Physical archives may require different preservation and retrieval attributes than those archives generated and preserved online.

Articles

An *article* is a word defining or modifying a noun. Articles include common words such as *a*, *an*, and *the*.

1. Definite articles.

A *definite article* describes use of "the" to identify a noun.

Examples, definite article 'the':

Please complete <u>the</u> report.
Provide <u>the</u> new employees with <u>the</u> orientation manual.
Let's add new topics to <u>the</u> meeting's agenda.

2. Indefinite articles.

The indefinite article consists of either 'a' or 'an.' This is indefinite because it generalizes the nature of the noun or adjective and action involved.

Examples, indefinite articles:

Should we set <u>a</u> time for the meeting?
Let's set up <u>an</u> organizational meeting to plan our new marketing campaign.

The first example of "a" is related to "time" but does not specify the time itself. The second example uses "an" which relates to the adjective "organizational" but is also indefinite because it does not tell when the meeting will take place.

3. Articles for unknown quantities.

Some articles are not limited to *a meeting*, *an answer*, or *the employee*. Misuse of articles in business documents is one of the most common forms of error (another being the use of excessive capitalization). The number of nouns or adjectives is not known or not specified. In this case, "some" or "any" may also serve as articles.

Examples of articles for unknown quantities:

We need to arrive at some solutions.

The meeting did not conclude with any recommendations.

The use of "a," "an," or "the" may also include unknown quantities.

Examples of "a", "an," or "the" as articles for unknown quantities:

They provided us with a number of possible answers.

In this case, an unusual set of circumstances affected the outcome.

What is the range of possibilities?

4. Articles are not used with possessive pronouns.

When a possessive pronoun is used in a sentence, articles are not needed.

Examples, incorrect article usage with pronouns:

The committee reviewed the our budget.

The managers met with a their board of directors.

Examples, correct usage with pronouns:

The committee reviewed our budget.

The managers met with their board of directors.

5. Articles are omitted in some situations.

In some usage forms, no article is needed. This is especially true when including an article makes the expression awkward or distracting.

Examples, unneeded articles:

We met with visiting executives for a dinner.

Employees were asked for the creative solutions.

Examples, excluded articles:

We met with visiting executives for dinner.

Employees were asked for creative solutions.

Artwork

Writing style for descriptions of artwork is relevant for many business applications. These include ad campaigns, logo design, or marketing initiatives based on the use of visuals.

The creative aspects of a visually-based presentation rarely stand alone, and need to be augmented with narrative descriptions. The narrative should be brief, descriptive, and may be of greatest benefit when it points out attributes that may not be obvious to an audience.

Examples, narrative pointing out hidden meanings:

The FedEx logo includes an arrow pointed to the right.

The Bronx Zoo logo consists of two giraffes in silhouette. But the space between the animals' legs also represents the famous New York skyline.

Wendy's shows a cartoon of Wendy's face, but on her collar, the word "Mom" is also shown, which is subtle but sends a clear message.

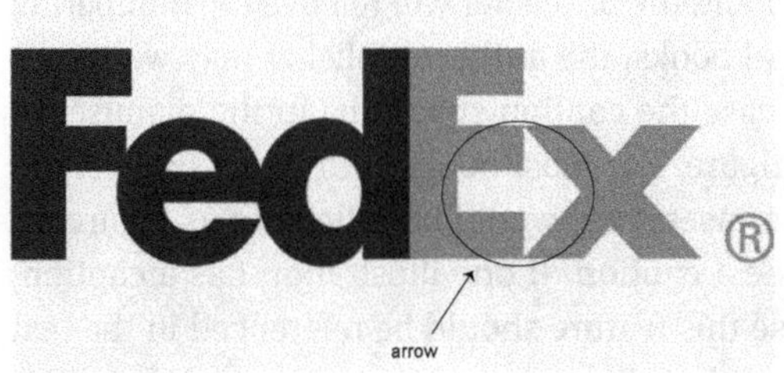

Figure A.1: FedEx logo

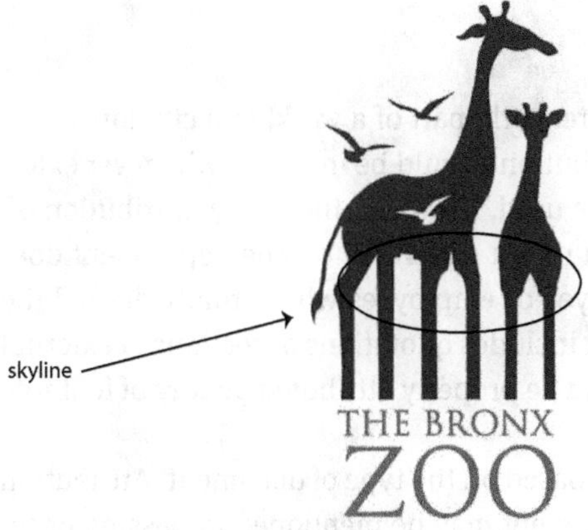

Figure A.2: Bronx Zoo logo

Figure A.3: Wendy's logo

In presenting a subtle or hidden symbol or other message, the narrative or verbal style should point out the items of interest. Effective presentation adds drama and significance to artwork. In an informal book, an *illustration* may be used where art is placed on a separate line. Generally, if there are more than one illustrations per chapter an author will submit an illustration numbered by chapter and the number within the chapter and the publisher will remove the numbering for the final book. In some informal books, the author/publisher may want captions but not numbering; in that case the caption should be in the manuscript under the figure, not *part* of the figure. For most books with many figures, the figures are numbered and in those cases, they would be called out as Figure 4.1 or Figure 4-1 and generally include a caption. If one illustration has a caption, they all should. All figures that use this feature should be referenced in the text and you should not say "below" or "above" as you are not guaranteed the placement of a numbered figure.

Attribution

Giving credit for the source of an entire work, part of a work, or a citation are all forms of *attribution*. In business, attribution should be included whenever external ideas, expressions, or concepts are used. However, internally, attribution often is not the custom. For example, a report generated by one department does not include attribution for the employee or employees who actually drafted the document. However, if that document includes quotations or sections of external articles, papers, or books, those should be properly attributed by way of footnote or in-text notation.

The form of attribution should be based on the type of document. Attribution for a large section of an external document may be mentioned in passing or referred to an appendix. Frequent usage may be summarized with an end-of-document "References" section and mentioned in text by the name of the author or authors, and year. A publisher may impose a style guide preference for the use of in-text attribution, and these may appear in many formats.

Examples, in-text attribution:

The test concluded that security systems were ineffective (Anderson, 2016).

Analysis demonstrated that "customer interest was not widespread even with the extensive promotional campaign" (Campbell and Nelson, 2013).

B

Backmatter

Material appearing at the end of a report, paper, or book is collectively classified as *backmatter.* This is distinguished from the main body of work as supplementary or supporting material.

1. **Epilogue, afterword, and postscript.**

   A final and often very brief concluding chapter to a book or report is called the epilogue or, less frequently, the afterword or postscript. The purpose to this section is to summarize and repeat primary points or conclusions in the body of the work, or to add additional thoughts not directly related to or part of the range of topics. For example, an epilogue concluding a book on accounting might include an epilogue stating several points, including:

   Incidentally, the long-standing application of Generally Accepted Accounting Principles (GAAP) has been under fire for many years, and in the near future may be replaced by the more practical International Financial Reporting Standards (IFRS).

2. **Extro (or Outro).**

   The rarely used *extro* is the opposite of an introduction. It is intended to serve a purpose similar to the epilogue, by providing a conclusion and summary of the longer work and its primary points.

3. **Appendix or appendices (also called addendum or addenda).**

   One or more appendices follow the body of a work, including reports, papers, and books. Appropriate items to include in the appendix are statistical summaries, study results, or extensive tables, especially containing numerical and financial data.

4. **Glossary.**

   A glossary is desirable when a significant volume of terms is used in the body of work and that may not be widely known to readers. Such terms are usually technical in nature and not part of a normal vocabulary outside of the document's primary topic. Glossary terms need to be precise. Publishers cite glossary definitions as a major source of error, demanding careful editing. For this reason, some publishers prefer to not include a glossary at the conclusion of a work.

DOI 10.1515/9781547400218-002

5. Endnotes.

Endnotes are fully cited references noted within sections of the report, paper, or book. While a common practice is to include endnotes in a single section at the end of the document, they may also be included at the end of each chapter or reduced to footnotes on each page. Publishers have preferences about placement and treatment of notes; the preferred format should be determined in advance.

6. Bibliography or reference list.

A bibliography summarizes sources referenced in the larger work. It is needed when sources are extensive. It may be subdivided into primary and secondary sources, or between type of source (books, articles, newspapers, broadcasts, reports, government sources, etc.).

A reference list is used primarily in published academic papers and appears as the final part of the paper itself. Within the paper, cross-reference is provided within the narrative or in the form of footnotes. When the narrative form is used, the author's last name(s) and year of publication is shown at the appropriate spot, and full citation provided in the reference list. The first reference usually spells out all authors' names when several names apply; and subsequent reference for three or more is shown with the last name of the first author listed, followed by *et al.* (Lt., "and others") and the publication year.

7. Index.

The last section of backmatter is the index. This is used in books or exceptionally lengthy reports or articles. The index consists of primary and secondary topics arranged alphabetically. A secondary topic is used when entries for a primary topic are extensive, requiring further explanation for the location within the document. Sub-topics are arranged alphabetically and indented under the primary topic heading.

Baseline

The *baseline* has several distinct definitions. In terms of business writing, three specific definitions are applicable: in statistics, budgeting, and as a legal concept.

1. Statistical baseline.

In statistics, a *baseline study* identifies a starting point or benchmark for measuring outcomes. This is expressed and documented in four separate types of descriptive statistics:

- Frequency measurement (percentage outcomes, number of occurrences, or counts of a particular type of response)
- Dispersion or variance (standard deviation, range or interval analysis, dispersion of results)
- Central tendency (mean, median, and mode)
- Position measurement (ranking by percentage or quartile, relative score rankings)

2. Budgeting baseline.

The budgeting baseline begins with the most recent year's budget and actual outcomes, notably in categories of expense and cost, or for forecasts or revenue. In describing and providing assumption bases for a budgeting report, the means of baseline budgeting should be clearly specified and explained, including justification for the underlying assumptions.

When a budget is based on the previous year's actual results, the baseline is historical. An underlying assumption is that actual expenditures provides the baseline for future expense and cost levels. When an annual budget begins with no assumption of past expense levels, but rather is constructed with a requirement that every expense level has to be justified independently from the past, it is termed *zero-based budgeting*. The assumption in this case is that relying on past expense levels builds in overspending or poor controls and lacks the ability to establish well-controlled levels based on newly developed assumptions, thus creating a new budgeting baseline.

3. Legal reference.

The *baseline* in law has several definitions. Overall, baseline is a starting point for making comparisons under prevailing law. It may also be used as reference to conditions that would exist in the event that a tort or other event had not taken place. Under this definition, the baseline describes the level of harm based on previous conditions (population, demographics, etc.). This "measure of harm" standard describes how an act or series of acts harms someone in relation to the circumstances that existed previously. The definition describes the harmed individual's or company's *positive entitlements* (rights and privileges) as the baseline to measure harm and to assign monetary value to the degree of harm occurring away from the baseline. This definition applies primarily within tort law.

Bibliography

A *bibliography* is an alphabetical listing of sources and references, placed at the end of a book or article. Format corresponds to style in use for citations (APA, MLA, or Chicago); however, page and section references are excluded in the bibliography.

1. **Listing and style.**
   List sources in the bibliography in alphabetical order and in the same style as citations throughout the work. Shortcomings of bibliographies draw attention away from the quality of research:
   a. **Outdated works.**
      When a bibliography is based excessively on older sources, it lacks the credibility gained from more contemporary or recently published sources.
   b. **Weak or inappropriate sources.**
      Weak sources include informal blogs, unpublished work, or self-citation. Inappropriate sources include unedited sources such as *Wikipedia* and other online opinion pieces that are not based on solid research, but solely on opinion. In a scholarly work, the use of basic sources (the "for Dummies" book series, for example) is inappropriate due to lack of academic quality and references.
   c. **Obvious bias.**
      A bibliographical listing of sources with a particular slant or bias, to the exclusion of opposing points of view, lacks credibility and portrays the work as one-sided.
   d. **Exclusion of important sources.**
      When a work is on a topic largely based on seminal previous works, excluding the primary sources from the bibliography makes it incomplete.

2. **Bibliographical essay.**
   An alternate form of bibliography is the bibliographical essay, which includes not only the sources but analysis of what they provided to help in structuring the work. To add value to the work, the essay should include the following attributes:
   1. Organization should follow a logical course and reveal how source materials were organized and applied in research.
   2. The flow of the essay should be logical even though it does not have to follow the sequence of the document.

3. A comparison drawn between several sources may lead to analysis of differences in opinion or confirmation of ideas.

   Example:

   In the analysis of stock market deceptions throughout history, reference has been made to irrational behavior, which "can be avoided by identifying and controlling the significant variables," according to Morton D. David (1983), *Game Theory*, Dover Publications. P. 72. However, this does not directly address the problem of "legal" but deceptive practices. For example, "The mumbo jumbo of open disclosure is a smoke screen which makes the no-load funds one of the neatest con games of the twentieth century" (David Sokol, 1972, *Today's Stock Market Scams* ... Sherbourne Press, p. 64).

In this section, the dissimilar sources address different aspects of the topic with analysis, enabling a reader to understand the referenced sources used by the author.

Blogging

Style employed in blogs tends to be less formal than elsewhere. To add value to a blog, follow these style guidelines:

1. Keep blog entry size relatively small. An entry of 500 words or less is preferable, since online readers tend to have a short attention span.
2. Cite sources under the same guidelines for other forms of communication. This adds value and credibility to the blog.
3. Follow general style guidelines of proper grammar and punctuation.
4. Unless language usage is intentionally unique for a particular blog, follow the usual rules for clarity of expression.
5. Avoid the use of slang, obscenity, and idioms not acceptable within the intended purpose of the blog.

Budgets and forecasts

The formats selected for written budget and forecast documents determine how well they are grasped. The usefulness of these documents may be determined by how well they are presented.

1. Set up explanatory narrative sections.

Budgets are primarily planning and control documents, estimates of the financial future, and explanations showing how those estimates were developed. Readers cannot comprehend numbers alone and need additional narrative summaries and explanations. Each summary should represent the major departments or divisions making up the entire budget. If you prepare the budget for only one department or section, you will need only one summary section. The summary section is most effective when limited to the following information:

1. A brief description of the department or section, its work and purpose, and how it works with other sections of the organization.
2. Methods employed in developing the budget, including basic assumptions concerning the financial direction anticipated during the budgetary period. Also describe policies or goals imposed on the section by management to the extent that those policies have affected the budget.
3. Major departures from budgeting assumptions used in previous periods, including a short explanation of the previous year's budget versus actual results. When appropriate, include methods employed to reduce the likelihood of errors in the current budget.

2. Provide clear, concise cross-references.

The budget is a complex document. Help the reader or reviewer by providing consistent and concise cross-references between sections of the report. Be especially thorough in documenting the budget summary to supporting documents. Organize the budget report with numbered pages, and use consistent titles for account categories.

3. Follow usual practice for organization.

Arrange the report in the following sequence:

1. *Table of Contents*
2. *Summary sections,* which present the overall budget plan in narrative form
3. *Budget summary,* showing the full budgetary period, preferably by month
4. *Supporting documents,* to explain the assumptions used to develop the budget; this section should include adequate month-by-month explanations, as it will later serve as the source document to explain budget variances.

4. Break down assumptions by source or type so that variations can later be identified in the same groupings.

Major segments of expenses should include newspaper ad, radio, printed material, and other related classifications.

Each of these groupings should be budgeted separately on the assumption worksheet, and the total used for the category's budget. Later, actual expenses can be compared in the same budget category.

In the case of income forecasts, include an adequate explanation of the assumptions used to develop each source of revenue. Attempt to tie revenue projections in your forecast to sources that can be monitored and identified.

5. Design the budget report with monitoring in mind.

Preparing the budget report is only the first step in the budgeting process. A properly used budget serves as the document against which each month's actual outcome is measured. The supporting document section of the budget should be organized and designed so that assumptions can be tracked and variances explained completely.

Bullet points

The effective use of *bullet points* breaks up narrative and combines outline style with running thoughts. When used appropriately, bullet points work as a form of strong emphasis. The bullet point in most word processing programs is added with a single click and adds automatic spacing and indenting as well.

Example of bullet points with subject line:

Procedures for new employees

- Employee policies are defined in the manual.
- Internal procedures require distribution of the manual.
- New employees are required to attend a half-day orientation.

The bullet points work best when the following guidelines are used:

1. When the number of outline points exceeds three to five, use numbering in place of bullet points.
2. Keep bullet points short, preferably one line or less; avoid turning bullet points into longer sentences or paragraphs.
3. End bullet points without punctuation or with a period. Do not use semicolons. Be consistent in how bullet points are ended. Keep punctuation consistent.

4. Be consistent in formulating bullet points as full sentences ending with a period; or as sentences or sentence fragments without ending punctuation.
5. Express the primary word or phrase as close as possible to the beginning of each bullet point.
6. Use this outline form only for directly related thoughts and ideas. Do not create a bullet point list for unrelated points.
7. Describe a list in the preceding paragraph or assign an applicable title so that a reader knows the subject of the list.
8. Keep the outline format throughout the list. Do not attempt to connect the lines with transitional linking words or phrases.
9. Use bullet points for efficiency and organization, but not for personal communications. Bullet points work in the proper places, but may be perceived as lacking a friendly tone.
10. Ensure consistency in form. Use the same indents, spacing, and font throughout the list.

C

Callouts and sidebars

The callout is used to highlight important aspects of a report or article, or to provide additional information (definitions, statistics, or resources for further information).

The callout or sidebar may be boxed off for emphasis and arrange so that text wraps around it. A lengthy sidebar may be converted to a footnote to avoid excessively long boxes or distracting volume of this feature (see also Annotations).

Guidelines for callouts and sidebars:

1. Limit sidebars to as few words as possible; these should be short and serve as emphasis.
2. Use sidebars only when the statement is related directly to the primary topic.
3. Use a frame or box, or set up callouts and sidebars in a different font, italics or boldface to separate it from the main text. Boxing off the area is preferable, as different fonts may be distracting rather than adding emphasis. If you are writing a book, ask your publisher about the use of sidebars. Callouts also refer to text used to identify items in figures.

Capitalization

A word is said to be "capitalized" primarily when only its first letter is capitalized. Commonly, *capitalized* does not imply that letters beyond the first letter are also expressed in capital letters. When a word is described as "all caps," every letter is capitalized. The editing abbreviation *u.c.* means "uppercase," or capitalize. The abbreviation *l.c.* means "lowercase."

The use of improper capitalization is the worst error in business documents. The rule is "Do not capitalize unless you *have to*. Readers will assume there is a meaning associated with capitalization.

1. Capitalize the first letter in a proper noun but not in a common noun.

Proper nouns are the names of people, places, and organizations. Whenever these nouns are used, the first letter in the word is capitalized. A generalized reference—a common noun—is not capitalized.

DOI 10.1515/9781547400218-003

Category	Proper Nouns	Common Nouns
Names and titles	Mary Adams	the woman
	Robert Brown	the man
	Dr. Anderson	a doctor
	President Connors	the president
Place names	Chicago	downtown
	Washington D.C.	the capital
	Lake Bethel	a lake
	Mt. Shasta	the mountain
Organizations	Alcoa Aluminum	the company
	University of Miami	the school
	Toronto Stock Exchange	the exchange
Brand names	Coca-Cola	a soft drink
	John Deere	the lawnmower
Days, months, holidays	Wednesday	today
	September	last month
	Memorial Day	a holiday
Historical references	World War II	the war
	Battle of the Bulge	a battle
Religious titles	Catholic Church	church
	God	the gods
Titles of publications	The Quest	a book
	The New York Times	a newspaper

2. Capitalize the first word of a sentence.

The first word of every sentence is capitalized. In an outline, the first letter of each subsection is capitalized. A quotation within a sentence begins with a capital letter unless the quotation begins in the middle of a sentence.

Examples:

The procedures manual states, "Reports will be due by the fifth day of each month."

The procedures manual states that reports "will be due by the fifth day of the month."

Exceptions: Some names, even though proper nouns, begin with lowercase letters or prefixes. These are capitalized when the name begins a sentence or when it appears as the first word after a colon.

Examples:

Roberto de Ignasio spoke at today's luncheon.

Marcus van Dyck published an article on a topic of wide interest: Van Dyck presented his theories of enlightened business management.

3. **Capitalize titles of books, magazines, and other published materials.**

Titles of books, magazines, and organizations should be capitalized. However, articles *(a, an, the),* coordinating conjunctions *(and, for, nor, or),* and prepositions under four letters are written in lower case *unless* they are the first or last word.

Examples:

New York Times Magazine [newspaper]
"Leadership: It's Not About You" [article]
Of Human Bondage [book]
"Muddling Through" [article]
International Business Machines [organization]

4. **Follow the rules for special situations.**

Special rules or style decisions have to be made when dealing with special situations.

a. **Geographic regions:**

Decide when to capitalize based on whether a specific region is meant (capitalized) or a general direction or area (do not capitalize).

Specific Region	*General Direction*
the East	heading east
the South	south of here
West Texas	western Texas

b. **Heading words:**

Capitalize headings unless they are articles.

Examples:

Audit-Proofed Data System
State-of-the-Art Automated Model

c. **Sections of documents:**
When sections are mentioned in text (Appendix 1, Figure 6, and Volume II, for example) they should be capitalized for emphasis.

5. **Use capitalization as a form of emphasis.**

In some situations, fully capitalized words are used to emphasize isolated words to draw attention to them. However, this technique, when overused, is distracting and may constitute a "shout" (excessive use of caps). Most publishers will switch to italic. All caps are extremely hard to read.

Examples:

The division reported a PROFIT this quarter.
Our goal is to NOT provide free services.

6. **Avoid overusing capitalization.**

Avoid overuse of capitals and all-caps in documents. Excessive use is distracting to the reader and does not add value to the message.

Examples:

The Division Reported A Profit This Quarter.
THE DIVISION REPORTED A PROFIT THIS QUARTER.

In both of these examples, capitals are used inappropriately and excessively.

Captions

Captions are brief descriptive phrases or sentences accompanying charts, graphs, photographs, and other visual representations in reports.

1. **Use descriptive captions to guide readers in interpreting visual information.**

Captions may be titles only or full sentences. When using a full-sentence, descriptive caption, end it with a period. Use descriptive captions to emphasize the key information presented in a graph or other illustration.

Descriptive captions:

The rate of profits has exceeded forecasts in every quarter.
The per-employee expense declined after our new budgeting controls went into effect.

2. Use only brief title captions in technical reports and appendices.

Some charts and graphs are self-explanatory and need only titles (but be sure to use a title). Use title captions when you do not want to editorialize beyond the presentation of data. In these cases, do not place a period or other punctuation at the end of the caption. Capitalize each important word in a title caption (do not capitalize conjunctions and prepositions with fewer than four letters).

Brief captions:

Rate of Profits
Per-Employee Expense

3. Place captions consistently.

Generally, captions for tables are used above the table as a table can continue on for pages. But graphics for figures are usually placed below as they generally fit on a page. Decide on placement, and be consistent throughout a single report or book. Always place full-sentence captions beneath the graphic.

4. Accompany captions with numbered references.

Graphics are effective ways to communicate information in reports quickly and effectively. The caption is especially useful when a report contains a large volume of financial information. Preface each caption with a reference—number a Figure (or Table) 1, for example—so that the reader can quickly find the graphic mentioned in the text. Be aware of guidelines for placement of text: above for tables or below for figures.

Case studies

Case studies may be informal or formal. An informal case study should be short and included within the narrative. Using real names and situations adds credibility, whereas a generalized and non-specific case study may not be as convincing.

1. Informal case study

The format of an informal case study should be conversational in tone, and restricted to as little space as possible. It is helpful to use real situations and names in order to avoid the appearance of a made-up case study.

Example, ineffective case study:

> One high-profile organization used the Six Sigma program to significantly change the culture within the company, improve managements' effectiveness, and turn the company back into a profitable venture.

Example, effective case study:

Jack Welch changed the culture at General Electric in 1995 by setting a five-year goal transforming the company into a Six Sigma-focused organization. The revolutionary changes launched Welch's reputation as an effective visionary and leader.

2. **Formal case studies**

The formal case study is likely to be lengthier than an informal one, and also will follow a structure. The structure is especially useful when a document includes several case studies.

The structure of a formal case study consists of:
1. Title page. This may include the name of the organization or individual at the center of the case study.
2. Key words. In case studies presented in the format of a paper, including a short list of key words orients the reader to the range of topics within the study.
3. Abstract. For a lengthy case study (appropriate in some situations) an abstract provides the reader with a summary at the beginning (see also Abstracts). This should be restricted to a single paragraph and define the primary points brought out in the details to follow.
4. Problem or situation. State the challenge or situation addressed in the case history. This may be a source of risk, loss, or poor morale fixed through the particular events in the case study. Not all case studies lead to solutions, however. The situation summary may describe a case study for an ongoing problem that has not been resolved.
5. The history. This section describes the precise details of how a situation developed over time, and how it was addressed (or not addressed).
6. Conclusion. This final section explains how an initial problem or situation was resolved or is ongoing. This section may also include instructive observations concerning the case and related topics.

Casual assertions and inferences

A casual assertion is distinct from a correlation. The casual assertion assumes a conclusion not necessarily contained within the statement. True correlation associates one fact with another. The casual assertion often lacks validity upon analysis. An observed conclusion may be invalid, intentional or otherwise, due to adopting a casual assertion. An intentional casual assertion requires interpretation of data in an inaccurate manner; unintentional casual assertions result from assumptions that are not fully true. A cause-and-effect relationship is required in order to prove correlation.

Examples of casual assertions:

> A business venture in a rural community failed, demonstrating that rural areas are high-risk for new products or services.
>
> Profits rose last year from 6% of revenue in the prior year, to 7% this year. This supports a forecast of 8% net return this year.

Examples of correlations:

> A business venture in a rural area failed, demonstrating that further study is required before entering into assumptions about products and services that consumers in such areas will want to buy.
>
> Profits rose last year to 7% from 6% of revenue in the prior year. This supports our belief that maintaining profitability between 6% and 7%, as expressed in the forecast, requires diligent expense controls.

These examples demonstrate that random assignment of conclusions is associated with casual assertions. This is likely to occur when research does not lead to supportable conclusions, and individual assumptions are used to replace valid proof.

An inference may be casual. Notably when a hypothesis is not tested fully, or when assumptions are not developed fully. Whereas a casual assertion is the result of erroneous combination of facts or beliefs, an inference develops from how information is combined to reach conclusions.

Examples of casual inferences:

> A business venture in a rural community failed, and rural communities often lack exceptional schools. This proves that unexceptional schools are the cause of business failures.
>
> Profits rose last year to 7% from 6% of revenue in the prior year. We also moved our headquarters to a more modernized building. The improvement in the headquarters building led to improved profitability.

While assertions and inferences are similar, both are based on flawed beliefs or conclusions. Statistical inference, deducing conclusions or properties based on samples, is in reference to testing and development of conclusions and is often based on a very small sample. Great care has to be taken to ensure that the sample truly is representative of the larger population.

Examples of statistical inference:

A new product test was conducted on 100 shoppers at 6 p.m. on a Friday. Results concluded that the new product was more desirable than the higher-priced and better known product.

Our last budget examined past pricing of supplies, and found that average prices rose by 3% over the previous year. This has been used as a baseline for annual budget increases for the same expense in the coming year.

Both of these inferences *may* be flawed, as the statistical base is not necessarily accurate for the conclusions drawn. Some improved inferences may include the following:

A new product test was conducted on 100 shoppers at 6 p.m. on a Friday. Results were deemed unreliable, since a majority of shoppers at this time were not likely to be primary shoppers for a family.

A budgetary process examined past prices of supplies, and concluded that averages rose by 3% per year. The budget may be adjusted based on an audit of usage, with the purpose of reducing theft and misuse of supplies. Improved comparison shopping is also justified, since a study of typical supply prices indicated that prices have not risen during the past year.

In both cases, the *assumptions* led to conclusions inferred by apparent facts. However, a more detailed examination revealed that the statistical inferences were misleading.

Charts and Graphs

Most business reports concern numbers—data concerning finances, profits, production, marketing, and other numerical information—that is best understood when displayed graphically. As a result, charts and graphs are valuable business tools. Readers understand information better and retain more of it when it is presented visually than when it is presented verbally or in print.

1. **Keep charts and graphs in scale.**

The *scale* is the value representation used in the graphic—for example, dollars, units of production, or employees. One axis of the graphic is used for the value and the other for a distinction, such as reporting periods (month, quarter, fiscal year), divisions, or companies.

The scale must be an accurate representation. For values, this means the baseline should be at zero. The graphic representation for information beginning above zero will appear inaccurate unless expressed in terms of relative change from the beginning of a period to the end. The graph should also be scaled to a size that is reasonable for the report and is easy to read. A square or a rectangle approximating a square is most practical in the majority of applications.

2. Keep scales the same throughout a single report.

Select a consistent scale and use it for reporting similar data throughout the report whenever possible. Otherwise, the relative value of similar information will be distorted. Dissimilar information invariably requires different scaling. Readers and reviewers are likely to make associations between graphs, assuming the scales are identical even when they are not.

3. Cross-reference charts and graphs to the text.

Graphics within the body of the report or appendices should be carefully cross-referenced to the page number in the report or the proper section of a larger report. Narrative that refers to charts and graphs should identify them by graphic number (e.g., "see Figure 3-1" for the first Figure in Chapter 3) and by location (e.g., "see below" or "see the next page").

4. Provide brief captions to distinguish graphics.

Captions should tell the reader at a glance exactly what the graphic shows. Even complex graphics can usually be reduced to a few words. The caption makes a distinction between otherwise very similar graphs in the same report or on the same page.

A brief descriptive caption can be used to emphasize the most important point of the graphic. For example, a graph can be labeled, "Sales and Net Profits," telling the reader precisely what the graph reveals. Captions may be longer than a brief title when appropriate. In this example, a longer caption could read, "The rate of net profits has increased during a period of rising sales volume."

5. Include the source.

At the bottom of the graph, identify the source.

Examples:

Source: New York Stock Exchange
Source: Prepared internally from data at National Business Forum
Source: Annual reports, three organizations

6. Strive for simplicity.

Graphics can show numerous results; however, simplicity makes the information more easily conveyed and, from the reader's point of view, much easier to understand and retain. A single graph can be designed to show yearly results in comparative form, for several divisions, and broken down by different product lines; however, much important detail might be lost. It may be preferable to break out some comparisons in several similar graphs, and discuss each one briefly in text.

7. Select the best graphic to convey information.

No one graphic is suitable for every situation. In a lengthy report containing a great deal of complex financial information, variety in style of presentation is desirable. Too many similar charts and graphs confuse the reader, specialized charts and graphs invariably improve the overall impression. Excessive volume of graphics can be simplified, or set apart and included in an appendix to avoid disrupting the flow of information.

a. **Chart or table numbered by chapter and item:**
Use charts and tables within a narrative section to highlight financial information.

A table:

Sales by division (in $ millions):

Description	Current Year	Prior Year
Durables	$1,244	$1,006
Parts	603	719
All other	154	89
Total	$2,001	$1,814

b. **Line graph:**
One of the most popular types of visual aids, the line graph, is most useful for showing two or more comparative values over a specific period of time–for example, actual versus budget in a yearly or quarterly summary; sales compared to forecasts, or sales in two or more periods over a year; and other comparisons of financial information over a time line. In the typical line graph shown in Figure C.1, the value is reflected from top

to bottom (the vertical axis), often meaning dollars or units of production; time is shown from left to right (the horizontal axis). This graphic is most commonly used for reporting business results and is the most compatible with accepted reporting methods, since dollar results are reported over a period of time in financial reports.

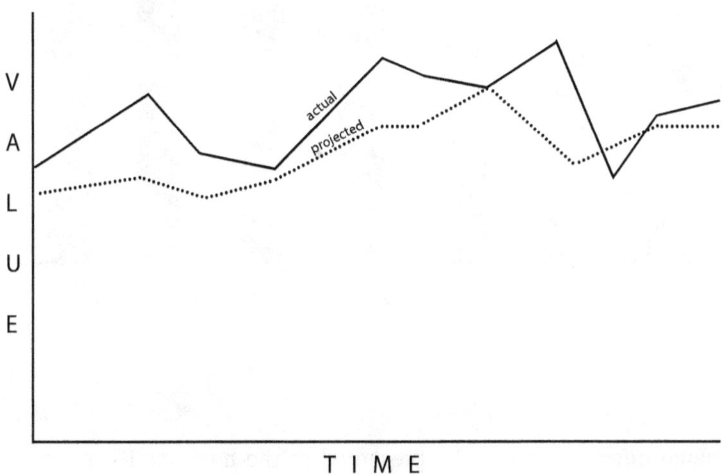

Figure C.1: Line Graph

c. **Bar graph:**
The bar graph is used for reporting comparative information in total or for a discrete moment in time (as opposed to a dynamic report in monthly, quarterly, or annual periods). Two types can be used. The vertical bar graph, shown in Figure C.2, is useful for demonstrating levels of financial information for a limited number of comparisons (departments, divisions, or areas, for example). Value (such as dollars) is shown on the vertical axis, and the comparative distinction is shown in the bars from left to right. A typical example would be total sales volume (value) by division (comparison).

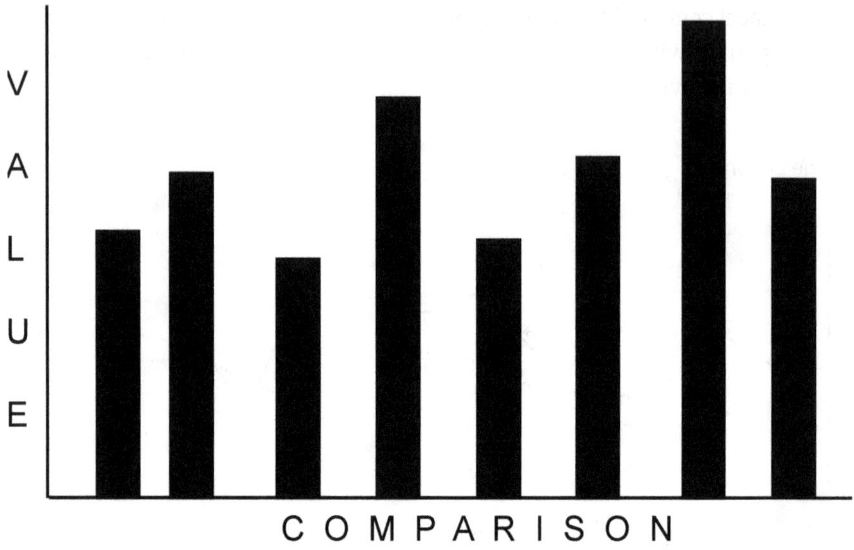

Figure C.2: Sample caption

The same information may be presented in the horizontal bar graph, which is useful when a larger number of factors are being compared. Because of its horizontal shape, a longer graph can be represented without exceeding the width limits of a standard-sized page. In Figure C.3, the value is shown on the horizontal axis, and the comparison bars are shown from top to bottom.

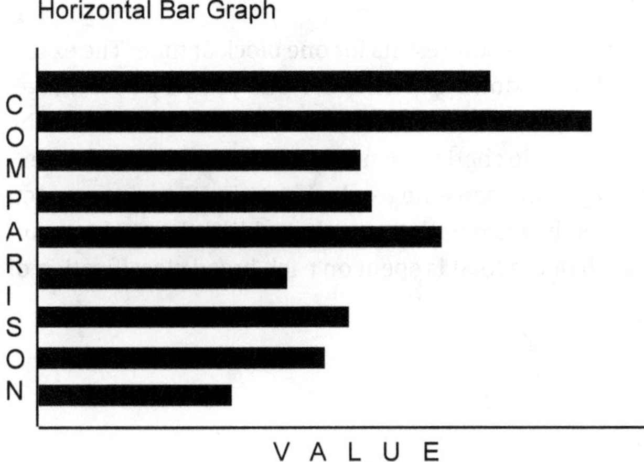

Figure C.3: Horizontal Bar Graph

When the value results are shown for several different comparisons, the bars themselves can be coded, as shown in Figure C.4. Sales results are shown for four different divisions in the same year, and each bar has a different color or shading.

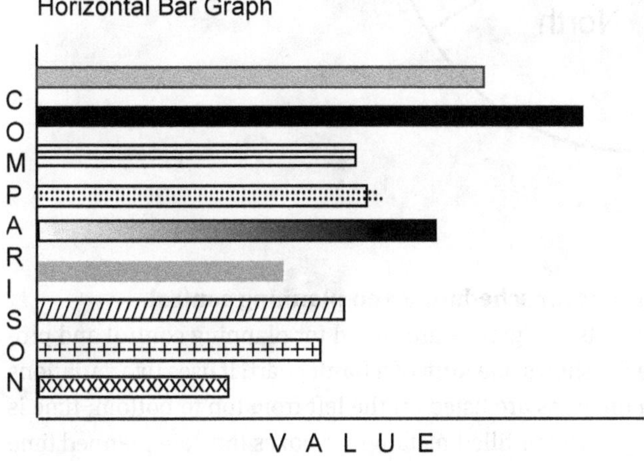

Figure C.4: Horizontal Bar Graph (coded)

d. Pie chart:

This chart is also used to report results for one block of time. The example in Figure C.5 breaks down expenses for one year, by percentage. While a line graph might show the relative dollar values of revenues by geographic region, the pie chart presents a visual breakdown of the entire year. Simply reporting percentages does not give the same impact. The pie chart makes the information visual, enabling the reader to understand how much of the total is spent on each broad classification of expense.

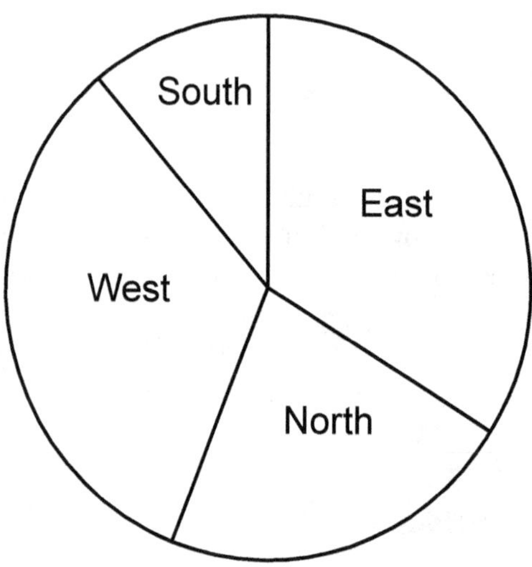

Figure C.5: Pie Chart

8. Use charts and graphs for scheduling and planning control.

Some specialized charts and graphs are suited for planning control and project scheduling. Figure C.6 shows one form of a Gantt chart; it uses two variations of rectangular boxes. Functions are listed on the left from top to bottom; time is reflected from left to right. The unfilled rectangular boxes indicate planned time required for each task, and the filled boxes are used for actual time. Because this chart allows you to see at a glance how planning and implementation are working, this technique is especially useful for complex projects requiring numerous functions. It helps you to anticipate time delays well in advance since many functions overlap in time.

Gantt Chart

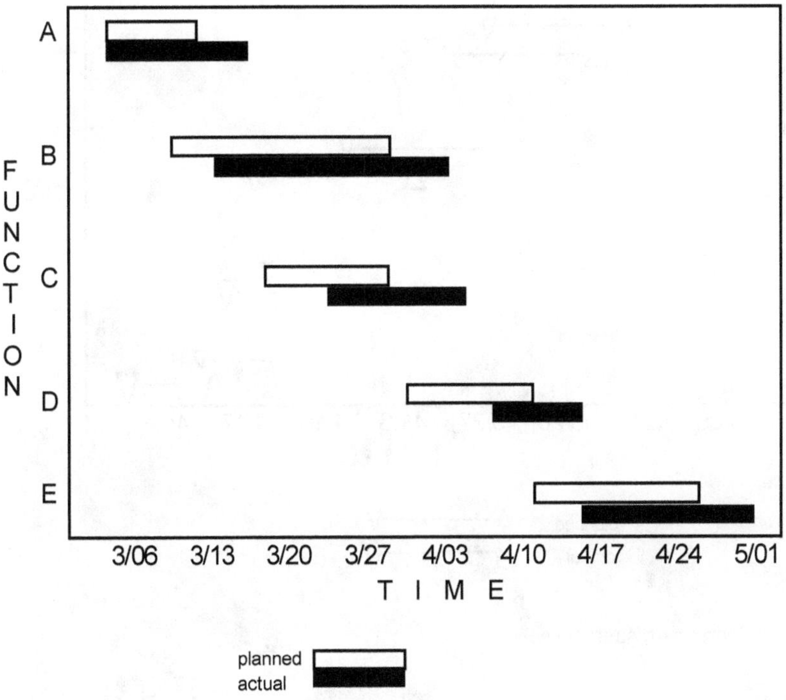

Figure C.6: Gantt Chart

An alternative method involves using blank or filled-in triangles to reflect the same information. In Figure C.7, a triangle pointing upward indicates the starting point; a triangle pointing downward is the planned or actual completion date. The advantage of this type of Gantt chart is that the planned and actual scheduling can all be placed on a single line.

Gantt Chart, Alternative Symbols

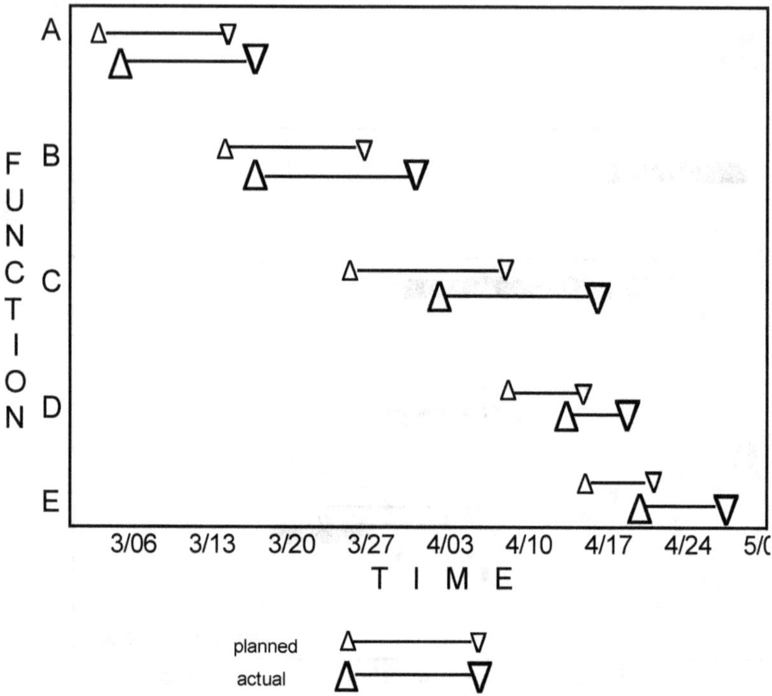

Figure C.7: Gantt Chart, Alternative Symbols

9. Use charts and graphs to improve presentations.

When making presentations at meetings, use charts and graphs to convey information clearly and effectively. Most people retain visual information more completely than they do written or verbal information.

Following are some guidelines:

1. *Keep it simple.* The more complex the diagrams, drawings, and other visual aids are, the less effective they are. Artwork should be extremely easy to grasp, and should be used to support a point you are trying to make. Think of the figure as a tool to improve conveying the information, never as an excuse for a complete, clear explanation.
2. *Keep words to a minimum.* Having too much to read on what is supposed to be a visual aid defeats the purpose. The fewer words, the better. Never use a figure that consists only of words.

3. *Keep all figures at the same scale when possible.* If you are conveying similar types of information through the use of figures, keep the scale the same whenever possible. If you are forced to alter the scale because of sizing and presentation, be sure to point out to your audience that what they are viewing is not comparable to other artwork.
4. *Two to three colors are enough.* With modern technology, the production of multicolor artwork is simple. Nevertheless, avoid overly colorful and elaborate graphics, which can be confusing or take too much effort to figure out. Simplicity is still the best way to convey information so that your audience's interest remains high.

Circa (ca.)

The term *circa* is Latin, used to describe a date or date range, and meaning "about." It is used when a specific year is not known. It is abbreviated "ca." in common use; and may also be abbreviated "c," "circ." or "cca."

Examples of circa reference:

The period of operations was c. 1910–1923. (1910 is "about" and 1923 is known.)
Founders first met from c. 1885–c. 1890. (Both years are estimates.)
The chairman and CEO was born ca. 1955.
Systems were first developed circa 1950.

Circular arguments

The *circular argument* (also called circular reasoning) describes a statement producing a logical fallacy, but no real information. This argument may appear true at first read, but contains the defect of relying on a false premise for the conclusion. This should be avoided in professional communication.

A circular argument arises when the writer believes the initial premise but is unable to prove it, or it is the result of unclear writing and poorly developed assumptions. A common form of circular argument declares that two separate facts support one another, but in fact they do not: "A is true because B is true" is the beginning of the circle. It is completed with the conclusion that "B is true because A is true." There is no basis to believe either statement; it is conclusion without basis. Another circular argument simply adds justification that is fallacious.

Examples:

We had a higher profit last quarter because the previous quarter's profits were lower.

The negative variance in the expense budget was caused by spending more money than the budget estimated.

The solution worked because it solved the problem.

A profitable quarter is defined as a quarter with profits rather than losses.

Watch for unintended circular arguments in writing and examine better methods for expressing ideas.

Citations

Some business reports, published papers, and correspondence refer to other works. In such cases, crediting the source is necessary. This is the case when:

1. The source is statistical, and citing it adds credibility to the report.
2. A quotation or conclusion makes a point for the report and the citation is necessary to verify information.
3. The information presented was developed by someone else or comes from a separate source, published or unpublished.

The citation acknowledges not only the source, but also authorship of material used from another source. It also enables readers to go to the original source and read further, verify context, and confirm the points made in the document.

This section describes the types of citations and their formats. A format should be selected for applicability to the document, and should be used consistently throughout. The three primary formats are APA (American Psychological Association); Chicago; and MLA (Modern Language Association).

APA is used for writing in the social sciences and business publications, and is most often seen in professional and peer-reviewed papers. Chicago style (also called Turabian) is also used for business publication and in the fine arts. MLA is most often used in the humanities.

Entries in endnotes (covered later in this section; see also Annotation, Endnotes) normally include page or section numbers in addition to author and publication; bibliography citations may or may not include page or section numbers, but it should be organized consistently (see also Bibliography).

1. **Cite your sources in a bibliography.**

The bibliography is a section at the end of reports, books, or memos that lists the sources used as reference material. It may contain a number of sources that are not specifically cited within the document, or specific references in text may be made by using footnotes to the sources. To ensure applicability of bibliographic entries, the material within the document should relate to each biographic entry by footnote, endnote, or in-text reference. Avoid including sources in the bibliography that are not related directly to the document's arguments or points.

a. **Book citations:**

The format for citation varies considerably, depending on the purpose of the document and the publishing medium; however, some general rules should be followed for all citations from books. Entries are organized in alphabetical order by (primary) author's last name. Each entry contains the title, the city of publication, the publisher, and the year of publication. Specific sequence depends on which style is used; however, a list of citations should use the same style consistently.

- Author. Author names are shown by last name and, depending on style, first name or first initial. When there is an editor rather than an author, the abbreviation Ed. is shown after the name. When two authors are credited, their names are listed in the same order in which they appear on the title page. When more than three authors are included, the first use of the citation includes all names; subsequent reference has the first author's name listed, followed by the abbreviation et al. (Lt., "and others").
- Title. The title of the book follows, and is placed in italics, ending with a period. If the title itself includes sentence endings other than a period (such as exclamation or question marks), those are used in place of the period.
- Place of publication. The city in which the book was published is listed next. If the city is well known (such as New York or Boston), no state is included in most instances. If the preference is to list city and state (or city and country), that style should be applied consistently. If the city of publication is obscure, the city name should be followed by a comma and the state abbreviation. The city of publication segment is ended with a colon.
- Publisher. Next comes the publisher's name. If the publisher's name includes ending terms like "and Company," "& Sons" or "Inc.," such

additions may be excluded or, if included, should be used consistently.

- Date. The entry includes the date, which appears within the citation depending on the style. A date may be restricted to the year (for books) or for a specific period (month, months, season, or day and month, for example).

For books, the following comparative listings for each of the three most common styles are shown for footnotes or endnotes (the entry for bibliography is identical but page numbers may be excluded):

APA

Evans, W. (1992). *Border Crossings*. Scarborough, Ont.: Prentice-Hall Canada, p. 16.

MLA

Evans, Wendy. *Border Crossings*. Scarborough, Ont.: Prentice-Hall Canada, 1992.

Chicago

Wendy Evans, *Border Crossings* (Scarborough, Ont.: Prentice-Hall Canada, 1992, 16).

In Chicago style, the footnote or endnote is as shown above, but the bibliography is different:

Chicago style bibliography entry

Evans, Wendy. *Border Crossings*: Scarborough, Ont.: Prentice-Hall Canada, 1992.

Entries are arranged alphabetically by the first-appearing last name. When three or more authors are involved, the first reference lists all three; subsequent references list first author's last name followed by *et. al.* Whenever "et al." or another author is listed, a comma must both follow and precede the first author's name.

When the book is not authored by an individual, list the organization's name as author.

Citation for a book authored by an organization: (Chicago style)

Consumer Guide. *Money-Saving Toll-Free Phone Book.* New York: Beekman House, 1983.

b. Magazine, periodical, and newspaper citations:

The format for citing articles in newspapers and magazines is similar to that of books, as are the rules for method of citation. The article's title or headline is included in regular text font and set off with quotation marks in some styles, as well as the main publication in italics. In addition, the publication volume number, month, and page numbers are included. For a newspaper or other periodical published other than monthly, the precise date is given.

Magazine and periodical citations:

APA:

Rindlaub, J. (July 1995). Steering to Prosperity. *Washington CEO*, 49.

MLA:

Rindlaub, John. "Steering to Prosperity." *Washington CEO*, (July 1995): 49.

Chicago:

John Rindlaub, "Steering to Prosperity," *Washington CEO* (July 1995): 49.

c. Unpublished works:

Follow the same format as for published works to the degree possible (author, title, source, year).

APA:

Brown, M. (February 24, 1996). *Solving the Automated Transition Problem*. Speech presented at Ames Corp. seminar.

MLA:

Brown, Martha. "Solving the Automated Transition Problem." Speech presented at Ames Corp. seminar, February 24, 1996.

Chicago:

Martha Brown, "Solving the Automated Transition Problem." (Speech presented at Ames Corp. seminar, February 24, 1996).

2. Place book citations properly.

Within the body of the report or book, specific reference to sources is given in one of several ways.

a. Within the narrative:

The author's last name and the publication date are given in some styles; in others, only a footnote or endnote number is given, and the full citation is included within the note itself but not in the text. The complete citation is given in the bibliography, and when page numbers are included in the note, the bibliography is more likely to refer only to the work but not to specific pages or sections.

Example:

A recent survey (Smith, 1996) reveals that the majority of such cases are not profitable.

The complete citation for Smith is listed in the reference section at the end of the paper. When a work includes multiple publications by the same author, they are distinguished by specifying the year: (Smith, 1996) versus (Smith, 1998). When both appeared in the same year the works are distinguished by letters: (Smith, 1996a) versus (Smith, 1996b).

b. **Footnotes and endnotes:**

An asterisk or numbered reference in the text is accompanied by a note at the bottom of the page, in one of two ways: (1) the author and year alone are given, as in [a] above; or the full author and book title are given in the first such reference, with the author's last name and a shortened title only in subsequent references.

Footnotes appear at the bottom of each page and commonly are used in reports or articles. Endnotes (end of chapter or end of book) are more often used in books. For e-book editions in which page numbers do not appear, endnotes may be converted to footnotes.

c. **Repetitive references:**

When the same source is cited more than once, an abbreviated form is used in footnotes and endnotes. When the source follows immediately, the term *ibid.* is used. This Latin reference means "in the same source (or place)." When the source is the same but the page is different, it is specified in the second entry.

Example:

(16) Hayakawa, S. I. (1964). *Language in Thought and Action*, 2nd ed. New York: Harcourt, Brace & World, p. 80.
(17) *Ibid.*, p. 102.

When the same source is used but does not follow the original entry immediately, the last name is followed by a comma and the term *Op. Cit.* (work cited).

Example:

(16) Hayakawa, S. I. (1964). *Language in Thought and Action*, 2nd ed. New York: Harcourt, Brace & World, p. 80.
(17) Berger, J. (2013). *Contagious, Why Things Catch On.* New York: Simon & Schuster, pp. 117–119.
(18) *Hayakawa, Op. Cit.*, p. 102.

3. Ensure accuracy in meaning and context.

Accuracy in citations is essential for a publication to be perceived as reliable and in proper context. By citing partially, inaccurately, or out of context, the meaning can be changed or distorted, or even changed entirely. Such practices should always be avoided.

a. Accuracy

An example of inaccuracy in a citation follows, in which the meaning of the full statement is changed by exclusion:

Original full statement:

> The financial obligations of an organization include not only accurate financial reporting, but should not ignore all material facts, which must be disclosed within footnote sections.

Inaccurate citation:

> The financial obligations of an organization ... [may] ignore all material facts ... within footnote sections.

b. Context

Beyond inaccuracy, the context of a citation should be appropriate and should apply to the discussion underway at the point of the citation itself.

Original full statement:

> With some exceptions, employees are required to report instances of safety violations or failure of internal systems. Compliance is the sole obligation of the risk management team, to ensure factory safety and quality control.

Out-of-context citation:

> employees are required to report instances of safety violations or failure of internal systems ... the sole obligation ... to ensure compliance with factory safety and quality control.

4. Use citation generators

Many online citation generators allow for selection of citation by style and may even look up publications and provide the proper citation format. These include:

http://www.citationmachine.net
http://www.easybib.com/
http://www.citethisforme.com/us/citation-generator
http://www.bibme.org/

Clauses

The use of independent and dependent *clauses* helps express thoughts clearly and ensures consistency and strength in the expression of ideas.

1. **Independent clauses**

An independent clause expresses a complete thought with a complete sentence.

Examples, incomplete clauses:

The teacher and the student

Managers and employees

Examples, independent clauses:

The teacher met with the student.

Managers and employees talked regularly.

2. **Dependent clauses**

The dependent clause consists of subject and action (noun and verb) but is not a complete thought. It begins with a marker word at the beginning of the clause, such as "when" or "if."

Examples, dependent clauses:

When the board met to discuss financial reports ...

If the budget variances are relatively low ...

The thought was incomplete in both instances and requires completion to create an independent clause. This requires a coordinating conjunction or marker word.

A coordinating conjunction sets up completion of the thought. Examples include "and," "but," and "so."

Examples of coordinating conjunctions:

The board met to discuss the financial report, <u>and</u> offered three suggestions.

The budget variations were relatively low, <u>so</u> no adjustments were made.

Marker words include "however," "also," and "therefore." These may be entered in the clause following commas or semicolons.

Examples of marker words:

The board met to discuss the financial reports, <u>also</u> to offer suggestions.

The budget variations were relatively low; <u>therefore</u> no changes were made.

3. Comma splices

Avoid the comma splices, which is the use of a comma to join two independent clauses. The replacement of a comma with a period is more effective in expressing the two ideas. Replacing the comma with a semicolon is appropriate when it transforms the independent clauses into a single dependent clause.

Examples, comma splices:

The newly hired manager changed everything, it was disruptive.

Reports generated from our department were routine, no one read them.

Creative ideas were stated in the marketing department, no one followed up.

Examples, comma splices corrected:

The newly hired manager changed everything. It was disruptive.

Reports generated from our department were routine; no one read them.

Creative ideas were stated in the marketing department, but no one followed up.

4. Run-on sentences

The longer the sentence, the harder it is to read. In a book avoid sentences more than two lines. In extreme cases, two independent clauses that are not separated with the use of punctuation, creates a run-on sentence This is grammatically incorrect, but is fixed easily with punctuation.

Examples, run-on sentences:

Our president is not involved in daily operations she is a big picture thinker.

Employees avoided overtime on weekends they preferred time with family.

Examples, correcting run-on sentences by separating independent clauses:

Our president is not involved in daily operations. She is a big picture thinker.

Employees avoided overtime on weekends; they preferred time with family.

Cleft sentences

Cleft sentences contain a main clause and a dependent clause. The same idea could be expressed with a simple sentence, but the cleft format adds emphasis and intonation.

Examples, simple sentences:

Our directors preferred a meeting away from headquarters.

The book's outline was executed by the ghost writer.

Examples, transformation into cleft sentences:

What directors preferred was a meeting away from headquarters.
It was the ghost writer who executed the book's outline.

A cleft sentence is formed with an initial word such as "what" or "it." Used properly, the cleft sentence adds variety and emphasis. Over-used, it may create an archaic tone to a professional document, so the cleft construction should be used sparingly.

The noun phrase is usually the point of emphasis in a cleft sentence. However, the same construction is accomplished through a prepositional phrase ("It was the desire ..."), an adverbial phrase ("What was hurriedly decided ..."), or an adverbial clause ("Because management was so concerned ...").

Clichés

A cliché is a form of expression familiar to people and identifies a range of sentiments. However, expressions classified as cliché tend to lose their meaning due to overuse. A cliché becomes an easy or even lazy method for self-expression.

1. Avoid cliché expressions.

Some writers fall into the habit of using clichés, hoping to convey an idea efficiently. Unfortunately, the use of clichés is distracting and reduces the effectiveness of writing.

A cliché:

We are in a "Catch-22" situation.

A better choice:

The negative outcomes are unavoidable.

A cliché:

It's six of one, a half dozen of the other.

A better choice:

It doesn't make any difference.

Cliché expressions common to business situations:

A-OK
add insult to injury
all and sundry
all things being equal
at the end of the day

back to the drawing board
back to the salt mine
be that as it may
beat a dead horse
beat around the bush
bed of roses
behind the eight-ball
beside the point
bird in the hand
bite the bullet
bottom line
brain trust
business as usual
cast pearls before swine
catch as catch can
child's play
clear the air
cold feet
conspiracy of silence
cream of the crop
cut-and-dried
damn with faint praise
dog eat dog
dot the i's and cross the t's
draw a blank
Dutch treat
dyed in the wool
easy pickings
eleventh hour
embarrassment of riches
enemy at the gate
explore every avenue
fact of the matter
fair and square
fair to middling
far and away
far cry
fat cat
feast or famine

feel the pinch
few and far between
fine-tooth comb
finger in every pie
first magnitude
fish out of water
fits and starts
fly in the face of
follow in the footsteps
for what it's worth
force to be reckoned with
fortunes of war
from A to Z
from bad to worse
full head of steam
get a handle on it
get a leg up on
get in on the ground floor
get to the bottom of it
give pause
go against the grain
go for broke
go hat in hand
go it alone
go time
grin and bear it
grist for the mill
half the battle
hand in glove
hand over fist
handwriting on the wall
hard and fast
head in the clouds
heads will roll
hem and haw
here and now
high and dry
high-water mark
hit or miss

hit pay dirt
hit the nail on the head
hog the limelight
hoist by his own petard
hold at bay
hold the fort
hold your own
hope against hope
huff and puff
if worse comes to worst
ill-gotten gains
in a nutshell
in a word
in hot water
in the bag
in the long run
ivory tower
jaundiced eye
keep the ball rolling
kid-glove treatment
know the ropes
knuckle under
last but not least
last legs
last resort
last straw
lay our cards on the table
leave no stone unturned
left hand doesn't know what the right hand is doing
left in the lurch
left to your own devices
lesser of two evils
let sleeping dogs lie
let the chips fall where they may
let's face it
letter perfect
lion's share
long and the short of it
long shot

long suit
looking down his nose
lost cause
loud and clear
low man on the totem pole
make a virtue of necessity
make ends meet
make no bones about it
man of few words
man of the hour
mark my words
mind over matter
mine of information
moment of truth
moral victory
more or less
movers and shakers
naked truth
needless to say
nothing to write home about
off and running
on the ball
on the carpet
on the level
on the ropes
open secret
out of the woods
out on a limb
pack it in
part and parcel
pay the piper
pay through the nose
penny wise and pound foolish
pick and choose
pick your brain
play it by ear
play with fire
point of no return
pound of flesh

powers that be
pull it off
pull out all the stops
pull strings
pure and simple
push comes to shove
put on hold
put on the back burner
put your best foot forward
quick study
rack your brain
rat race
read the tea leaves
rings a bell
roll with the punches
rule of thumb
run of the mill
saving face
second to none
see it through
see red
see the light
sign of the times
sit tight
sitting pretty
six of one, half a dozen of the other
sixth sense
sky's the limit
smoke it out
snow job
so far, so good
sooner or later
spill the beans
steer clear of
straight from the shoulder
take it or leave it
take it with a grain of salt
taken to the cleaners
tell tales out of school

tempest in a teapot
that being said
then and there
there's the rub
throw caution to the wind
tighten your belt
time and again
tip of the iceberg
tit for tat
toe the line
too many irons in the fire
too much of a good thing
tough nut to crack
tower of strength
truth be told
turn a deaf ear
turn back the clock
turning point
two sides to every question
unwritten law
up to snuff
uphill battle
vested interest
vicious circle
watchful eye
wave of the future
wearing two hats
well and good
when all is said and done
whys and wherefores
win hands down
wing it
wishful thinking
word to the wise
world of good
year in and year out
you get what you pay for

Coinage of words

In organizations, internal style often includes coined words and phrases unique to that organization (or department). For example, an organization based in Australia with an office in Japan adopted the use of Japanese words for "one" (*ichi*) as well as "one, two, three" (*ichi, ni, san*) in internal discussions and memos.

Examples, coined words:

We will address these concerns *ichi* by *ichi*.

Let's follow the process correctly, *ichi, ni, san*.

Another example used a nickname for the chairman of the company ("Bud") to describe situations requiring approval at the top level.

Examples, nicknames to coin a phrase:

Was this proposal Bud-verified?

The larger budget will require an Act of Bud.

Many commonly used words originally were coined by authors in published works. Examples include *Yahoo*, invested by Jonathan Swift's 1726 book, *Gulliver's Travels*. The Yahoos were a race of violent people. It soon became incorporated as a coined word to describe anyone who was violent or uncultured.

The word *freelance* is used popularly to describe independent contractors or experts for hire, versus employees; it is most often used to describe independent authors or journalists working as stringers. This term first appeared in Sir Walter Scott's 1819 book, *Ivanhoe*. The term described a mercenary soldier or knight offering to fight for payment without allegiance to a political or national cause.

More recently, the term *nerd* first appeared in 1950, in the work by Dr. Seuss entitled *If I Ran the Zoo*. The word was a made-up reference without a specific definition:

> "And then, just to show them, I'll sail to Ka-Troo/And Bring Back an It-Kutch, a Preep, and a Proo,/A Nerkle, a Nerd, and a Seersucker too!"

Colloquialism

Usage of informal language or phrasing, which adds color and variety to expression of ideas, is generally described as *colloquialism*. This is not always appropriate in formal business style, but may be used to enliven reports or memos. This form is more often used in speech and less in the written word.

The derivative of the term is from *locution* (regarding idiom or style of expression), but often is mistakenly thought to mean *location* (a style of speech unique to a region or area). A colloquial expression is distinguished from jargon or slang, and refers to "natural" language and usage versus formal or grammatically rigid methods of expression.

Examples, colloquialism:

The con man bamboozled the unsuspecting consumers. (deceived)
That employee went bananas and had to be discharged. (insane or angry)
The department is suffering from the blues. (low morale)

Compound Words

A compound word is a term formed by two or more other separate words. It may be expressed as a single word *(workplace),* a hyphenated word *(mind-set),* or two words *(task force).* Often there is an authoritative source for using the word, such as a dictionary, but for many words, especially adjective forms, rules of usage depend on the circumstances.

1. Start by consulting a dictionary.

Determine whether there is an established style—single word, hyphenated, or two words—for a particular compound word. This is often the case for nouns.

2. Follow common usage.

Hyphenate a temporary compound word that is not in common usage or when custom does not dictate the creation of a single word. Many compound words that were originally hyphenated lose the hyphen with common usage. The current trend is to use fewer hyphenated compounds and more single words.

Examples:

The computer-literate group has a competitive advantage.
A craze-for-profits mood does not always mean good news for the customer.
Our make-do culture enables us to change with changing conditions.

3. Hyphenate adjective forms before a noun but not after.

Adjective form before a noun:

best-equipped department

Adjective form after a noun:

department is best equipped

4. **Be consistent in form.**

Strive for consistency of form within a document. When you are uncertain whether a compound word should be hyphenated or kept separate, choose a form and use it consistently throughout the document.

5. **Learn the rules of usage for hyphens.**

   a. **Use hyphens when the compound word takes the form of an adjective.**

      Examples:

      near-perfect marketing plan
      slow-profits year

   Do not hyphenate when the first half of the compound word ends in -ly.

      Examples:

      nearly perfect marketing plan
      disappointingly slow year

   b. **Do not use a hyphen when the compound word is a verb.**

      Examples:

      Be sure to follow up on the assignment.
      Let's run through the presentation.

6. **Close up words without hyphens when compounds are formed with prefixes.**

   Examples:

   antedate
   overflow
   biweekly
   postscript
   cooperate
   underreport

Conclusions

Conclusions are appropriate in reports, articles or books and serve one of several purposes: to summarize main points, to make recommendations, or to arrive at a logical belief.

1. Summarizing main points

A report that simply presents facts or research but fails to summarize the main points may be confusing and create a sense of incompleteness. A conclusion can be brief but add dramatic emphasis by summarizing the main points of the document. This may be accomplished in a narrative style or through a limited number of bullet points.

2. Make recommendations

A document may present a series of facts describing conditions or a situation, and conclude with recommendations based on a defined problem with one or more possible solutions.

3. Arrive at a logical belief

Another form of conclusion is the arrival at a logical belief. For example, based on revenue trends, a report could conclude that “distance from headquarters determines the rate of annual growth in revenues and profits.” This is a *logical* belief as long as the body of the document provides proof for the expressed belief.

Copyright

The *copyright* of material is the exclusive legal right of the originator of a work to its use and distribution. It is distinguished from a trademark or patent. Copyright is granted for intellectual property, and protects an expression of an idea but not necessarily the underlying idea itself.

1. Copyright notices

To claim a copyright, a notice of copyright should be affixed on a published or distributed document. A document originally published without this notice may be granted the same level of protection as a document containing the notice, even if the notice is later added.

A copyright may be held by an individual, several individuals, or an organization.

Example, summarized copyright notices:

© 2018 Andrew Smith

The initial notification can be expanded by describing that the claim of copyright is not limited. The term “All rights reserved” is found in documents making this claim. This can be further expanded with a more detailed explanation.

Example, expanded copyright claim notice:

> All rights reserved. No part of this publication may be reproduced, distributed, or transmitted in any form or by any means, including photocopying, recording, or other electronic or mechanical methods, without the prior written permission of the publisher, except in the case of brief quotations embodied in critical reviews and certain other noncommercial uses permitted by copyright law.

A copyright cannot be claimed for product names, organization or group names and titles, pseudonyms, the titles of books and other works, mottoes, slogans, or advertising catchphrases, or ingredient listings on products, in formulas, or in recipes. Documents produced by a government cannot be copyrighted.

2. Fair use doctrine

In writing a business document, copyright does not prevent the use of material developed by other people or organizations. Fair use applies, but in different degrees, in the United States, United Kingdom and Commonwealth countries, the European Union, and elsewhere. Fair use applies based on the purpose of use, the amount of copyrighted material used or cited, and any effect on the marketability of an original work due to secondary use. As a result, non-commercial use of certain formats is not protected by copyright law. The number of copies distributed, either through hard copy or electronically, may further limit fair use of material.

Fair use has to be limited in terms of the percentage of a work used. A brief citation that credits the original work is allowed under fair use, but song titles or lyrics, and lines of poems usually cannot be used even if only a limited portion is copied and cited. In cases of fair use, no permission is required in advance, but proper and complete source credit should always be given.

In education, a common percentage cited for fair use is 10 percent or less. In book publishing, the limit of 5 percent is often cited. For example, a book of 200,000 words could be the source for the use of 10,000 words or less under the fair use doctrine if the five percent rule applied.

Because copyright law and fair use are legal concepts, style based on extensive citation should be subjected to legal review if and when a document will be published and made available to a wide audience of readers.

Cross reference

Documents, articles, and books make frequent use of cross referencing. However, it is easily overused, making it more difficult for readers to track the text. As a first consideration, cross reference should be used only sparingly and only when necessary.

Cross reference takes several forms. It may be confined to a page source:

Budgetary variance explanations should be short but concise (see page 32).
They may include more detail: (See page 32, "The variance explanation")

Other forms of cross reference may be to an index, footnote, endnote, or other document.

1. General guidelines

Avoid excessive use of cross reference. When a brief explanation provides the same benefit, use that in place of a cross reference notation.

Example, cross reference:

Budgetary variation explanations should be short but concise (see page 32).

Example, in-text explanation:

Budgetary variation explanations should be short but concise. A one-sentence statement is adequate, such as "Original budget did not consider additions of personnel in the department."

Include the reason behind a cross reference rather than just the notation by itself:

Example, inadequate cross reference:

See Section 4

Example, cross reference with reason:

Further definitions of budgetary formats are found in Section 4.

2. Cross reference within the same document

When referring to another section of the same report, article, or book, be clear in the cross reference itself.

Examples:

Refer to "Budgetary formats," Section 4.
For expanded explanations, refer to Page 32, "Variance reporting."
A detailed example of variance reporting is provided in Appendix B.

When referring to other parts of the document, capitalize the cross reference: Section, Page, Appendix, Chapter, Paragraph, Figure, Table. Do not abbreviate these parts when used as cross references. Do not cross reference when the material is on the same page or a following page. In such cases, refer in a different manner (see below, see next page, or as shown above).

3. Cross reference to another document

When referring to a different document (report, book, or paper), cross reference has to be more specific. Include the title of the publication as part of a generalized reference format, followed by specific location within that document (chapter, page, section). Use consistent formatting for multiple references to other documents—cite in the same manner as elsewhere, and use consistent citation style.

D

Dangling modifiers

A *dangling modifier* is a word or word phrase modifying a word that is not made clear. The expression of an action must be identified clearly in order for an expression to be understood.

Examples of dangling modifiers:

After finishing the draft of the report, it was turned in.
Having entered the department, work assignments were given out.

In the first example, it is not clear who took the action of turning in the report. "After finishing" is a dangling modifier because it lacks identification. In the second example, "Having entered" is similarly lefty unassigned.

Corrected sentences:

After finishing the draft of the report, I turned it in.
Having entered the department, our manager gave out work assignments.

To correct a dangling modifier, these changes accomplish the corrections:

1. Name the person or other entity taking action.
2. Combine the phrase and clause into a single, connected expression.
3. Change the dangling modifier into a complete introductory clause.

Data analysis

In any presentation (in the form of a report, article, or book), a data set may be required to make a case. It is not adequate to express opinions or assume that conclusions are obvious. Data analysis is the process of critically evaluating a range of issues in order to determine validity and, as a result, to draw accurate and supportable conclusions.

A document lacking data analysis is subject to question if differing opinions about the meaning of the data set are presented. In order to respond to criticisms, the "body of evidence" supporting conclusions should be organized and expressed to make the case.

DOI 10.1515/9781547400218-004

1. The data matrix

Organization of data into a *data matrix* is a method when data consist of numerical and statistical information. Unlike citations in which other authorities are cited in support of a hypothesis or statistics, numerical information often is difficult to express without data matrices. In cases when conclusions are arrived at by analysis of a series of outcomes, the conclusion itself may be more powerfully articulated when the matrix is included (either within the narrative or as appendix material).

For example, a report concerning revenue, profits, and net return over a 20-year period will reveal a trend. Rather than merely stating the trend and discussing its significance, a 20-row table displaying all the results (and perhaps accompanied with a graph revealing the slope of the trend) strengthens the case. A table without interpretation has limited value; the interpretation of data—the data analysis—is where conclusions are reached, based on what the data reveal. In order to measure numerical outcomes, four specific statistical methods are useful:

1. **Ratios** express the significance of larger numbers to one another when the numbers themselves may not present the relationship clearly.
2. **Nominal** distinctions of data are essential in order to explain data. These distinctions may include financial values, divisions of an organization, and time periods (months, quarters, or years, for example).
3. **Ordinal** values are used to set sequences of data. For example, a series of financial outcomes for 12 regions of the country may be organized geographically, but that provides less impact than the ordinal arrangement from best to worst, or newest to oldest, for example.
4. **Interval** values are organizational but do not add to statistical significance. For example, in a lengthy data set, the lists may be assigned numbers beginning with "1" or "a" for the purpose of distinguishing them from one another.

2. Distributions of data

An *empirical frequency distribution* is required for statistical data when a listing of outcomes contain values and variables, not only based on outcomes but in relation to one another. For example, a ratio analysis could assume the expected outcome of 8% net return. Not only is a list of outcomes compared to that standard, but to one another as well.

In other forms of data, outcomes may be based on variation among observed events. For example, product tests in several locations are not expected to be identical, but should fall within a range of distributed outcomes. The data analysis relies on this expected range of outcomes to validate the assumptions of a test.

The *relative frequency* organizes frequency distribution into a summarized ratio or percentage to provide relative meaning to the outcomes. Each instance is divided by the total to develop a ratio of the outcome to the whole, or a percentage of outcome parts per 100.

3. Central tendency

The distribution of data sets contains a *central tendency*, or either a mean or average of the entire population sample. Identifying this mean or average is essential in evaluating data sets, because it describes the expectation that will be applied against outcomes, notably against those outcomes far removed from the center.

a. Mean

The *mean* (average) in its most basic form (simple average, or A) is derived by adding together the values in a field (V), and then dividing the result by the total number of values (n):

$$(V_1 + V_2 + ... V_n) \div n = A$$

The simple average (A) is the most rudimentary version of the mean. This may be further modified by weighting the latest entries, with a more complex version called exponential moving average (EMA).

To ensure accuracy of the calculated mean, exceptional spikes, or values outside of a typical or representative range, may be excluded to avoid distortion of outcomes. Removal of these outliers, or spikes, results in a *trimmed mean.*

b. Median

The *median* is the value in an outcome that represents the midpoint in the full range. Half of the outcomes should be above, and the other half below the median. This is a variation of the central tendency based on the *range* of the distribution rather than on its mean. When the number of values (n) is odd, the median (M) is found by adding "1" to the total, and then dividing by "2":

$$(n + 1) \div 2 = M$$

For example, in a field of 99 values, median is calculated as:

$$(99+1) \div 2 = 50$$

When the number of values (n) is even, the median (M) will be a partial number and is calculated by adding "1" to the total, dividing by two and then finding the central value. For example, when the median is halfway between 50 and 52, the median is 51.

c. **Mode**

The third variety of central tendency is *mode*, which is the value appearing most often. This may not be central in the same sense as mean or median. For example, in a series of recent property sales, the average sales price was $415,000 but one price—$419,500—appeared three times and no other prices appeared more than once. The value of $419,500 is the mode. When one value appears the same number of times, it is called a *unimodal* outcome. When two or more different outcomes appear the same number of times, the result is a *multimodal* outcome.

The mode is most useful in statistical analysis when several choices are presented. For example, in a survey of 200 customers, a product was presented and several choices were given in response: Prefer, do not prefer, uncertain, and no opinion. The results:

Prefer	63
Do not prefer	41
Uncertain	40
No opinion	56

In this case, "Prefer" was the mode. The fact that this response occurred 31.5% of the time is not as conclusive because there were four choices and the range of outcomes was not itself significant. In drawing a conclusion, the mode serves a different purpose than mean or median.

4. Data reliability

Another aspect of analysis is the determination of *data reliability*. This is determined by testing for consistency. When a wide range of outcomes occurs, it draws reliability into question. Statistical measurements of samples versus larger populations may reveal a lack of reliability caused by poor sample selection. For example, a survey of customers may not consist of "typical" customers based on location, time of day, and questions posed. The analysis of reliability often is overlooked, but may represent the most crucial determining factor for reliability of results.

A related factor is *validity*, which expands on reliability to ensure that the sample tested is representative of the greater population. Reliability refers to the applicability of samples and statistical methods. Validity refers to whether the correct set of assumptions was applied in data analysis. For example, in surveying employees in six operating sectors, respondents were asked to critically evaluate management's effectiveness. If the results are anonymous, they may be more valid than when respondents are identified. Fear of retaliation for a negative report will tend to distort the validity, since respondents are less likely to provide honest responses.

Databases

A database is a collection of related data in one or more forms. A database management system (DBMS) is an automated application that enables data to be arranged and sorted for retrieval based on one or more key fields within the database.

The database may exist in a simple format such as a document file or spreadsheet; or it may be a more complex program enabling end users to execute functions. The functional groups within a software-specific database should be defined to include data definition (specific attributes that describe the organization and relationship of data); method and timing of updates (additions, deletions, and modifications of data); retrieval methods (methods for manipulating or entering selections and key fields); and methods for administering and securing the database (monitoring users, allowing and limiting access, developing controls and security measures, and backup systems to offset corruption or system failures).

These primary elements are included in written descriptions and design of database systems. A non-technical business writer developing documentation for database processes and controls will coordinate the effort with technical experts, programmers, and database designers to ensure that complete systematic procedures and security protocols are put in place. Among additional considerations in writing procedures and controls are performance capabilities, need for training, scalability of the database, resilience of software, and methods of access.

Data collection methods

The initial test of data value is found in *correlation* among results. When results from several sources are similar, it tends to validate the quality of methods; when results are poorly correlated, there is a greater likelihood of less value in the method. This may lead to evaluation of initial data collection methods and adjustments required to improve correlation.

Data collection methods rely on the accuracy of testing—questions in a survey, for example. If questions are leading or incomplete, the method will be flawed. A high correlation of outcomes from different sources confirms validity, whereas a largely variable outcome indicates poor correlation. For example, a test for a new food product showed high approval when tests occurred in supermarkets between 5 p.m. and 6 p.m. on weekdays; and very low approval rates in midday and weekend tests. Analysis revealed that the primary shopper (shopping at midday or on the weekend) applied more critical tests of ingredients and price, and non-primary shoppers (for example, a spouse stopping at the store for milk on the way home) was more interested in taste. Consequently, the two sample groups were dissimilar. The lack of correlation revealed that emphasis of days and times should have focused on the primary shopper.

A similar range of qualifications apply to data collection methods of all types. For example, a test designed to determine why a second shift in a three-shift factory had a much greater error rate than the other two shifts was inconclusive at first. Assumptions ranged from poor supervision to differences in performance at various times of day. Once the data collection methods were more closely evaluated, the reason was clear. The second shift was used for all trainees, where a higher error rate was expected.

Data matrices

Many internal reports and other business documents show conclusions or give scant coverage to the source data. Consequently, a reader cannot know whether the report is based on valid analysis or even a detailed data set.

Including *data matrices* within a document (if brief) or in an appendix (if extensive) adds great value to the document. This applies when numerical information is included. For example, in a financial report comparing four divisions and their operating results, a statement may be included that "only the Midwest division showed improvement; the other three divisional results were flat or declined." This conclusion provides no proof of the outcomes and does not articulate the degree of outcomes in comparative form. A multi-column table showing the revenue, direct costs, gross profit, expenses, operating profit, other income and expenses, and net profit for each of the divisions (with additional columns for each line's percentage to revenues) supports the conclusion and provides the reader with an accurate data matrix of the results (see also Data analysis).

The need for data matrices is especially crucial when involving financial information, which represents a large proportion of internal reports. Too often, the report explains the results without showing them, so that a reader has to rely on the report writer's interpretation. This may lead to inaccuracies. For example, a report concludes that "the Western division was the worst performing, with revenue at only 70% of the average of the other three divisions." However, the report did not include a data matrix summarizing this. It also failed to realize that the Western division suffered a catastrophic fire and was down for four months. By annualizing the outcomes during fully operational months, the conclusion would have been quite different (for example, 70% of the average yielded over eight months would be annualized as 105%, or far better than the average: *70% ÷ 8 months * 12 months = 105%*). This could be documented within a data matrix, so that outcomes would be clarified.

Dates and times

The expression of dates and times should be made consistently within a document. Although this may seem obvious and simple, the selection of style for dates and times is complex and many choices are available.

1. **Dates**

   The use of dashes and number of digits to employ in expressing years, months, and dates is made complex when multiple date ranges are involved.

   a. **Year**

   When expressing a range of dates, use a connector word (between, or, from/to) or a dash, but not both. Never use a slash to reflect a date range.

   Example:

   From 1999–2006 (incorrect)
   Between 1999–2006 (incorrect)
   1999/2006 (incorrect)
   From 1999 to 2006 (correct)
   1999–2006 (correct)

   Use the same number of digits to reflect year range. The full four-digit format is preferable.

   Example:

   2001–03 (incorrect)
   2001–2003 (correct)

   b. **Month and year**

   Be consistent in reporting a combination of month and year. Spell out months when used on both sides of the expression:

Example:

Dec 2007 to Jun 2009 (incorrect)
December 2007 to June 2009 (correct)
Between Dec 2007–Jun 2009 (incorrect)
Between December 2007 and June 2009 (correct)

Months may be expressed in a similar manner. For example, March–June is appropriate but Mar–Jun is not. The months are spelled out.

Months also may be abbreviated numerically. January 4 may be reported as 1/4 or 01/04 in common usage. Three formats are in use:

YMD (year, month, day) – 2016/04/15
DMY (day, month, year) – 15/04/16
MDY (month, day, year) – 04/15/16

Usage varies by country.

Examples:

Germany, United Kingdom, India: YMD or DMY
United States: MDY
France, Brazil, Russia: DMY
China, Japan: YMD

c. **Days**

Reporting days within a date should also be consistent. Day-to-day reporting employs several formats.

Example:

5–10 February, 2011
January 5–10, 2016
13 June 2006 – 17 February 2011

Days of the week are always capitalized, either when spelled out or abbreviated. When using the abbreviated form, place a period after the day:

Sunday or Sun.
Monday or Mon.
Tuesday or Tue.
Wednesday or Wed.
Thursday or Thu.
Friday or Fri.
Saturday or Sat.

d. Approximate dates

Report estimated or approximate dates with the use of c. (circa), but avoid use of ca. Use c. 1650 but not ca. 1650.

When a range of dates applies, use the same rules for connectors. For example, c. 1650–1685 but not ca. 1650–1685. When both dates are estimates, use the distinguishing label for both. For example, c. 1650–c. 1665.

It is also acceptable to estimate dates based on known limitations. For example, "before 1650" or "after 1685." When specific dates are not known, a rare but acceptable qualifier is fl. Meaning "flourishing" during a known period. For example, name (fl. 1650–1685).

e. Seasons

Season names are not capitalized in most applications: summer, not Summer. This is an inconsistency of style, since days of the week and months are capitalized. The exception is when the name of the season appears in personalized form. In this instance, subsequent seasonal references are also capitalized:

Example:

Summer Olympics are followed by colder Autumn weather. (correct)

Summer Olympics precede fall weather changes. (incorrect)

The connector with capitalized proper nouns (Summer Olympics) carries over to the later reference to another season.

f. Decades

Four digits are always used when referring to decades. For example, 1990's is acceptable but not the 90's, the 1990s' or 1990-ies. Under both APA and Chicago style, no apostrophe is used before the 's' when expressing a decade. When referring to part of a decade, hyphenate before the numerical portion: mid-1990s or post-1980s.

It is also acceptable to spell out the name of a decade: Nineties, Eighties, or Seventies. However, for the first decade of a century, the proper usage is unclear. The decade between 2000 and 2009 may be called the naughts, aughts, or zeroes, but these are awkward. It is preferable to specify the decade numerically in this case to avoid confusion.

g. Centuries

When referring to centuries in the current period (AD, or *Anno Domini, year of our Lord*). This may also be referred to as CE (*Common Era, Cur-*

rent Era, or *Christian Era*). As a general guideline, if a year occurs between zero and the current time, it is not necessary to specify it as AD unless other references to the prior period are also involved.

References prior to the current era are abbreviated as BC (*before Christ*). This also may be called BCE (*before Common Era*, *before Christian Era*, or *before Current Era*).

The distinctions may be placed either before or after the year, and no periods are included.

Examples:

462 BC (correct)
462 B.C. (incorrect but often used)
AD 315 (correct)
BC 462 (incorrect)

References BC, BCE, and CE appear after the year. However, AD should appear before the year because it is an abbreviation of a Latin phrase. Placement ahead of the year makes this distinction.

When referring to specific centuries, do not use Roman numerals. Either spell out the name or use numerical abbreviations.

Examples:

XVII century (incorrect)
Seventeenth Century (incorrect)
17th Century (correct)

When the century is referred to as a hyphenated expression, it is not capitalized. For example, "seventeenth-century governments" or "14th-century literature" are correct expressions.

2. Times

In expressing time of day, a 12-hour mode requires identification of the period from midnight to noon (a.m., or *ante meridiem*) and from noon to midnight (p.m., or *post meridiem*). An exception occurs when other clarifications are included to describe time of day.

Examples:

We will meet at 10 this morning.
The event is scheduled for 6 this evening.
The afternoon appointment is for 2 o'clock.

The use of "o'clock" is not required, however, and is becoming less common.

a. Time modes

The 12-hour time mode is most often used in the United States, Canada, and Australia.

The 24-hour clock is used in most other parts of the world and in the military. It is also called the "International Standard" for reporting time. This eliminates the need to clarify a.m. or p.m. since none of the specific hours are repeated in the 24-hour clock. The conversion from 12-hour to 24-hour involves adding 12 for all p.m. hours, as shown in the table below.

12-hour time	24-hour time	12-hour time	24-hour time
1 a.m.	01:00	2 a.m.	02:00
3 a.m.	03:00	4 a.m.	04:00
5 a.m.	05:00	6 a.m.	06:00
7 a.m.	07:00	8 a.m.	08:00
9 a.m.	09:00	10 a.m.	10:00
11 a.m.	11:00	12 p.m.	12:00
1 p.m.	13:00	2 p.m.	14:00
3 p.m.	15:00	4 p.m.	16:00
5 p.m.	17:00	6 p.m.	18:00
7 p.m.	19:00	8 p.m.	20:00
9 p.m.	21:00	10 p.m.	22:00
11 p.m.	23:00	12 a.m.	00:00

In the 24-hour clock, the hour is always expressed with two digits. Thus, "02" is correct but "2" is not. Minutes and seconds, when applicable, are also two digits each. The expression "02:15:00" is correct but 2:15 (used in the 12-hour clock) is not correct in the 24-hour clock. The latest time reported will be 11:59:59, followed by midnight, or 00:00:00. The next increment in 00:00:01 (one second after midnight).

In some applications of the 24-hour clock, the colon is omitted and the word "hours" added at the end. For example, 02:15 (2:15 a.m.) becomes 0215 hours. This method is most often used in military applications. Another abbreviated use is to reduce the time to two digits followed by "h" as in "open 8h-17h" (8 a.m. to 5 p.m.).

The 24-hour clock clarifies scheduling, especially for travel. A train leaves at 8. Does this mean 8 a.m. or 8 p.m.? If clarified as 08:00 or 20:00, confusion is avoided on the part of the traveler. However, in a business application, reference to an hour may be obvious since offices may be open only during the day. Referring to the "meeting scheduled for 8" clearly means 8 a.m. However, the use of a.m. or p.m. as a matter of consistency is preferred even when the actual time is obvious.

b. **Time zones**

When referring to a time among individuals in different time zones, clarification is the key. The correct time zone to use is the location most affected, such as the time when an event occurred or is scheduled to occur. A phone conference for an organization based in Chicago will take place at 2 p.m. (CST) even though participants may be located elsewhere. The correct full expression of time, time zone, and date is: 2 p.m. Central Standard Time on February 10, 2017 (3 p.m., EST).

Daylight saving time (DST) is grammatically correct when standard time does not apply. The term "Daylight savings time" is grammatically improper. To avoid confusion between "standard" and "daylight" designations, the matter is simplified by referring to the time zone without specifying which version applies: Pacific, Mountain, Central, and Eastern Time, for example.

Decimals, fractions, and percentages

Business communication involves extensive use of numbers and numerical values. Clarity in documents depends on the ability of the writer to select the best method of explanation. Decimals, fractions, and percentages are different methods for expressing the same values, as shown in the table below.

Decimal	Fraction	Percent
0.5	1/2	50%
0.75	3/4	75%
1.2	1 1/5	120%
3.667	3 2/3	366.7%
4.3	4 3/10	430%

1. **Decimals**

The decimal point divides a value into whole and partial sides. Values to the left of the decimal point are whole numbers; values to the right are partial values (less than one). The number of digits to the right indicates the number of zeros following "1" in the denominator (see Fractions, below) of an equivalent fraction: Determining the number of decimal places depends on circumstances.

a. **Decimal value with no whole numbers**
When expressing a decimal value that consists entirely of partial values and no whole values, add a zero to the left of the decimal.

Examples:

0.25 (correct)
.25 (incorrect)

b. **Decimal expression for dollars and cents**
In the United States and Canada, decimal points are used to separate dollars and cents. Elsewhere, the comma is in use. When the expression consists of dollars and cents, limit the decimal places to two values (cents as portions of the whole dollar).

Examples, U.S. and Canada:

$0.25 (not $.02500 or $.25)
$3.16 (not $3.1600)
$67.00, not $67 (although $67 is an acceptable expression, when preparing a financial report, the two digits to the right of the decimal should be left in place consistently for all values being reported).

Examples, elsewhere:

$0,25 (not $,02500 or $,25)
$3,16 (not $3,1600)
$67,00, not $67 (although $67 is an acceptable expression, when preparing a financial report, the two digits to the right of the decimal should be left in place consistently for all values being reported).

The financial report for dollars and cents should be aligned on the decimal point or comma, and a monetary sign should be used for the first time and the total, but excluded on all other lines.

U.S. and Canada, example, incorrect:

$0.25
$3.16
$67.00
$70.41

U.S. and Canada, example, correct:

$ 0.25
3.16
67.00
$70.41

Elsewhere, example, incorrect:

£0,25
£3,16
£67,00
£70,41

Elsewhere, example, correct:

£ 0,25
3,16
67,00
£70,41

c. **Exceptionally large decimal places**

To manage large numbers of decimals, separate into groupings of three. The lack of separation is acceptable in some forms of expression. Never include commas as part of a decimal expression.

Examples, incorrect:

78.356979493 (in some applications, this is acceptable)
78.356,979,493

Examples, correct:

78.356 979 493

d. **Avoid beginning sentences with decimal values.**

The preferred use of decimal values occurs within the sentence and not at its beginning.

Incorrect use:

75.3 customers enter our store each day.

Correct use:

Daily visits average 75.3 customers.

2. **Fractions**

Fractions, like decimals, are methods of expressing portions of a whole. A fraction contains a top and a bottom number. To convert fractions to decimals, divide the top number (the numerator) by the bottom number (the denominator).

Example:

3/4 = 3 ÷ 4 = 0.75

Rules for expression of fractions include clarification about when to spell out the value and when to use the numerical version.

a. **Spell out fractions in narrative.**

Fractions in narratives are usually spelled out and hyphenated.

Examples:

one-fifth

three-fourths

If the use of hyphenated fractions is awkward, convert to decimal or percentage form.

Examples of awkward hyphenation:

Fifteen-three hundredths (preferred 5 percent *or* 0.05)

Ten-eightieths (preferred 12.5 percent *or* 0.125)

b. **Avoid using complex fractions.**

Avoid using excessively long fractions. As a guideline, any fraction that is difficult to imagine should be converted to decimal form.

Example:

23/1000 (complex)

= 0.230 (preferred, conversion to decimal)

c. **Do not spell out fractions when expressing units of measurement.**

Use fractions in text when they are expressed with units of measurement. In these instances, do not spell out the fraction.

Examples:

4 1/2 hours

3 1/2 feet

3. Percentages

Percentages are alternative forms of expression for decimals and fractions. A percentage is a portion of the whole. In business, percentages are commonly used to describe segmentation of overall values: profits, sales, employees, markets, and budgets. Just as common is the use of percentages to describe degrees of change (percentage of increase or decrease in financial value, for example).

a. **Use the proper format for communicating percentages.**

In sentences, spell out the word *percent* rather than use the symbol.

Example:

Sales volume grew by 14 percent last year.

In tables and reports, use the percentage symbol rather than the word. When percentages appear in a column, only the first line and the total should be accompanied by the symbol. An example is shown in the table below.

Region	Amount	Percent
West	$ 23,851	8%
East	107,900	37
North	42,830	15
South	118,347	40
Total	$292,928	**100%**

b. Select proper instances for using percentage or decimal combinations.

When the percentage is less than 1 percent, express it in decimal form.

Example:

0.5 percent of employees [this is equal to one-half of 1 percent]

c. Strive for clarity in communication.

A percentage expression is often more effective than decimals or fractions. Use percentages to clarify the message.

Decimal expression:

Sales were 1.2 times greater.

Fraction expression:

Sales were 1 1/5 times greater.

Percentage expression:

Sales were 120 percent greater.

Definitions

In writing *definitions*, certain standards may be applied to ensure simplicity, consistency, and relevancy of the items included, based on the purpose and technical levels addressed. The development of one or more definitions is based on three criteria:

1. The word or phrase to be included and defined.
2. Need for a definition based on audience and technical knowledge.
3. The limitation of definitions based on the class or concept and the characteristics that differentiate this grouping from others.

1. Time and place for definitions

Definitions are required whenever the audience for a document might not be likely to understand a class of terms; when a word or phrase has variable meanings and needs to be defined in a limited and particular way; and when the etymology of a word or phrase expands a point raised or adds to the interest of a discussion.

2. Writing effective definitions

Avoid unnecessary adverbial phrases; define nouns with other nouns and verbs with other verbs.

Example, poorly constructed definitions:

Annualized yield is when a one-year period applies.

Budget variances are where assumptions were incorrect.

Examples, improved construction:

Annualized yield is the yield earned as if the investment were held for a full year.

Budget variances are differences between actual and estimated expense totals.

Also avoid a circular definition.

Examples, circular definitions:

Narrative reports consist of the use of narrative sections.

Management by exception means acting only when an exception occurs.

Examples, improved construction:

Narrative reports primarily consist of written words, without artwork.

Management by exception is a hands-off style.

3. Use familiar terms to define less familiar ones

Using overly technical terms does not clarify the definition, but only adds to confusion. Use non-technical and familiar terms in the definition.

Examples of overly technical terms:

Laissez faire, from Latin second person imperative, passive attitude of governance.

Artificial intelligence, a form of machine functioning enabling perception of the immediate environment in imitation of cognitive reasoning.

Examples, improved construction:

Laissez faire, Latin "let them do as they wish," an attitude of passive governance.

Artificial intelligence (AI), machine-based reasoning in contrast to natural (human) intelligence.

Denotation and connotation

The literal meaning of a word is its *denotation*, or what it denotes or refers to. A *concrete word* identifies a specific, tangible person, place, or thing (e.g., typewriter, New York City, Bob). A *relative word* describes qualities or degrees, or modifies another word (e.g., red, high, low, hot, cold, impossible). Finally, an *abstract word* refers to an idea or concept without specifying one type or example (e.g., ability, intelligence, ambition, idea).

The implied meaning of a word is its *connotation*. When the denotation of a word is understood, the next step is to express the broad range of connotations that a word carries. For example, the word *hot* may mean *spicy*. However, it can also refer to the weather, demand of a product with customers, one's appearance or clothing, or a fit of temper. Many words have a wide range of connotations. Even a fairly straightforward word or phrase may have connotations that are implied in the context of use, without being specified. Consider the following applications of the phrase *big business:*

I want a career in big business.

The environment has suffered because of the practices of big business.

We're going into town today to conduct some big business.

The actual meaning of words involves both denotation and connotation. The subtlety of style and expression depend on the proper use of phrases. Everyone has seen examples of writing that is factual, yet places a specific slant through connotation.

Example:

The business interests of some out-of-town investors have led to development pressures in the area. There can be no doubt that these interests are guided by the profit motive. Because these investors do not live here, they are not as aware as we locals are of our heartfelt concerns.

This paragraph is loaded with connotation. There are no factual errors or lies within the statements themselves, yet the writer is clearly opposed to the "outsiders" and their motives.

Writers deal with style decisions in everything they create, all in an effort to find the most suitable way to express their ideas. There is no one right word for every situation; many words may contain the right denotation yet not convey an idea as accurately or as precisely as another choice. The writer's skill and vocabulary determine how an idea is conveyed.

Derivative work

Any work drawn from another work is termed a *derivative work*. This may involve copyrighted or uncopyrighted underlying material. An adaptation, summary, or expansion (forms of transformation) often are used in business writing. Credit should always be given to the original author even when the work is not copyrighted, or when only a limited amount of material is used under the fair use doctrine.

Descriptive statistics and inference

The term *descriptive statistics* refers to numerical values containing and articulating the properties within a population or sample. It is used to summarize variables and to point out the key takeaway from a statistical analysis. This includes inferences gained from the data and the significance they reveal.

Examples:

Results show that customers display a preference for quality over price.
Current period budget overruns point out the failures in our process.
Losses reveal that our supply chain risks are poorly insured or mitigated under current risk management processes and systems.

The danger in inference is in whether sample results are truly representative of the larger population. For this reason, descriptive statistics may be properly set up to explain how a statistical conclusion was reached and why the inference is realistic and accurate. Sample parameters may not be representative of population parameters.

Inference may be based on testing of hypotheses, resulting in conclusions about the larger population—customer preferences, budgetary shortfalls, or demographics, for example. Statements based on this should be correlated and supported by the data. A second form of inference is based on estimates, which is used when the population parameters are unknown. For example, investor behavior in the event of a sudden and unexpected market correction cannot be known based on behavior in past corrections. The variables include root causes, domestic and global factors, and the degree of the correction. The *statistical significance* should be identified as part of the estimated inference analysis.

Desktop publishing

The creation of documents online, or *desktop publishing (DTP)*, requires page layout and design and is based on software applications. The ability to self-publish or to publish in a short timeframe is a great advantage over publishing standards in existence prior to automation. The range of self-publishing may include promotional materials such as newsletters, press releases, and even magazines or books produced and marketed online.

Desktop publishing combines the word processing capabilities of a desktop computer with software for the design elements. These software products range widely in terms of cost and sophistication. In whatever format desktop publishing takes place, style standards apply.

1. **Pay attention to the overall design and appearance.**
   With a wide range of possibilities available for desktop publishing, it is easy to overlook the importance of the overall design and appearance. Too much variety in style, graphics, borders, and other visual elements reduces professional quality and appearance.

2. **Limit fonts and text size.**
   Select one font as the primary font for the published item. Vary text size only for headers and subheads. Also reduce instances of emphasis, avoiding excessive use of boldface, italics, and all-caps. Excessive emphasis translates to no emphasis, and excessive variety of font or style is distracting to the reader.

   Readers want to be able to read documents without being distracted. A subtle form of emphasis is to highlight limited text with shades and variations other than black text color. The typographic color variation is more effective than boldface, italics or all-caps because it is not as obvious as a form of emphasis. However, it has the same effect, drawing the reader's attention to a subtle difference from the overall body of narrative and the color variation employed.

Dictionaries

Works intended to provide alphabetical definitions of words or terms are called *dictionaries*. These are distinguished from glossaries because they are likely to be more extensive and may include sources and pronunciation rules.

A general dictionary is likely to include definitions of all words in a language, and a specialized dictionary is limited to one field or science. A definition should use well understood terms rather than replacement of one technical term with another. Using the word being defined is also ineffective (for example, "Current Assets: assets that are current" is a poor (circular) definition, compared to "Current Assets: assets in the form of cash or conversion to liquid form within 12 months" which provides meaning to the term).

Double negatives

The use of *double negatives* in most forms is improper grammar. This usage causes confusion and may have two completely different intended meanings. There are exceptions, and in some non-English languages a double negative is acceptable form.

Example, improper double negatives:

The department doesn't not do this work.

Preferred forms:

The department doesn't do this work. (negative meaning)
The department does this work. (positive meaning)

In some forms, a double negative is used affirmatively.

Example, affirmative double negative:

I am not uncertain. (meaning "I am certain")

Dysphemism

A term that portrays a negative opinion or an unpleasant connotation is a *dysphemism*. This should be avoided in business writing with few exceptions. When citing a source and quoting something precisely, a dysphemism will reveal the extent of a negative expression. For example, if a journalist writes a negative story about an organization that unfairly describes them, it is acceptable to quote the source as part of a report explaining the extent of an unfair description, a libel, or an untrue statement. The original source's personal opinion probably is part of the statement.

Example:

The company's management should be in the nut house.

In this expression, no support is provided for the claim of management's failures, and the use of "nut house" is an example of a derogatory term. In writing directly, a dysphemism should never be used as a means to strengthen a personal opinion.

Example:

Church elders disagree with our selling birth control drugs because they are on a witch hunt against us and other pharma companies.

In this case, the use of "witch hunt" portrays the Church negatively. This form of expression does not advance an argument effectively and does not belong in professional reporting or correspondence, without exception.

Some journalists and writers resort to dysphemism with a claim of free speech. However, a distinction should be made between free speech and offensive expressions. This extends to another form of dysphemism that is also destructive, the use of taboo language. The extreme form of expression in this realm includes offensive racial words, expletives, references to intoxication, immoral behavior, and bodily functions. None of these forms have a place in business communications. They may be used to release personal feelings toward others, but they do more harm than good.

As with all forms of dysphemism, when citing what someone else has said, it may be appropriate to accurately quote the source. However, a compromise is appropriate to avoid using the offensive term by giving the first letter with ellipses or dashes. Everyone will understand the word or phrase being cited without needing to see it spelled out.

E

Editing and proofreading

Editing is a process of review of written material to check for clarity, grammar, accuracy, and problems in expression considering the audience. Effective editing requires correction of problems so that the written message is clear and concise and conveys ideas well.

Proofreading is a process undertaken to ensure that a copy reproduces correctly the original material from which it was transcribed. A proofreader ensures that all words (and numbers) are correct and that all spelling is correct. Also to be checked are any corrections indicated from the original draft.

1. Editing

A careful, considerate, and insightful editor is at least as valuable to the finished product as a competent writer. The editor's function is an important contribution to the overall quality of communication.

a. Understand the true meaning of the message.

An editor is responsible for ensuring that the writer's message is expressed properly and clearly. The meaning of a document can be unintentionally altered with careless writing and, equally, with careless or incomplete editing.

Editing most often requires simplification of text to bring forth the message.

Original text:

Managers responsible for filing such reports should be aware of the deadlines and of related fines imposed on the company for missing them.

Poorly edited text with distorted meaning:

Managers who file reports may also impose fines on the company for missing deadlines.

Effectively edited text:

Managers filing reports should be aware of deadlines and understand that fines are imposed on the company if those deadlines are missed.

DOI 10.1515/9781547400218-005

While the differences in these versions are slight, the correctly edited version clearly expresses the message and conveys the essential information.

b. **Edit to simplify.**
Good editing clarifies and simplifies. Avoid editing excessively so that a message is made less clear. In many cases, removing words or phrases is the best way to simplify a message.
Original text:
Budgetary considerations are to be prepared, analyzed, and articulated with consideration for accessibility and retrieval.
Editing that simplifies the message:
Budgets should be prepared for ease of accessibility and retrieval.

c. **Respect the writer's style.**
When editing someone else's work, respect that person's style and method of expression, unless they are clearly inappropriate for the audience. The editor's job is to fix, not to change, the document. When the style is inappropriate to the degree that the entire document has to be rewritten, the editor should provide guidelines to the writer.

d. **Remember point of view and voice.**
Business documents should contain the proper point of view and voice. In formal reports, personal opinions and the first person *(I, me, my)* are rarely used. Second-person (you) is also not appropriate in most business reports and communications other than email and other one-to-one correspondence. Third-person voice (they, them, their) is preferred.
First-person voice:
I recommend this course of action.
If it were up to me, I would reject that idea.
My opinion is that we should take action.
Second-person voice:
You should take this course of action.
Your idea is incomplete; you may want to reconsider.
You need to take action.
Third-person voice:
This course of action is recommended.
Their idea should be rejected.
Taking action is the best course.

2. Proofreading

The purpose of proofreading is to check for errors or confusing expression. It is difficult for anyone to proofread their own work. A fresh set of eyes is more likely to identify problems and correct them.

a. Determine the level of proofreading required.

The proofreading task may occur on several levels. *Basic* (*standard*) proofreading consists of checking for spelling, punctuation, and grammar. *Editorial* proofreading adds elements to make voice consistent and to ensure clarity of expression. *Detailed* proofreading is a proofread that may also require reorganization of material or extensive rewriting.

Example, original text:

The weekly meeting is sheduled for 9 o'clock a.m. and will take place according to usual procedure in the conference room on the 2nd floor. Attendee's have been sent a agenda for review.

Basic proofreading:

The weekly meeting is scheduled for 9 a.m. and will take place according to usual procedure in the conference room on the second floor. Attendees have been sent an agenda for review.

Editorial proofreading:

The weekly meeting is scheduled for 9 a.m. in the conference room on the second floor. Attendees have been sent an agenda.

Detailed proofreading:

The weekly meeting will be held at 9 a.m. in the second floor conference room. The agenda has been sent to all attendees.

b. Proofread carefully and consistently.

Check the document for consistency in voice and method of expression. Also ensure that the tone of the message is appropriate. In a business communication, tone is all-important and makes an impression, whether appropriate or not.

Example, incorrect tone:

Hey dudes, don't forget to chip in for the mega-surprise birthday celebration for the big cheese. Lunch room. 12 noon, Friday. We all said no presents so keep it simple.

Example, correct mode of expression:

To all employees: The surprise birthday celebration for Bob takes place in the lunch room at 12 this Friday. As agreed, we will not bring presents.

c. **Mark up the document to correct problems in spelling, grammar, or the sequence of words and phrases.**
Markup should be clear and when required, explanations should be included. Online documents may be proofread with Track Changes in Word, for example. This allows for highlighted changes as well as comments.

Example, comments:

The expression "powers that be" is replaced with "managers"—powers that be is cliché and unnecessary.

e.g. and i.e.

The Latin abbreviation *e.g.* is from *exempli gratia*, meaning "for example." The term is found in academic writing as well as in business reports and other documents.

Example, use of e.g.:

Management proposed a series of internal controls, e.g. automation of purchasing order procedures.

Competition has initiated several measures to attract customers, e.g. discounts on purchases and free shipping.

The abbreviation i.e. has a separate use. It means "that is" and also is used in many variations of business correspondence. The use of a comma appears at times for these abbreviations, but is not required in general use. Likewise, some publications italicize these, but this is also unnecessary.

Examples, use of i.e.:

Management proposed one idea in particular, i.e., automating the system.

Competition is attracting customers with a lower cost measure, i.e. free shipping.

Electronic mail (email)

Modern methods of communication are dominated by email, largely replacing previous written methods. Email is used for correspondence, conveying reports and memos, attaching electronic files, and communicating with groups of people.

1. **Document communications decisions.**

One potential flaw with any system that eases workload is the tendency to overlook important procedural steps. Document communications carefully using logs, saved files, and cross references. You need to be able to (1) rebuild the sequence of communications; (2) list those with whom you have shared your files; (3) recreate and retrieve important paperwork; and (4) update files without also losing the originals.

2. **Don't overlook the need for face-to-face meetings.**

The popular use of electronic systems and other time-saving technologies does not entirely replace the need for face-to-face meetings. The human element can never be replaced entirely, and some matters are most effectively dealt with in meetings. Avoid the temptation to replace direct contact through electronic alternatives completely.

3. **Design messages according to the situation.**

Just as meetings are sometimes necessary, not every form of communication is best handled electronically. Some problems are readily solved with a personal discussion rather than through the exchange of written messages.

4. **Write subject lines correctly and completely.**

Due to the popularity of email, your message will have to compete with numerous others. The subject, or "entry," line for each message should be designed with these guidelines in mind:

   a. **It should briefly and clearly state what the message contains.**
   A short, concise message is always more desirable than a longer, complex subject entry.

   b. **It should get the reader's attention and interest.**
   Be a bit creative so that the message draws attention to itself.

      Humdrum topic lines:

         Upcoming budget review meeting
         Fiscal analysis report, personal finance

      Possible alternative:

         Making the numbers work
         "Last chance" budget review, Tuesday, 10 a.m.
         Report: How *you* can save money

5. **Apply the basics of good communication.**

   Electronic messages, like handwritten ones, are best when designed with consideration for the basic requirements of style:

   Be brief and straightforward, with an emphasis on clarity.

   State early on the audience and purpose of the communication, and end with an action plan, a request for response, and a signal that the message is over.

   If you are communicating with more than one person, limit and identify the audience.

   Avoid the temptation to clutter the email of those who have no real interest in your message.

6. **Edit prior to transmission.**

   Check your message before sending it. This review should not be limited to running it through a spell-checking system, although that is advisable as well. Read over what you have written, edit out any unnecessary parts, and look for ways to improve the style and clarity of your message.

7. **Use proper grammar and punctuation.**

   With email, it is easy to overlook the importance of the impression your messages make. Misspelled words, poor grammar, and abbreviations make a poor impression in professional correspondence, including in email. Such abbreviations include "u" in place of "you" and other shortened or phonetic words and phrases; and well-known slang lettering representing a series of words such as BRB (be right back). Do not exclude punctuation, this can create misunderstandings.

   Example:

   > A manager wrote a message to another and received the reply, "no thank you." Not sure what this message meant, the manager thought it sounded like a rebuff. In checking the original message, the real meaning became apparent. He had concluded the message with "thank you." The response lacked punctuation and emphasis. It was intended to say "No, thank *you*.

Electronic mail formatting guidelines

Formatting email should conform to the basic standards of formatting any and all business correspondence. These standards include:

1. Use salutations for the person addressed. If more than one but fewer than four recipients, list all names. If more than four, use a generic salutation, such as "To all concerned."

2. Break the message into paragraphs to aid in reading.
3. Identify all attachments.
4. Check spelling and grammar before sending.
5. Ensure consistency in voice (first or second person preferred).
6. Vary sentence length to improve rhythm.

Emphasis

Writers use emphasis to draw attention to key points in reports, letters, memos, and other documents.

1. Placement is the key.

The decision to place ideas within a sentence provides an opportunity to emphasize what you consider most important and to subordinate less important ideas. The key ideas should be expressed so that the reader understands.

Poor placement:

The department has several tasks, including compliance, timely reporting, employee training, and, most important of all, cost controls.

Better placement:

Cost control is the most important task in the department. Other tasks include compliance, timely reporting, and employee training.

In the second example, the item identified as most important is brought to the start of the message, emphasizing it. Mentioning the key item first is not the only way to organize the sentence. In some cases, placing the key item elsewhere is just as effective.

Example:

The department has a number of important tasks. However, every department has one job in common: cost control.

The concept of subordination is of equal importance in placement. Discussion of several items might obscure the point the writer is trying to make. By subordinating less important items, the writer allows the reader to concentrate on the major point. To subordinate a less important list, mention them after discussing the important or main point, or include the secondary items in parentheses or as a footnote.

2. **Use repetition as a powerful expression tool.**

The technique of repetition is extremely useful in conveying ideas. If overused, it becomes irritating, but selective emphasis of very important points is greatly aided by repetition.

Effective repetition:

Two-thirds of all customers stopped at the promotional display. Two-thirds.

Our stores, like real estate, succeed or fail for three reasons: location, location, location.

Repetition of rhythm is another effective way to emphasize critical points. A three-point argument is a popular device, often used in promotional literature and annual reports. When you want to emphasize these points, use repetition and rhythm for maximum effect.

Three point repetition of rhythm:

We care about cost. We care about profit. We care about quality.

The organization aims to reduce cost, improve profit, and ensure quality.

A similar device to achieve emphasis is the contrary, or offsetting, statement.

Contrary statement:

We need to control our market, rather than allowing the market to control us.

Quality produces profits. Profits reflect quality.

3. **Organize opening and closing ideas.**

Writers can use a technique public speakers practice to ensure that the important ideas are conveyed: open and close with the most important message. Some speakers subscribe to the three-step method.

1. Tell them what you're going to say.
2. Say it.
3. Tell them what you said.

This might seem too rudimentary for reporting within the business environment, where brevity is appreciated; however, the technique works well, especially in training environments.

Example:

Customer loyalty is key. Once the customer accepts the pricing, service, and quality we provide, we earn that customer's loyalty. However, if we establish that and then betray the customer's faith, we will never recapture it. We have to deserve loyalty, and we have to keep it. That loyalty is key.

4. **Be aware of the appearance of your message.**

The way you design your message has much to do with how it is received. Like other techniques of emphasis, overuse destroys the intended result. Some of these design elements include:

s p a c i n g
italics
underlining
CAPITALIZATION of entire words
Capitalization Of Every Word
words in "quotation marks"
boldface
changing font size

You may also isolate a limited amount of text and enclose it in a box as a sidebar to a report, as a form of emphasis.

Just changing the margins and spacing of a single sentence achieves the same result.

If you attempt to emphasize too much of your message, you lose the effect. Also avoid using too many stylistic methods for emphasis within a single report or letter. When a single **report** contains too many STYLE t y p e s, forms of emphasis, or excessive emphasis, the reader will be distracted.

Examples:

Too many style types in one sentence.
Odd s p a c I n g or CAPS or "quotes" to emphasize.
Capitalizing Every Word

The point is that excessive emphasis means no emphasis. It is also a distracting method of communication. Limited use of emphasis is best, and draws attention to the *main point*.

5. Insert headings for emphasis.

In preparing reports, label sections clearly as a form of emphasis. Many people on the distribution list will not want to read the entire report but might be interested in selected portions. By providing headings, you make their task easier.

You may also provide headings in letters, memos, and other documents. They break up lengthy documents into smaller sections and help the reader quickly identify the sections of the document. For especially long documents, include a Table of Contents at the beginning and, when possible, cross reference to page numbers.

6. Use visual aids effectively.

Charts and graphs are efficient devices for emphasis. Important statistical information can be reduced to a half-page in the form of a graph, and the point can be conveyed instantly to the reader. Without visual aids for such key information, the reader will need to visualize and translate narrative information without help. The message may not be conveyed at all.

The use of color is an additional way to emphasize a key point. This may include colorized charts and graphs or the use of a highlighter pen.

7. Insert lists and outlines to break up text.

Business reporting is concerned more with agenda items and priorities than with narrative and descriptive text. Accordingly, lists and outlines are appropriate forms. These techniques also provide excellent opportunities for emphasis. When dealing with several important topics in the same report, use the outline form in the report's body to lead the reader through. Use lists to draw attention to the critical and major elements in a decision.

With a large number of lists or outlines, notably for financial information, add emphasis with selective use of percentages to accompany dollar values.

Example:

Revenue	$635,401	100%
Direct costs	306,993	
Gross profit	$328,408	52%
Expenses	293,801	
Operating profit	$ 34,607	5%

8. Insert dashes, commas, and parentheses for variety in emphasis.

Be aware of the relative degree of emphasis achieved in selecting methods for asides or secondary thoughts. The greatest emphasis is achieved by setting material between dashes; commas provide somewhat less emphasis; and parentheses tend to downplay the separate word or other material, providing the least amount of emphasis.

Examples:

During the period of civil unrest—four days—our stores were closed by government decree.

The results of the survey, while impressive and promising, were nonetheless conducted in a flawed manner.

Our entire purpose (increasing market share) was shattered by the competition's development of a cheaper, better product.

9. Design sentences to achieve clarity and emphasis.

The construction of a sentence determines its clarity. Edit your writing to clarify the intended message. When a sentence's meaning is unclear, chances are it should be broken into two sentences or that some words can be removed without losing the meaning.

Unclear message:

Priorities within the department itself can be categorized in two major groups, immediate and long term, both of which depend on budgetary constraints and approval from top management before we can proceed.

Clearer message:

Departmental priorities depend on budgetary constraint and approval from top management. These restrictions apply to both immediate and long-term priorities.

A second feature in the construction of sentences is *rhythm*. When a reader is exposed to a long paragraph containing sentences of the same length, the monotony may cause a lack of concentration and perhaps inability to retain the information fully.

Monotonous rhythm:

Every division has experienced budget problems. Attempts at solving them have had mixed results. New controls are probably called for. Centralized management has not been effective in this effort. More action is needed at the divisional level.

Variations in rhythm:

Every division has experienced budget problems, along with mixed results in attempted solutions. New controls are required, but centralized management has not been effective in this effort. Divisional-level action is the answer.

Vary the length of paragraphs to achieve the same variety in rhythm. When paragraphs are consistently seven to eight lines long, the entire document becomes a difficult-to-read, monotonous reading chore. Consider a one-sentence paragraph to add high emphasis to a key point. (Note: As a general rule, a true paragraph should not contain only one sentence. As a technique for achieving emphasis, that rule can be broken occasionally.)

Example:

Every division has experienced budget problems, along with mixed results in attempted solutions. New controls are required, but centralized management has not been effective in this effort. Divisional-level action is the answer.

Divisional-level action.

Empirical approach

In an analytical report, especially one involving statistics, it is useful to begin a discussion with the hypothesis statement. This is the basis for a study, consisting of a belief based on limited evidence, further investigation, and a conclusion.

The hypothesis statement should be expressed using the *empirical approach.* This may be an assumption based on limited data, not generalization about what should be the case.

Examples, generalization:

Every division should be able to control expenses and yield net return of 8%.
Employees always challenge a new manager until authority is established.
Regulators start out assuming the worst.

Examples, empirical statements:

Net return of 8% per division is a starting point for setting annual goals.
New managers may need to establish their authority within the department.
Regulators may be suspicious of the organization until facts are presented.

The empirical approach overcomes a tendency to include *generalization* in a statement, based at times on a study but not necessarily always true. A generalization is resolved through the use of *plausibility*.

Examples, generalizations:

The analysis proves that divisions never reach goals without oversight.
Employees are not cooperative until strong leadership is imposed.
Regulators do not understand how businesses operate.

Empirical plausibility:

Divisions are more likely to reach goals with central oversight.

Strong leadership leads to higher levels of employee cooperation.
Regulators may need to be helped to understand operational standards.

The empirical approach is not only intended to soften or qualify conclusions. It also is based on application of the scientific method. This is the process of basing conclusions on proof and outcome of experimentation, versus intuition, assumption, or generalization. By observation, those employing the scientific method may prove or disprove a hypothesis with factual results, adding credibility to empirical statements.

Empirical knowledge based on the scientific method involves a specific series of steps: identification of a problem, hypothesis, research and testing, decision. Great confidence is gained from empirical statements because they are based on this set of steps. The alternative—speculation, assumption, generalization—results in unproven and at times false conclusions.

Endnotes

Endnotes include citations and other source references within a document. The endnote may appear at the end of each chapter or section (in a book) or as a set of references at the end of an article or report (see also Backmatter; Citations).

Endnotes are first referenced in text with a single numeral or symbol. In a word processing program, this occurs with automatic placement. The selection of numeral or symbol is made when the document is set up. The endnote is an expansion of the footnote.

et al.

The abbreviation *et al.* is from the Latin meaning “and others.” Its use, often seen in academic and other cited works, is used when more than one author is being cited.

In the first instance of citation, all authors’ names should be given, followed by the year. For example: Brown, Covey & Smith, 2016. In subsequent references to the same work, list only the first author followed by *et al.*: Brown *et al.*, 2016.

When only two authors are involved, use of *et al.* is not appropriate since the term is plural. The full terms are found in three different genders, all plural: *et alii* (masculine), *et aliae* (feminine) and *et alia* (neuter).

Euphemism

A word substituted for another word or term, intended to soften its bluntness or harsh meaning, is a *euphemism*. In business correspondence, this occurs often.

Examples without euphemism:

We are heading for bankruptcy unless we change course.
The current quarter's results were disastrous.
Customers think our products are awful.

Examples with euphemism:

Steps will have to be taken to avoid dissolution.
Revenues and profits for the current quarter did not meet forecast levels.
Customer preferences do not favor our products.

Note the differences between "bankruptcy" and "dissolution," for example. Softening the message may not always be appropriate, but there are instances in which standard methods of communication—especially internally—rely on selective use of the euphemism.

F

Fact checking

In any form of writing involving citing of facts or quotations from outside sources, *fact checking* is essential to ensure fully accurate use of material. This may be performed by the author of a report or paper, but more often is undertaken by someone else, an editor or proofreader.

When fact checking has been completed, the individual performing this check may indicate completion by writing or entering 'CQ' on the document or section of a document. This is an abbreviation of the Latin, *cadit quaestio*, meaning "the question falls" (or, is no longer in doubt).

False subjects

A false subject is an abstract pronoun. Often found at the beginning of sentences, false subjects weaken the tone of the message. A false subject damages the sentence; it replaces the intended subject with an indefinite article. Occasionally, however, there are reasons to use a false subject deliberately.

1. Identify false subjects.

Know how to recognize a false subject. Being able to spot their use helps break bad habits, and helps to avoid them.

False subjects:

It is our intention to meet this afternoon.

This *report* is the most critical.

Actual subjects:

The entire team intends to meet this afternoon.

The budget summary report is the most critical.

2. Edit out the false subject.

Correcting the problem of false subjects invariably involves removal of unnecessary words. Accordingly, the task is fairly straightforward compared to other editorial problems. Look out for sentences beginning with phrases such as *It is, It was, There is,* and *There was.* The indefinite pronouns in these examples (*It* and *There*) are readily identified false subjects. Writing style will improve dramatically when false subjects are deleted from the beginnings of sentences. False

DOI 10.1515/9781547400218-006

subjects also appear in the middle of sentences, so merely looking for the problem at the beginnings will not capture all instances.

Mid-sentence false subjects:

We decided that it would be necessary to prepare a written explanation.

Improved sentence:

We decided to prepare a written explanation.

3. Leave in false subjects when necessary.

Sometimes false subjects have to be left in a sentence because of the way they are used. The language allows for some appropriate false subjects, a feature that maintains its richness and variety. In editing, recognize that some false subjects should be left in place.

Necessary false subjects:

It was five p.m., so work stopped for the day.

There is no evidence to support that theory.

Figure of speech

Business writing may include many *figures of speech*, which consists of words or phrases with specific meaning beyond literal interpretation. This serves as a form of emphasis or clarity within a document, but should be used in a limited manner. Excessive figures of speech may become cliché or may distract the reader.

1. Variations in figures of speech

A figure of speech can involve alliteration, hyperbole, metaphor, simile, oxymoron, or synecdoche.

a. Alliteration

Repeated use of words with the same first letter is a literary tool emphasizing key points. It may more properly belong in promotional materials such as annual reports or advertising, than in business correspondence.

Examples:

definition, decision, delegation

products, people, profits

b. Hyperbole

An exaggeration of fact is hyperbole and should be avoided in most business venues. For example, “up to our elbows in profits” overstates the facts, when less hyperbolic statements would be as descriptive and more appropriate. Another example, “a dizzying array of poor choices” is not specific enough to explain the meaning of the phrase, and is more distracting than it is intended to be.

c. **Metaphor**
A creative combination of phrasing may be creative or cliché depending on how and why it is used. For example, "food for thought" is intended to describe an idea as intriguing but it is overused and may also be considered a cliché expression.

d. **Simile**
When two separate references are combined, a simile may result. A metaphor makes a statement, whereas a simile draws a comparison. For example, describing someone as "wise as an owl" or "dumb as a stick" paints a picture of extremes and may or may not be appropriate in business communications.

e. **Oxymoron**
The oxymoron—a contradictory reference—is properly used in only limited applications. For example, in describing a period in which profitable outcomes were accompanied by decline in brand reputation, a description of "painful profits" is an oxymoron that accurately describes the circumstances.

f. **Synecdoche**
The synecdoche may be ironic or sarcastic, depending on where and how it is used. For example, referring to a committee of talented managers as a "brain trust" is meant to describe exceptional collective abilities. Likewise, the term "clown car" to describe a department or a competitor is intended to deride a group of people.

File naming

Conventions for naming of files, whether hard copy or automated, should follow basic guidelines for ease of location and retrieval. Thus, "Receipts" does not reveal enough information, whereas "Receipts, 2013–14" tells not only what the file contains, but the date range as well. The label "Receipts 2013/14, C+3" adds more information, that records should be retained for the current year plus three years.

Online files should be named with the same rationale, for ease of retrieval. For example, a file of email correspondence is most efficient when labeled by the individual, department, or organization for which email was received or sent. Arranging a series of files by date would make it necessary to examine all files to find those email documents for a particular source.

Financial reports

The most common form of reporting in business is financial. A reliable way to measure performance is through analysis of profit and loss, cash flow, and the relationship between assets and liabilities. A manager seeking approval for new equipment or a change in processes has the highest probability of success when presenting arguments based on financial projections. Organizations make great effort in budgeting and forecasting and on monitoring results to check the accuracy and reliability of those budgets.

Accountants deal with the major financial reporting and budgeting functions in most companies, but all managers and employees can improve their skills in communication by mastering the style points for financial reporting.

1. Avoid excessive narrative discussion of numbers.

Reports often attempt to combine large volumes of numerical data with accompanying narrative explanations. Some report writers make the mistake of believing the narrative sections should repeat the numbers, even though the numbers are plainly evident. Use narrative sections to discuss ideas and goals or to explain to the reader the nonnumerical aspects of the case while avoiding redundant references to charts, graphs, and tables.

Redundant narrative:

The accompanying table reports that $362,805 was paid out in salaries, out of a total of $771,900 of total expenses.

Concise narrative:

Results for the year (see Table 1) break down the gross profit by category. The most significant expense was for salaries, representing 47% of the total.

2. Use charts and graphs to make financial reporting arguments visual.

Large volumes of numbers are difficult to explain; no one readily perceives the real significance of long columns and rows of numbers unless they are extremely familiar with the issue, and many readers of reports do not have the benefit of such knowledge. The report writer has to determine the most efficient style for conveying information.

The use of percentages accompanying the numbers, notably when highlighting the most significant results, draws attention where it is needed and clarifies the important message behind the results.

3. Use tables with text, and discuss their significance.

Charts and graphs can be used to reduce a full page of difficult-to-understand numbers to the essential conclusions they show. The visual representation is invariably more effective than any narrative. Reserve narrative sections to interpret what the numbers reveal.

4. Emphasize important conclusions.

In narrative sections, convey conclusions rather than passively repeating numbers. When you do need to discuss values, however, express them as percentages rather than numerically.

Numeric expression:

Sales last quarter were $1.65 million, and net profits were $115,500.

Clearer message using percentages:

Net profits last year were 7 percent of sales.

5. Follow reporting conventions.

Financial reporting follows a standard format, both in reporting style and in the arrangement of reports and accompanying charts and graphs. Because of the precise nature of the accounting report, these formatting conventions and styles need to be followed strictly.

This does not mean, however, that the report should be unnecessarily technical or difficult to understand. The reader is not always well-versed in accounting terminology or style. Additional suggested guidelines to add to the clarity of financial reports:

1. Attach explanatory notes for the reader who lacks an accounting background and who may need to be oriented to essential, important information.
2. Use footnotes when appropriate to draw the reader's attention to unusual or especially significant information.
3. Use financial reports as tools that enhance a less formal verbal report, which is always preferable when communicating numerical information.
4. Encourage everyone in the organization to use financial terminology in a consistent manner. If necessary, publish an internal summary of special jargon to help clarify communication.

Flowcharts

Processing information at the departmental level requires complete documentation of procedures: instructions for reporting, use of forms, departments and individuals to use as sources and to whom results are sent, the reporting chain, and numerous other related ideas. Department supervisors are invariably responsible for setting up a system to document the processes completed in their department. Part of that assignment includes listing the steps and routines related to every task and procedure. One tool that is useful in this task is the flowchart.

1. **Use the rudimentary single-process flowchart for single-process ideas.**
   The basic format for flowcharting follows one line of steps. For this reason, it is referred to as the *single-process flowchart* (Figure F.1). This format became popular in the 1960s and 1970s, when flowcharting became associated with computer science. Because a computer executes only one function at a time within a single routine, the flow of logic is best shown with a single-process flowchart.

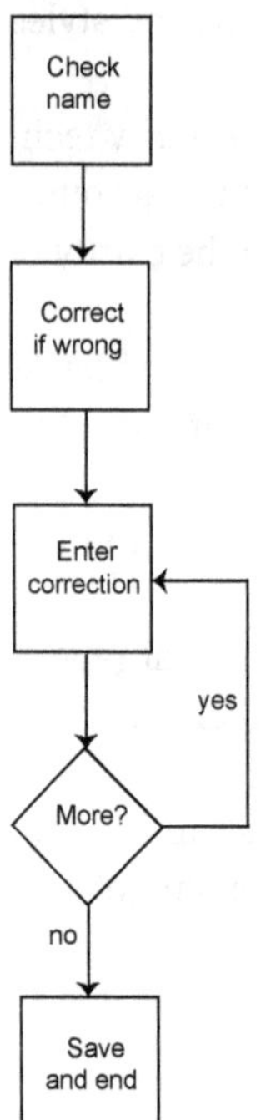

Figure F.1: Single-process flowchart

The decision box is shaped differently from others and represents the point in the process where a loop occurs. In this example, a "yes" answer to the question returns the flow to the previous box. When a "no" answer appears, the flow continues onward.

2. **Use differently shaped boxes to represent different functions.**

A variety of box shapes were developed within the computer industry to represent different functions. Use differently shaped boxes in the single-process flowchart for the same purpose, but limit the number of varieties to avoid confusion. You may need different shapes for process steps, decisions, documents, and start or finish.

3. **Use the dynamic flowchart for multi-process ideas or when multiple departments are involved in the flow.**

While computer programs execute steps in order, human processing is vastly different. In the business environment, managers and employees rarely work in isolation. Typically, several people in different departments contribute segments to a larger process. In documenting human processes, the *dynamic flowchart* makes more sense (Figure F.2).

Dynamic flowchart

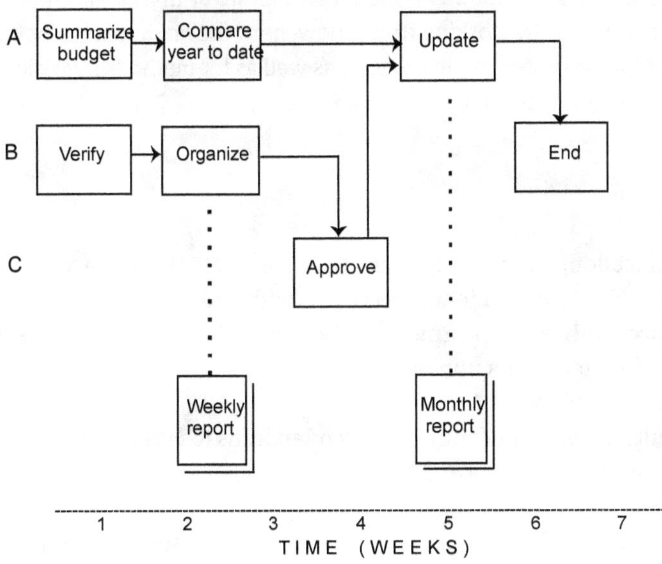

Figure F.2: Dynamic flowchart

This format presents a practical style for documenting processes in the noncomputer world. The same chart shows three different departments, labeled A, B, and C, each executing a number of steps in the process. There is interaction among the departments, shown by the sequence lines and arrows. Also shown are the documents produced as part of the process, represented by the dotted lines below the departmental flow, and the time line indicated along the bottom. The advantages of using the dynamic flowchart include the following:

1. The processes in different departments are shown in relation to one another.
2. Interaction among departments is documented. These are the most likely points for breakdown in procedures, so this feature is especially valuable.
3. The documents produced as part of the procedure are important to the trainee and to the manager responsible for producing reports, forms, and other types of documents.
4. The time line allows a reviewer to comprehend the importance of interdepartmental flow in the context of deadlines.

4. Design procedures manuals around the flowchart.

The dynamic flowchart is an excellent tool for the development of thorough documentation. When developing a procedures manual, begin with the dynamic flowchart, and then add narratives to support it. This method is preferable to the more common one of developing manuals with narratives only, making it difficult for employee trainees to comprehend the larger picture or timing and interaction between departments. By working from a flowchart, the manual developer is forced to account for every step in the process, as well as for methods by which information flows among departments.

Footnotes

Footnotes add clarification, representing comments relevant to the primary topic though not part of it. The format of footnotes begins with a reference in the text, usually superscripted; with text appearing at the bottom of that same page. Notes may be denoted by an asterisk or a number.

Anecdotal information:

The difficulty of communicating directly often leads to less direct means of expression. *

---

*One manager, cited by Harmon, 2013, got the message across to a chronically tardy employee by locking the door from the parking lot at five minutes past starting time.

1. **Insert a footnote to the source of specific information or when you quote from another source.**

   Statistical information supporting a comment in text:

   The majority of managers cite the problem of absenteeism as their primary concern in the department. [1]

   ---

   1. Survey of 126 managers, University of Saratoga, 1994.

   Source material for a quotation or fragment, or a limited fact:

   The "frustrated manager" expresses his frustration not overtly, but in other ways. *

   ---

   * Harmon, 1993

   A recent study revealed that a scant 13 percent of business managers had even read the procedures manual.[11]

   ---

   [11] Ames, 1995

2. **Footnote (or endnote) in published papers**

The practice for footnotes or endnotes (references) in published papers is to list the last name and year in text, and include the full citation at the end. This would reflect credit to the appropriate source (Sloan, 2016) within the document.

The reference at the end spells out a full citation based on the citation style being used.

3. **Use footnotes only when they are absolutely necessary.**

Footnotes are useful and interesting when appropriate; they can be entertaining as well, and can be used effectively to break up the rhythm of a report or study. However, excessive footnoting can also become disruptive and distracting to the flow of the document.

G

Generalizations

A generalization at times is useful as a broad observation. At other times, it should be avoided, notably when not supported by findings or statistical analysis (see also Empirical approach). A generalization results from the abstracting of properties in a set of circumstances, which may not be applicable. The resulting *deductive inference* is not proof, and often is in error.

For a generalization to be true, the parts of an observation have to be in agreement. If that connection is not present, the generalization will not be true. An example of a true generalization is the mathematical relationship between unspecific values A, B, and C:

$$\text{If } A = B \text{ and } B = C, \text{ it holds true that } A = C$$

This is a mathematical generalization that is easily proven. However, in non-mathematical generalizations, elements of opinion, interpretation, and inference make it less certain. If a generalization is not supported by the facts, it should not be included.

1. Appropriate generalizations

An observation of fact helps center an argument and may add value to the document.

Examples, appropriate generalizations:

A training program adds value for existing and new employees.
Ensuring continuation of a positive trend is not always possible.

2. Inappropriate generalizations

An inappropriate generalization is a conclusion reached from a misunderstanding of data or from incorrect interpretation of statistical findings.

Examples, inappropriate generalizations:

The competition reported 12% net return, so we should expect to match or beat that outcome.
Last year's portfolio return was 6% and this year's was 8%. Based on these results, we project a 10% return next year.

DOI 10.1515/9781547400218-007

Gerunds

Gerunds are verb forms that become nouns in sentences. This is the result of adding a suffix, usually "ing" to the verb. This practice is common in business writing.

Examples of sentences with verbs in verb form:

Work is a satisfying activity.

Analysis provides clarity in the meaning of data.

We eat lunch together every day.

Examples of sentences with verbs converted into gerunds:

We enjoy working.

Clarify results from analyzing data.

Eating lunch together is a daily routine.

Glossary formatting

A glossary is a summary of key terms, and may be constructed for a book or article, and even for a report when several technical terms are used. The general rule should be that glossary terms are included when the reader is not expected to know the definition of those terms. Avoid using terms in common usage.

1. Write a list of terms to include.

The glossary is arranged alphabetically. Begin by selecting terms to include. Avoid terms with commonly known meanings.

2. Develop a definition that is as brief as possible.

Avoid lengthy definitions; these belong in the body of the work. A way to avoid excessively long definitions is by referring broadly to what the terms mean, rather than including all the details.

3. Do not define terms with other terms.

Too many glossaries—especially on technical topics—define terms with other terms that might not be understood by the reader.

Example, overly technical definition:

Standardized terms—The option attributes including option type, strike, underlying security, and expiration. All must be present. For example, the underlying security is not interchangeable with other securities.

Improved definition:

> **Standardized terms**—The four essential attributes present in every option contract. (*See also* option type, strike, underlying security, and expiration).

The improved definition refers to the specific terms in the "See also" addition, while keeping the definition very brief and straightforward.

4. Capitalize the first letter of each term and boldface the entire phrase.

Use first letter capitalization and boldface to distinguish the term from its definition.

5. Alphabetize consistently.

Use either letter-by-letter or full-word systems to alphabetize the glossary. Be consistent once a style of alphabetizing has been selected (see also Alphabetizing).

Graphics

Select a form of graphic presentation appropriate for the type of document. PowerPoint presentations contain graphics mixed with text. The most effective use of graphics (preferred over excessive use of bullet points) is to display the screen and discuss it. Too many presentations consist of reading what is visible on the screen. This is not only a poor presentation method; it also fails to take advantage of widely available graphics.

A graphic may consist of a chart or graph, table, symbolic representation, or creative expression for a core idea.

1. Use appropriate, brief captions.

Select captions that describe broadly what some graphic reveals. Be creative. For example, in a graph that shows a pie chart for division of current quarter general expenses, consider the following ineffective versus effective captions:

Example, ineffective captions:

> Expenses, current quarter
> Percentage breakdown of expenses

Examples, effective captions:

> Where the money goes
> How we spend our money

2. Include annotations to highlight key points.

In setting up charts and graphs, use annotation to draw attention to important details. This can be as simple as one or two words and an arrow pointing to the section of a line drawing or bar chart. Annotation should be additive, providing more than what is shown on the graphic (see also Annotations).

Consider expanding annotated sections by including web links, references to other parts of a report, or emphasis for the primary point you want to convey to your reader or attendee.

3. Select graphics for specific reasons.

The graphic in a report or article should serve a specific purpose. This may include *descriptive or educational* aspects of a tangible product or asset (for example, in marketing a product sold by your company, a graphic is used to explain how it works). In a similar manner, a descriptive or educational graphic is used to explain a procedure or process.

Numbers often are the central theme in a report or article. Graphics are effective as representations of *numerical information.* In place of a passive listing of financial results, these can be converted to different formats, including bar charts, line drawings, or pie charts. These are easily constructed using Excel, Word, or Illustrator features.

H

Headings

Reports and other documents longer than a single page are often difficult for readers to absorb or to understand in context. Not all of the material is of interest to everyone; and time limitations may prevent the reader from devoting the time necessary to the entire document. Headings break up the text and allow the reader to concentrate on selective parts.

1. **Provide a guide to the sections.**

When presenting complex material in a report, break it down into logical components, and give each section a meaningful heading. Use a Table of Contents for long documents, including page numbers.

In lengthy reports, wide-ranging subject matter requires headings and a Table of Contents. This enables a reader to immediately find sections of greatest interest. A reader who is interested in only certain parts is more likely to look at the report if it has numbered pages and provides convenient cross references.

2. **Use headings for documents that are several pages long.**

Headings help readers when the document exceeds a few pages. Even a single topic can be broken down into logical sections. Readers like heading breaks because the segmentation enables them to absorb the subject and scan or skip discussions of no immediate interest. Heading breaks are similar to chapter breaks in a book.

3. **Use headings for multiple ideas.**

Headings make particular sense when a single document discusses more than one idea—headings alert readers that the subject is changing. If the reader has to read back over material to figure out what is being discussed, it will usually be at the expense of comprehension.

4. **Use emphasis and placement to draw the reader's attention to headings.**

Headings can be expressed in several ways. When you have a large number of headings, they may be numbered or given alphabetical distinctions. Placement and style also make the heading distinctive. Centering and boldfacing the heading in the report ensures its identification as a heading. If you have both primary and secondary headings, treat each type consistently.

DOI 10.1515/9781547400218-008

Heading treatment:

The Quarterly Budget
THE QUARTERLY BUDGET
The Quarterly Budget
The Quarterly Budget
T h e Q u a r t e r l y B u d g e t

For secondary headings, vary the treatment but keep this treatment consistent throughout the report.

Examples:

Primary heading
Secondary heading
Minor heading

5. Keep titles of headings brief but informative.

Avoid overly long headings. A heading exceeding one line (or is close to a full line in length) loses its distinctiveness. If such length is unavoidable, center it on two single-spaced lines, and break the lines in a way that makes sense.

Example, overly long heading:

Quarterly Budget Variances, Analysis and Proposed Solutions
Comparative Quarterly and Annual Financial Statements

Example, shorter headings:

Budget Variances
Financial Statements

Shorter headings are invariably better choices. The heading does not have to cover the topic comprehensively; it just needs to provide a guideline of the general concepts involved. Keep the details in the narrative. Readers want to be able to skim through the document and concentrate on areas of particular interest. The shorter the heading is, the easier this task will be.

Highlighting in text

Emphasis requires drawing attention to a word or phrase within the text. Methods of highlighting include capitalization, boldface, italics, and underlining. These are forms of emphasis, and should be used sparingly.

1. Capitalize for selective emphasis.

Use all caps for single words only, and apply this method only in rare cases. Excessive use of capital letters ("shouting") creates the appearance of alarm, in some cases, even appearing as a form of exaggeration. In addition, lengthy passages in all caps can be difficult to read.

Example, excessive use:

This year's NET PROFITS are HIGHER than projected.

Preferred, limited use:

This year's net profits are HIGHER than projected.

Use of capital letters should be extremely limited. The most common purpose is for acronyms.

Acronym expressions:

The company's stock is listed on NASDAQ under the symbol ABBS.
Our financial statements were prepared under GAAP standards.

In word processing, small caps can be selected, which are less offensive and easier to read than all caps in headlines or titles. Do not, however, use the small-caps feature for acronyms.

Small caps:

MARKETING DEPARTMENT BUSINESS PLAN

2. Employ boldface.

Using **boldface type** is a better way to emphasize than capitalization. Word processing systems will allow set-up and printing in boldface type. Use boldface for the following reasons:

1. Highlighting of key words or limited phrases.
2. Distinction between different levels of headings and subheadings when working in outline form.

3. Employ italics and underlining.

Like boldface, word processing systems allow set-up and printing in *italic type*. When working with fonts lacking italic style, underline words in text.

a. Use italics or underlining to provide special emphasis to part of a quotation.

When adding italics within a quotation, indicate that *you* are adding italics.

Example:

The article pointed out that "the study found *no instances* of failure in the marketing plan [italics added]."

b. **Use italics or underlining to emphasize a single word or short phrase in a report or letter that requires special attention from the reader or that you want to point out.**

Example:

Our division is *not* considering the plan.

c. **Use italics or underlining for foreign words and phrases that are not part of the everyday English language.**

Example:

The team leader has veto power *ex officio.*

d. **Use italics or underlining for words used as examples within text.**

Example:

How should we distinguish between the words *farther* and *further* in our reports?

4. **Apply general guidelines for emphasis.**

a. **Restraint:**

Use highlighted words and phrases selectively. Overemphasizing distracts the reader and destroys the desired effect. Excessive emphasis creates an impression that the author is not confident that text expresses the message clearly. Self-edit to improve text before resorting to highlighting for emphasis.

b. **Consistency of form:**

Use highlighting consistently within a single document. Do not switch between boldface and italics for similar or identical phrases used several times within one report. Select one style of highlighting.

c. **Choice of form:**

Pick the form of highlighting that works best for the type of document and the type of use. If you think boldface will appear excessive, select italics or underlining.

Boldface for key word emphasis:

Seminar topics include **management** and **leadership** in a remote office environment.

Alternative:

Seminar topics include *management* and *leadership* in a remote office environment.

d. Singularity of form:
Avoid combining two or more forms of highlighting. Readers are distracted by combined uses. A properly used highlighting technique should appear logical and correct within the text and should not unduly draw the reader's attention.

Homonyms

Words that sound alike, or that are spelled alike but have different meanings, are called *homonyms*. This is not to be confused with similar distinctions:

Homographs are words spelled the same but with different meanings, such as "bark" (a dog sound or skin of a tree) or "bow" (several different meanings). In the first instance, both definitions are pronounced in the same way; in the second, pronunciation is different.

Homophones are pronounced the same but are spelled differently. For example, "there" and "their" have identical pronunciation. However, the first refers to placement and the second is a possessive.

Hyperbole

Exaggeration, especially in the extreme, is called *hyperbole*. It is best to avoid hyperbole in business documents, as it creates the impression of a poor writing style. However, in some instances, hyperbole serves a purpose. For example, as a rarely used form of emphasis, a hyperbolic statement may draw attention to a main point.

1. Hyperbole as creative expression

Some forms of writing use hyperbole as a tool for emphasis through creativity. This is not normally appropriate for business writing.

Examples of hyperbole for emphasis:

We have been over this a million times.
I have tons of work.
They have money coming out of their ears.

2. Hyperbole for advertising and promotion

Many forms of advertising and promotion depend on hyperbole, and this has become accepted practice. However, the same techniques are not as appropriate in other professional business documents.

Examples:

See 100% improvement in computer speed.
Nothing else compares.
GE brings good things to life.

3. Hyperbole and cliché

Many examples of hyperbole are represented in the form of cliché expressions. As these are not strong expressions of ideas, they should be avoided.

Examples:

Fit as a fiddle
Dumb as a stick
Hot as the sun

Hyperlinks

Style for writing text with hyperlinks is specific because any additions or deletions may change the linkage to a site.

1. Do not add punctuation to an existing hyperlink, even at the end of a sentence.
2. 2. Do not add quote marks to a hyperlink.
3. 3. When URL addresses are exceptionally long, replace with an abbreviated version, such as those available at www.tinyurl.com
4. Line breaks for URL addresses cannot always be controlled. When possible, attempt to line up the line break at a rational point and not mid-word. Do not add hyphens to a line-broken URL address.

Hypothesis formulation

The hypothesis is a statement meant to indicate a theory or belief, that when subjected to testing can be proven or invalidated. The *hypothesis formulation* is the starting point in this process.

Formulation includes development of an empirical statement, generality and plausibility, specificity, and testability.

1. The empirical statement

The starting point in hypothesis formulation is development of a concise expression of the idea. This should not be based on assumptions of what an outcome should be, but rather of the idea to be analyzed and tested. For example, the statement that "Every product we produce is superior to the competition" is an *opinion* but not a hypothesis. An alternative may be: "Through research and design, it is possible to create a superior product." This is a hypothesis than can be analyzed and tested, with the desire to prove or disprove its validity.

2. Generality and plausibility

A statement of *generality* allows the analyst to determine whether underlying assumptions can be accurately used to test the hypothesis. For example, "Product testing leads to improvement in overall quality" is a generality that can be quantified by comparing extensively tested products with relatively untested products and then review market successes or failures.

A related concept is *plausibility*, the assumption that a hypothesis can be confirmed or disproven through analysis and testing. For example, the hypothesis statement that "Conservatives are better investors" is subjective. The terms 'conservative' and 'better' are both overly vague. In comparison, a plausible statement may be clarified. For example, "Conservative risk tolerance leads to safer levels of risk and opportunity" can be subjected to testing, assuming that conservative risk tolerance is distinguished from other modes of risk, and that "safer levels" can be quantified.

3. Specificity

An expectation of relationships between two or more variables allows a hypothesis to be tested with articulated outcomes. For example, the statement that "better educated consumers buy more of our products" may be difficult to prove or disprove because it is not specific. An alternative: "Testing our products in regions with dissimilar economic levels better defines our target consumer."

4. Testability

The ultimate test of hypothesis formulation is whether or not the idea can be tested. For example, the statement that "employee attitudes toward management are based on distrust" cannot be tested in order to draw a conclusion. In comparison, the statement that "surveys of employee attitudes may indicate how relations with management can be improved" is more testable. The statement points the way to a process that is likely to provide insights, rather than starting out with the conclusion.

I

Ibid.

The Latin abbreviation *ibid.* stands for *ibidem*, meaning "in the same place." It is used in citations, endnotes, and references when the source is the same as the preceding source. When exactly the same, the term *ibid.* stands alone. If the source is the same but the page is not, add a reference to the applicable page or pages.

Examples, use of ibid. in endnotes:

(**14**) Smith, J. (2015). *Proper citation guidelines*. New York: Citation Publishing, 237–243

(**15**) *Ibid.*, p. 246 (references same work and different page)

(**16**) Anderson, L. (2011). *Style guide comparisons*. Chicago: Chicago Writing Guide, p. 15

(17) *Ibid.* (references same work and same page)

Idiom

The *idiom* is a device (word or phrase) that is meant to convey an idea, but should not be taken literally. It may combine hyperbole or irony as well as cliché expressions and jargon. The use of idiom in business communication should be limited as it is an informal style of expression.

1. Personal idioms

References to individuals or groups of people (common or personal idioms) refer to characteristics.

Examples:

He has a chip on his shoulder.
I cannot come to work today, as I am sick as a dog.
She used language that rubbed me the wrong way.

2. Action-based idioms

Idioms referring to a course of action tend to illustrate traits or behaviors.

Examples:

Lacking growth in revenue, we have to face the music.
Slow down, you are getting ahead of yourself.
Let's set a goal and stay on the same road.

DOI 10.1515/9781547400218-009

3. **Idioms using references to color**
   Visualizing a message is accomplished with idioms using color.
   Examples:
   We are operating in the red.
   The news of a merger came out of the blue.
   In the market, that big decline is called Black Monday.

Imperative sentences

Imperative sentences consist of commands, requests, or suggestions. A subject may appear missing since the sentence often begins with the verb, but the subject is the individual to whom the imperative is directed.

Examples, imperative sentences:

Have the report on my desk in the morning.
Follow the guidelines we provided to you.
Remember to sign the form before submitting it.

As a matter of style, imperatives should be used cautiously. An unintended negative tone may be conveyed if an imperative sentence is not structured or designed properly.

Examples, negative imperatives:

Don't forget to prepare the report today.
Do not overlook the guidelines.
Never send in the form without a signature.

An imperative sentence may also take the form of an imperative and a tag question, in which case the command or request is followed by a comma.

Examples, imperative questions:

You will prepare the report today, won't you?
The guidelines are available, aren't they?
Your manager remembered to sign the form, didn't she?

Some variations of the imperative sentence take other forms as well.

Examples, imperative sentences with other forms:

Do prepare the report in a timely manner.
Check the guidelines, and use them.
Fill out the form, sign the form.

Indexing

Creating an index involves many complexities. An index is created for any work lengthy enough to require a guide to key terms. The index consists of an alphabetized list of primary entries within a work, and when several instances of a word or phrase appear, a sub-entry is also included.

1. Main entries

The main entry is normally a noun or noun phrase, unless reference is made to an activity. For example, "Trading" may constitute a main entry even though a verb, as long as the reference is found within the work as a primary topic. The main entry is capitalized.

2. Sub-entries

When a main entry appears more than five to 10 times in a work, a set of sub-entries should be included. These are listed with an indent, alphabetized within the entry, and may or may not be capitalized. The style should be consistent.

Sub-entry style should be related to the main entry.

Example, incorrect style:

Risk:
  Liquidity, 201–203
  Market risk, 119
  Trading problems and risk, 304

Example, correct style:

Risk:
  Liquidity and, 201–203
  Market, 119
  Trading problems caused by, 304

3. Locator conventions

The reference from an index entry to the specific location in the book normally involves a page number or range of numbers. These *locator* references follow the entries and a comma.

a. **Avoid listing all pages for a continuous occurrence.**
   The proper style for multiple-page locators is 169–171, not 169, 170, 171.

b. **List page ranges when not all-inclusive with the use of passim ("scattered").**
   When a range of pages serves as locators for a term, but not all pages are relevant, avoid listing all. Do not use the style "163, 165, 167–168, 173." As an alternative, the entry may be set up as "163–173 passim."

c. **Include locators in footnotes and endnotes by use of "n" or "f."**
When an entry is located in an endnote, list it as 169n. However, if it appears in both text and endnote, list the page only. A footnote receives the same treatment. For example, 169f indicates the topic is located in the footnote only. Exclude references to endnotes or footnotes in a range of page locators.

d. **Make multiple page references consistently.**
A consistent method of locator references is desirable. Spelling out the full page is a standard often used. For example, 166–169 is preference over 166–9 or 166–69. If the abbreviated version is employed, full pages are spelled out when the second to last digit changes. In both styles, 169–171 is the correct style.

Roman numerals are always spelled out in full. For example, when the locator in is frontmatter, the correct style is x-xiii, not x-iii.

4. Cross reference

In some situations, the index includes reference to other entries. This may apply to related terms, alternate or related meanings, different spelling, clarification of abbreviations, and pseudonyms.

Examples:

Market risk, *see* Risk, Market
First person, *see* Voice
Behaviour, *see* Behavior
Generally Accepted Accounting Principles, *see* GAAP
Clemens, Samuel, *see* Twain, Mark

When a reference appears in close proximity, the "see" reference can be replaced with the variant included in parentheses. For example, an entry may be written as: Behavior (Behaviour) rather than including both spellings next to one another.

5. Alphabetizing

Consistent alphabetizing style should be applied. Word-by-word is preferred over letter-by-letter style in most index applications, as this is the method readers will be likely to employ in looking for terms. Articles (the, a, an) should not be used at the front of a term and may be excluded. In titles of works, place articles at the end following the title and a comma. Titles should be italicized to set them apart from other alphabetizing entries, such as names of organizations.

Examples:

Financial summary (not "A financial summary")

President's Choice, The (not "*The President's Choice*")

Commerce Department (not The Commerce Department and not italicized)

6. **Numerical entries**

Entries beginning with numerals should be placed as though spelled out. Automatic alphabetizing systems within word processing programs do not adjust for this treatment in every case, so numerical references may need to be moved after a sort command.

Example:

Total reporting system

2017

Tyson Foods

Introductions, forewords and prefaces

Introductions, forewords, and prefaces are placed at the beginning of a book. The introduction is likely to be the sole form of frontmatter in a report. The three sections have clear distinctions and characteristics.

1. **Introductions**

The introduction explains the purpose and scope of a book or, in a report, serves as a summary. This summary may include key conclusions, findings, or recommendations.

a. **Keep the introduction short.**
   Introductions are not intended to become a major section of the report. They should be kept as short as possible and limited in scope. Long introductions will not be read all the way through; most readers want to get to the heart of the report as quickly as possible.
b. **Use introductions only for long documents.**
   If you have prepared a relatively short report, no introduction is required. Also avoid introductions for documents other than reports. They are useful only for orienting readers of longer reports, procedures and policy manuals, and studies.
c. **Summarize critical information.**
   The introduction is the best place to list information you consider the most critical.

i. **The conclusion or major recommendation:**
Start a report with the most important conclusion. The reader is then prepared to look through the report to examine supporting documentation, methods, and other material. Be sure to repeat the most important conclusion in the first section in case the reader skips the introduction, a not-uncommon situation.

ii. **The statistical or research methods used:**
Any report drawing conclusions should document the sources used. You may have developed your own research or used statistical information from other sources. In either event, briefly summarize these facts in the Introduction. For extensively used statistics or research, plan to provide greater detail and supporting information in an appendix to the report.

iii. **The reason for the document's preparation:**
Readers who are unfamiliar with your purpose or intention might not immediately grasp the purpose of the report. Explain this in the introduction. Assume, for example, you are preparing a report to ask management to purchase a new machine for your department. You prepare a report proving that the investment will save time and money, enabling the company to recapture its investment in a short period of time. Set out this purpose in the introduction.

iv. **Special considerations important to readers:**
Some reports contain information, sources, or statistical studies not commonly used, or they may involve an unusual method. In such cases, be sure to summarize these considerations for the reader.

v. **Scope of the report, if exceptional:**
Some reports are very limited in scope, prepared on assignment for one individual. Others are distributed to a wide array of readers. Explain the scope of your report in the introduction.

vi. **References to other important documents:**
Reports may refer to other reports prepared within the company; to material prepared by other companies or by government agencies; or to published material in books, research magazines, or trade publications. Refer to these in the introduction if they are limited in scope. If you have used a wide range of sources, explain the range in the introduction and include a bibliography of sources at the back of the report.

vii. **The involvement of other individuals or departments:**
If the report is a multi-departmental effort, be certain to acknowledge the participation of all others in the project. This is a courtesy to the others who worked on the report; it may also be important information, letting the reader know that more than one point of view was considered by the report preparer (see also Acknowledgments).

d. **Write the introduction last.**
Regardless of the sequence in which your document was prepared, the introduction should be written last. Only upon completion of the report will you know all of the critical points that should be contained in the introduction.

2. **Forewords**

The foreword normally is part of a book and is written by someone other than the primary author. This may be an expert in the subject matter, and generally extends only a few pages. It should also list the writer's credentials and title.

3. **Prefaces**

Some crossover is found between the preface and the introduction. It is likely to see one but not both appear in a book. The preface explains the purpose for the book or other document and may be used by the author to explain research methods or expertise that led to the document. The preface or introduction are the author's opportunity to sell the reader on the value of a book. If there are ancillary materials to the book, they should be mentioned, especially if some are for sale. The longer the preface or introduction, the less likely a reader will read it. Because the preface or introduction may not be read, any material that the reader absolutely needs to know about the book should be found in the main body of the book.

Irony

The use of rhetorical reference is a literary technique known as *irony*. Often associated with sarcasm, it may consist of a statement obviously untrue, as a means for focusing on the truth (opposite of the ironic statement).

Some forms of irony also serve as similes ("ironic similes") or as forms of sarcasm.

Examples:

Clear as mud.
The silence is deafening.

I haven't had this much fun since my dog died.
A net loss is just fine; our stockholders don't care about profits.

An ironic statement often is based on contradiction.

Examples:

I cannot discuss my own humility.
These words say nothing.
Sound and fury signifying nothing (Shakespeare, *Macbeth*)
Water, water, everywhere, Nor any drop to drink. (Coleridge, *Ancient Mariner*)

J, K

Jargon

Jargon is highly technical or specialized language unique to a special profession, such as the law, engineering, and accounting; or even development of unique phrases and expressions within a single corporation or office. In the business world, using words and phrases excessively or poorly is a language trap. This tendency leads to poor style habits.

In books, creating new words generally backfires. The occasional successful adoption of a word has made it more popular with authors, but attempts at the practice are very rarely accepted, excepting of course terms in primary works in the sciences were definition and naming is required. In such cases, before you do so, consider whether there is already an existing name that fits and also consider the future usage of the name (avoid unnecessary capitalization, words with related meanings, and so on).

a. Be aware of the dangers of excessive jargon.

Employees in an organization spend most of their time with fellow employees and develop certain words and phrases as a kind of shorthand. Be aware of which terms may be unique to the organization. If they are used outside the immediate organization, communication may be impeded.

b. Create a glossary for highly specialized terms.

When developing training materials, reports to those outside the occupation (including management), and even reports to fellow employees, define terms that may be unfamiliar to the reader. If your occupation uses jargon extensively, compile a glossary and distribute it to others. Avoid the consequence of unexplained jargon: a tendency to isolate yourself from all others who are not in your occupation.

Jargon generally does not translate well. Global companies such as DHL, employ people using a wide array of languages and so have created dictionaries for their employees of terminology that would not be found online or in a book.

c. Define technical terms when they first come up.

A solid practice is to define technical terms the first time they are used in reports, letters, and other documents. Definitions can often be inserted in text without distracting the reader or taking up excessive space. This practice clarifies the

DOI 10.1515/9781547400218-010

report for the reader. First mentions of defined terms are italicized in many applications, but thereafter are expressed in Roman style.

d. Avoid technical terms as much as possible.

When preparing a document for an individual outside your occupation or when writing a letter or memo for wide distribution, avoid using special terms or technical expressions. Such terms are developed for the convenience of those working in the field, and outsiders cannot be expected to comprehend them. Avoiding technical terms and striving for clarity of expression will benefit your readers. Excluding part of the audience in technical books and other documents decreases the overall value; in contrast, avoiding technical terminology does not take anything away from the message.

e. Recognize obscure expression.

A related problem the use of obscure terms. Even those who are not technical writers may fall into this trap. In the interest of clarity, the less obscure your writing, the better. Jargon develops as a bad habit because, in the corporate environment, the practice of communicating indirectly becomes easier than making short, direct statements.

An obscure statement:

> Departmental management contends and establishes its position that investment in this program will contribute to the development of greater profits in the immediate future.

A clearer message:

> The manager proved that investing in this program will be profitable within a year.

f. Find the shortest way to say it.

Editing for brevity is one method for avoiding obscure statements. As a general rule, the shortest way to say something is also the clearest way.

Unedited statement:

> If your schedule is not otherwise committed at this point in time, I would be interested in arranging for a midday respite meeting with you on the first day of the coming week.

Shorter, clearer statement:

> Are you free for lunch on Monday?

g. Self-edit for clarity of style.

Get into the practice of editing your own work before sending it to others. Use these methods to improve clarity:

1. Seek the shortest word with the same meaning.
2. Limit letters and memos to one page when possible.
3. Remove any material not essential to your message.
4. In a report, remove highly detailed discussions and, if they are necessary, put them in an appendix.

L

Legends, titles, and labels

The use of identifying information, especially on charts and graphs, should conform to a few essential rules of style: they should be brief, descriptive, and clear.

1. Legends

The legend usually appears below the illustration and explains either the meaning of the information, sources or special terminology.

Illustrations, overly complex legends:

Annual percentage growth in revenues, excluding discontinued segments

Comparison between revenue and net return divided by operating units and by geographic regions

Improved legends:

Annual revenue growth

Revenue and net return comparisons

When qualifications are important (such as exclusion of operating segments that have been sold or discontinued), this can be explained in accompanying text. The goal is to keep illustrations as simple as possible and to exclude unnecessary text.

2. Titles

Titles of graphs in reports and other documents should be limited to a single line of text, and shorter titles are preferred. Avoid the use of numbers, abbreviations, or acronyms; and in most cases, punctuation is not included in the title of an illustration.

Examples, complex or lengthy titles:

Summary, annual revenues and profits by year and by geographic region, including annualized partial year operations

Revenue growth rates among operating segments from base year of 2014 through fiscal 2018, 5 years

Examples, improved titles:

Annual revenue and profits

Revenue growth rates

The excluded information in these examples is apparent in properly labeled axes of the illustration, and can be excluded from titles.

DOI 10.1515/9781547400218-011

3. Labels

On illustrations, labeling should clarify what sections or parts of a graph reveal. For example, on a two-line chart, each line may be labeled to explain what it represents. On a bar chart, each bar may be labeled to distinguish it from other bars.

Labels should be as brief as possible, and are meant to explain the illustration. Longer explanations or highlights should be provided in accompanying narrative sections of the report, article, or letter.

Letters

The primary method for communicating in the business world traditionally has been the letter. Although letters still are used, online messaging via email has replaced a large segment of the letter-writing world. However, an email should be treated as a form of letter and the style rules still should be applied.

Letters make a first impression and introduce the organization, department, or individual. When the first contact an outsider has with a company is a letter, the writing style, spelling, and grammar convey an immediate impression. A single error or careless statement can destroy goodwill or create suspicion and mistrust. In contrast, a well-written, clearly expressed message strengthens the company's reputation, as well as the reputation of the writer.

1. Take special care with outside communications.

The business letter is the first impression you make for your organization. Whenever you correspond, the way you express yourself and the appearance of the letter together create an idea in someone else's mind about your company and you. If that image is positive, it benefits the company; if negative, it can do permanent harm.

As a rule of thumb, assume that individuals outside the organization will send a copy of your correspondence to your company president. Would you worry about the impression you create? Or would you be confident that the way you express yourself and the appearance of your letter make the best possible impression?

2. Arrange the letter correctly.

Many style points have to do with the kind of impression your letters make. Seemingly small matters in a physical letter, such as the size of columns and space left at the bottom of the page, make a big difference in how a letter is perceived. Someone who receives a letter from you consciously or unconsciously makes an immediate judgment about you and your organization based on the overall appearance of the letter. All of the details that go into proper construction of the correspondence matter, because each adds to the overall impression: construction and style, spelling (especially the name of the person you are writing to), the size and amount of margins allowed in the letter, and where on the page you place the address, the date, and the salutation.

Arrangement also refers to the contents of each segment. Deferring for the moment a discussion of the set-up, consider the importance of the three sections in the body of the letter:

a. **First paragraph:**
   The opening paragraph determines whether the reader will go through the entire letter and to what degree your message will be well received. The first paragraph should summarize your key point, attract the reader's interest and attention, and explain exactly the letter's topic.
b. **Body of the letter:**
   Within the main body of the letter, provide specific recommendations, requests, ideas, and other important points. All letters should be only as long as they need to be. As a rule, any business document has a greater chance of being read if it is short. A single page is ideal. For email, conforming to the rule of "shorter is better" also applies.
c. **Last paragraph:**
   Reserve the last paragraph for your closing argument: a request, a question, a promise, or a summary of important information. If the letter's intention is to ask for something, ask the question here.

   Poorly constructed last paragraph:

   In conclusion and to respond to your inquiry, our company's products are summarized in the enclosed catalog. We hope you will find it interesting.

   Improved last paragraph:

   Our catalog is enclosed. I hope you will look at it right away, and I appreciate your interest. Would you like to place an order?

3. **Select the right length for the letter.**

Every letter has its appropriate length. When the length begins to exceed three or four pages, it might be a report rather than a letter, meaning it should be organized in a different format and accompanied by a relatively short introductory letter.

The most desirable length for a letter is one page or less because the reader is less likely to read longer letters. Any message can be expressed briefly as long as supporting materials can be enclosed separately. Where letters exceed a single page, strive for clarity of expression. Where possible, summarize multiple-part discussions in outline form so that the reader will be able to seek out specific points or tell at a glance the points your letter makes.

Letters can be kept fairly short even for complex topics. Enclose supporting material to keep the letter brief and directed. In hard copy letters, these can be separate appendices or documents. In email, they can be added as attachments. For example, if your letter is on the topic of an eight-point argument based on a series of statistical tests, summarize the eight points in the body of the letter and refer to the supporting material. The letter is most effective if it is used to direct the reader to the most pertinent sections of the enclosed or attached material. It will be least effective if the same space is used to try to summarize a complex series of arguments.

4. Observe style conventions consistently.

A variety of style choices are possible in setting up letter formats. However, some conventions are more widely accepted for professional correspondence.

a. Address and dates

Placement of addresses and dates, as well as other margin alternatives, depend first on letterhead style. If your company's letterhead is arranged on the left top side of the page, the letter will appear more balanced if the date is indented on the left. If letterhead style takes up the entire top or is centered, you have greater flexibility in style.

Block style is the most conventional letter form: all material in the letter shares a common margin on the left side of the page. That means that the date, address, salutation, each paragraph, the closing, and the signature block have the same left margin. If the company's logo or name lines up to the left, the placement of the margin should conform to the left edge of that printed material.

The correct format for dates is as follows for Germany, the United Kingdom, and India:

Year, month, day: 2018, January 16 *or* Day, month, year: 16 January, 2018

The correct format for dates is as follows for the United States:

Month, day, year: January 16, 2018

The correct format for dates is as follows for France, Brazil, and Russia:

Day, month, year: 16 January, 2018

The correct format for dates is as follows for China and Japan:

Year, month, day: 2018, January 16

b. The year, expressed in numerals, is not abbreviated; use all four digits

Incorrect date styles:

Feb 16, 17
8 Jan. 17
March 23, '17

Correct date styles:

16 February, 2017
January 8, 2017
23 March, 1997

On all pages beyond page 1, blocks at the top of the page may include the name of the person to whom the letter is addressed, the date, and the page number. The date may be spelled out (e.g., September 19, 1996) or abbreviated in numerical form (e.g., 9/19/96).

Address blocks contain the full name and title of the person to whom the letter is addressed; the full address on the second line; the city, abbreviation of state, possession or province, and postal code on the third line. When abbreviating states, possessions, and provinces, use a two-letter abbreviation in all-caps; do not punctuate with periods.

c. Attention line

Some letters are addressed to an organization rather than to an individual, with an "attention line" directed to a department, a title, or an individual. This is the appropriate format to use when the person's name is not known or when you know the name but prefer to address your letter to the department. In the name and address block, the company name is listed but no individual or department. Follow this with the attention line.

Examples:

Attention: Customer Service Department
Attention: J. Davis, Account Supervisor
Attention: Vice President, Sales

d. Reference line

After the address, the subject of the letter is summarized in the reference line, a brief descriptive phrase advising the reader of the letter's topic.

Examples:

Re: Budget Committee report
Re: Sales meeting agenda
Re: Coding errors, acct. 4475

e. Salutation

The proper form for salutation in letters differs from that used in memos, notes, and other forms of correspondence. The letter normally is addressed to the individual by name, preceded by the word *Dear*. In a formal letter, include the individual's identifying honorific: *Mr.*, *Mrs.*, or *Ms.* After the name, place a colon.

Formal salutation:

Dear Mr. Sanders:
Dear Mrs. Adams:
Dear Ms. Thomas:

The use of "Dear" before names is not applied universally. A less formal style allows the use of other formats.

Informal salutation:

Mr. Sanders:
To Mrs. Adams:
Greetings Ms. Thomas:

Use first names in most instances when you are on a first-name basis with the individual. Conventions in some applications allow the use of first names; in those instances, also sign the letter or email with your first name as well.

First name salutation:

Dear Bob:
Dear Amy:

In some cases, you may be unsure whether an individual is male or female, either because the name may be either or because only initials are provided. In these cases, the salutation should include the entire name.

Salutation when gender is not known:

Dear Leslie Black:
Dear M. W. Haroldson:

When writing to a group of people rather than to an individual, make the salutation all inclusive.

Salutation to a group:

Dear Gentlemen or Ladies:
Dear Finance Committee:
Dear Executive Committee:

f. Closing and signature line

The closing segment of the letter is a short section of one to four words followed by a comma, intended to end the letter with the right tone or flavor to the message. The closing should be appropriate for a business communication and is based on the formality or informality of the relationship. If you, as letter writer, are a peer and close friend of the individual to whom the letter is sent, the closing can be correspondingly informal.

Informal closings:

As always,
Your friend,
All my best,

However, if the letter is to a superior, an individual or a group outside the organization, or someone you have not met, a more formal closing should be used.

Formal closings:

Sincerely,
Cordially,
With regards,

Your name should be given and aligned directly under the closing. In a hard copy letter, leave adequate room for your written signature, usually about four spaces. Put your name only without any punctuation. Whenever practical, sign the letter yourself. Avoid the use of rubber stamps or having someone else sign your name and placing their initials after the signature. That is a proper practice but not very personal, and could convey the idea that this letter was not important to you.

The closing and signature should be put at the same margin with the date and address blocks. When using block style, this would be at the far left margin on the page.

Electronic signatures are becoming widely used in online correspondence, including for contracts, letters of engagement, and letters. The E-signature is legally recognized in most applications, including legal documents filed in court. The ESIGN Act of 2000 (full name, Electronic Signatures in Global and National Commerce Act; June 30, 2000) was passed into law to recognize widespread use of electronic signatures and records.

Online services such as DocuSign enable sharing and electronic signing of documents without the need to pursue alternatives (such as printing out documents, signing them, and scanning the signed results to send back).

g. Letterhead and envelope

For hard copy letters, always use a business envelope and business letterhead when corresponding in the name of the company. Internal correspondence can be executed far less formally and in the form of a memo, but all letters sent outside the office should be done on preprinted letter and envelope forms. If email is set up to also reflect company logo and letterhead styles, external email should always use that format.

The address on the envelope for hard copy letters should always be generated via word processing, never handwritten, centered in the middle of the envelope and identical to the address as it appears on the letter. Several formats may be used (for letters *and* envelopes) when directing the letter to the attention of one individual within an organization or department. The style should match on both letter and envelope.

Address formats:

Ms. Marjorie Abbott, Manager
The Ames Company
804 Third Avenue
New York, NY 10022

The Ames Company
Attn: Ms. Marjorie Abbott, Manager
804 Third Avenue
New York, NY 10022

The Ames Company
804 Third Avenue
New York, NY 10022
Attn: Ms. Marjorie Abbott, Manager

h. Block style

Block style is the most common format for business letters and, in many respects, the most desirable. Because it is commonly used, others may expect to see a clean, professional, and simple format in which all lines, including each paragraph, are aligned to the left.

For this style, do not justify the right margin, even if you are using a word processing system that provides the justifying feature. Justification on both right and left tends to give the letter too much of a cubed appearance. Styles with indented paragraphs may seem to take on an improved appearance with justification, but the block style does not.

With block style, paragraphs are not indented; a line is skipped between paragraphs. Similarly, all other segments of the letter—date, address, attention line, reference line, salutation, closing, and signature—are aligned on the same left margin.

i. Modified, semiblock, and simplified styles

Modified block style follows most of the same rules as the standard block style, except that date, reference lines, closing, and signature are placed to the right of the page's center. The effect is still block-like, but the left margin paragraphs are offset by these other items, giving the page greater balance.

The semiblock style also calls for placing some segments to the right of page center, as with modified block. However, paragraphs are indented rather than a line being skipped (the indent is normally five spaces).

Simplified style is rarer. The salutation and closing lines are excluded altogether, so that the letter lacks even the minimal effort at adding a personal touch. Modern custom rarely calls for the use of simplified style except in email and internal memos.

j. Punctuation guidelines for letter style

For standard style, only absolutely necessary punctuation is used. A colon (or sometimes a comma) is placed after the salutation. A comma is included after the closing and before the signature space. In the letter itself, standard punctuation rules apply.

Closed style is an outdated convention in which all punctuation is included, including periods after dates and commas after each line of the address. Closed style draws attention to itself and gives a letter an unprofessional appearance.

k. **Margins and spacing**

Margins on the left and right should be about the same width. They can be set permanently for all correspondence. A margin of 1 1/4 inches provides enough white space to give the letter a professional appearance. The margin size is sometimes dictated by the company's letterhead design and logo placement. If the preprinted matter begins one inch from the far left edge, a one-inch left margin might provide a better appearance. Thus, a one-inch right margin would be necessary as well.

The bottom-page margin should be the same size as the side margins. If your company-s letterhead includes any printed matter at the bottom, the margin should be calculated from the top edge of the printed material rather than from the bottom edge of the page.

Spacing for business letters is invariably single. Double spacing or triple spacing is rare, although some modified spacing can be used for extremely short letters or as a form of emphasis for limited material. Use spacing as a means for centering a one-page letter on the page to avoid a distorted appearance.

l. **Continuation page heading**

When letters exceed a page, continuation pages should contain three forms of information: (1) the full name of the person to whom the letter is addressed, (2) the date of the letter, and (3) the page number. These headings can be set up in several ways; however, the format should conform to the margin formats used throughout the letter. For block style and modified block style (the most common formats), set up the continuation page headings on three lines, either on the far left or far right of the page.

Block style continuation line:

Mr. Robert Smith
October 9, 2017
Page Two

If the letter is using other than a block style, the headings can be set up in a modified form. The name may be aligned with the left margin, page number in the middle, and the date on the right.

Modified continuation line:

Mr. Robert Smith
-2-
October 9, 2017

Continuation headings sometimes repeat reference lines from the first page. This is not usual practice. However, if more than one letter is sent to the same person on the same date, they may be distinguished with an additional line on continuation pages.

m. Enclosures

If the letter is accompanied with enclosures, those should be identified beneath the signature block at the end of the letter. Several acceptable formats are used to indicate enclosures.

One item is enclosed. Spell out the full word or provide an abbreviation beneath the signature block.

Examples:

Enclosure
Enc.

More than one item is enclosed. In this case, indicate the number of enclosures only or list them with a brief description.

Examples:

Enclosures (3)
Enc. (3)
Enclosures:
(1) Budget report
(2) Projection worksheet
(3) Revision recommendations

Material is sent separately and is of interest to the reader. In this instance, indicate that related materials were mailed separately.

Example:

Enclosures:
(1) Projection worksheet
(2) Revision recommendations
Sent separately:
(3) Budget report

n. Carbon copy notation:

Letters are often sent to people other than the person to whom the letter is addressed. The list of those copied is often more important than the contents of the letter, since you are showing the letter's recipient the names of others who will receive the same letter. For example, when complaining about poor service at a store, you might write to the store's manager and send a copy to the vice president of marketing at the company's headquarters.

The term *carbon copy* is held over from the days when all letters were typed and before word processing was in common use. A file copy as well as several carbon copies were created on a typewriter using carbon paper. Today, of course, this method is rarely used. The "cc:" notation is still in use but is often referred to as a "courtesy copy" or "correspondence copy."

The indication "cc:" is placed below the signature block and, if applicable, below the enclosure notation. Following the "cc:" the name or names of all people receiving copies are listed. The indication may be given in several ways.

Examples:

cc:
copy to (one copied only)
copies to (several people copied)

Following the notation ("cc:" is most common), list the name or names of all others receiving copies. If the recipient of the letter and the "cc" list are all within the same organization, their titles are not necessary. However, titles should always be included if the "cc" list goes to people in different companies.

Example:

cc: Fred J. Green, President, Markets Co.
Andrea Smyth, Vice-President, Markets Co.
Susan Howard, Manager, Markets Co. Store 113

In some instances, a copy of a letter to someone may not include that person's name on the cc list. In that case, type or write the person's name on his or her copy only, under the notation *bcc* (originally meaning "blind carbon copy").

Example:

bcc: Mike Bandor, Customer Service, Markets Co.

o. Postscript:

A postscript is an afterthought placed at the very end of the letter. In some applications, a postscript is used intentionally to emphasize a key point or, in sales letters, to place the actual closing. The notation should be limited to one or two lines, following the indication, P.S.

Examples:

P.S. Please call by Friday, I will be out of town all of next week.

P.S. If you act before January 10, your first year's fee will be waived.

5. Set high standards for correct spelling.

All letters leaving the office under your name should be checked and rechecked for spelling. With spell-checker available in virtually all word processing systems, this is a simple procedure and one that should be executed without fail. Pay special attention to the correct spelling of names, especially the name of the person to whom the letter is addressed.

Lists

Business applications for lists are virtually endless. Lists are used in reports, budgets, memos and letters, and project schedules.

1. Employ parallel structure in lists.

A list should always be structured so that every item has the same grammatical format. The most preferable format is to begin with a verb. If a list is constructed with items consisting of full sentences or phrases only, all items on the list should follow that same format. Strive for lists beginning with verbs and containing full sentences. A numbered list is also called an *ordered* list. (A list employing bullet points is called an *unordered* list.)

Improperly constructed list:

1. Define responsibilities for the committee.
2. Task and deadline definitions.
3. Progress review (weekly).
4. Compile and merge information.
5. Final report.

Properly constructed list:

1. Define responsibilities for the committee.
2. Assign tasks and deadlines.
3. Review progress every week.
4. Compile and merge information.
5. Prepare the final report.

2. Observe the rules for lists within paragraphs.

Some lists come at the end of a paragraph, while others are contained within a paragraph. If the list is short, it should be contained without any special indentation. This is called an enclosed list.

An enclosed list:

> Our committee will (1) define responsibilities, (2) assign tasks and deadlines, (3) review progress every week, (4) compile and merge the information, and (5) prepare the final report.

An alternative format is to indent the list. This *displayed list* has the advantage of drawing attention to it and providing emphasis at the same time. It is the right choice for longer lists and lists with sub-lists.

Displayed list:

> Our committee will:
> (1) define responsibilities;
> (2) assign tasks and deadlines;
> (3) review progress every week;
> (4) compile and merge the information; and
> (5) prepare the final report.

Leeway is allowed for rules of punctuation in displayed lists. The only absolute rule is consistency. In the example above, each entry on the displayed list ended with a semi-colon; the second-to-last was followed by "and"; and the final entry ended with a period. Note the following differences between the enclosed list and the displayed list:

The displayed list is broken off from the paragraph by a colon after the word *will.*

The short action statements all begin with a verb but, because they are not full sentences, are not ended with periods. If the items were full sentences, ending each item with a period would be appropriate but not necessary.

The word *and* is included before the last list item in the displayed form.

3. Designate list items consistently.

The use of numbers, letters, dashes, or bullets sets off the items on a list. None of these methods has special value over the other. Consistent selection of list numbering is recommended when more than one list appears in the same document.

Determine a series of list rules for your own use. Following are examples of such rules:

Use numbers as the first level for lists, with letters for sub-lists.
Use numbers to identify priorities or sequences.
Use bullets or dashes for lists in which all steps have equal importance or when the order is not important.
Lists break up text, especially in books, and are likely to be read due to the emphasis a list adds. Use lists to bring emphasis to the message.
Capitalize the first word of each list item as a form of style consistency.
Avoid ending list items with commas; leaving off grammar is cleaner and easier for readers to comprehend.
Prefer setting lists apart versus enclosing them within paragraphs. This clarifies the message and purpose of the list itself.
Do not overuse lists. As emphasis, these are powerful tools, but when overused, they lose their impact.

4. Apply uniform treatment throughout the list.

The only hard and fast rule for lists is to be consistent, although there are general guidelines.

a. Capitalization

Capitalize the first word of every item in an enclosed list (or a displayed list) when all items are complete sentences.

b. Parentheses

Enclose the identifying number of list items in parentheses for all enclosed lists. For displayed lists, parentheses can be used, but the preferred method is not to use parentheses and to insert a period after the number or letter.

Enclosed list:

The steps are (1) prepare the initial report, (2) submit it for review, and (3) redraft.

Displayed list with parentheses:

(1) Prepare the initial report.
(2) Submit it for review.
(3) Redraft the report.

Preferred form for displayed list:

1. Prepare the initial report.
2. Submit it for review.
3. Redraft the report.

c. Colons

Do not use a colon to introduce an enclosed list when it is within a continuing sentence. In most instances of enclosed lists, items follow verbs or prepositions.

Enclosed lists:

Our marketing plan identifies (a) markets, (b) competitive forces, (c) projected revenues, and (d) profits.

Our marketing plan is designed to (a) define markets, (b) identify competitive forces, (c) project revenues, and (d) estimate profits.

Colons are used to introduce displayed lists.

Displayed list:

Our marketing plan has four goals:

1. Define markets.
2. Identify competitive forces.
3. Project revenues.
4. Estimate profits.

d. Periods

End each item in a displayed list with a period when it is a complete sentence. Some lists set up in displayed form are, in fact, one sentence; that is, each item is part of a continuing sentence. In this case, each item concludes with a comma, and a period is placed at the end of the final item. This technique should be used only for short lists. The use of lists helps avoid overuse of commas, and this should be applied consistently. The word *and* is used in the next-to-last item. Effectively, this is an example of a displayed list using the rules of an enclosed list. The list is improved by removal of dashes and use of capitals at the beginning of each item.

Example, poor list style:

We will implement our plans with

1. complete market analysis,
2. analysis of customer patterns, and
3. product introduction.

Example, improved list style:

1. Complete market analysis,
2. Analysis of customer patterns, and
3. Product introduction.

When selling a book, buyers pay attention to non-text items. The clearer, simpler and more consistent they are, the better the book will sell.

5. Distinguish between lists and sub-lists.

When a list includes sub-lists, distinguish them by different numbering and lettering systems. Use the displayed list format when sub-lists are needed. The usual convention is to use numbers for the main list and lowercase letters for the sub-list.

A list with sub-lists:

1. Prepare the budget worksheets:
   a. Format
   b. Responsibility
   c. Uniformity
2. Complete the worksheets:
   a. Centralized control
   b. Departmental input
   c. Deadlines
3. Review preliminary work:
   a. Task force membership
   b. Meeting schedule
   c. Authority for changes

The use of greater margins between primary and sub-list identifiers aids in emphasis in the use of a sub-list. But consistency counts as well, so be aware of the worst case and adapt accordingly.

Distinguish between the list and sub-list within a report or memo and the outline, which stands alone and is intended to present a course of action, priorities, or steps in a process. The outline is a detailed list complete with sub-lists (possibly on more than one level).

When a list becomes too complex to use within the body of another document, set it aside and refer to it as an attachment. In these cases, it is generally possible to break lists into more than one list. So rethink the presentation. That helps avoid overly long memos and letters. It enables the writer to use the space to describe key points rather than presenting too much detail. A list should be short enough to include within the body of another document, without distracting the reader.

M

Manuscripts

Manuscript is derived from the original meaning of handwritten script. The manuscript is a semifinal draft of a document being prepared for a final version. Manuscripts include long reports, brochures, articles, or books produced within an organization or association; or published either independently or through a publishing company. Final copy is prepared from the manuscript in bound form, with properly typeset narratives, photographs and graphics, and bound in adequate numbers for distribution.

1. **Use the proper paper for editing.**

   Some publishers require hard copy, usually as well as electronic files. However, these cases are becoming rarer.

   When paper copies are required, always use plain white paper, 8 ½ by 11 inches, for preparation of a manuscript when a hard copy is required. Never use erasable or onionskin bond paper. If you submit a photocopy, ensure that the quality is adequate so that an editor can read the text without having to contend with high contrast.

2. **Follow guidelines for text preparation.**

   If you are provided with manuscript guidelines, read them thoroughly and follow all directions.

   a. **Spacing:**

      Manuscripts should always be double-spaced (some sources will require triple-spaced manuscripts), to provide adequate room for making corrections.

   b. **Numbering:**

      Pages should be numbered consecutively, beginning with page 1 for each chapter or section.

   c. **Page headings:**

      Page headings provide important information. Word processing systems enable you to preset page headings automatically as *headers*. The header should contain enough information to identify the topic of the entire manuscript and the source, or author. A popular format is to include the title and author at the left and the page number at the right top of each page.

DOI 10.1515/9781547400218-012

Example:

Marketing Plan   Page 62
John Green

d. Ancillary material:

When graphics, tables, and photographs are part of the manuscript, clearly label each one, and indicate its placement in the final version. Prepare graphics in a format consistent with a publisher's guidelines.

Example:

(Insert Photo 3-18 here)

3. Follow indicated standards for corrections and editing.

Make all corrections to your manuscript using the proper editing and proofreading marks. Track changes enables editing without needing to hand-insert corrections, as these may be entered within the track changes feature.

Before editing make sure that all people involved in the project are agreed on (1) responsibility for editing at each phase, (2) deadlines and methods, and (3) authority for changes and final approval.

4. Properly cross-reference the manuscript.

Manuscripts should be prepared with thorough cross-references between text and graphics or between text and material in appendices (see also Cross reference). Select the cross-reference standards. For example, standards may specify:

1. All charts and graphs are to be numbered by chapter. For example, Chapter 6 illustrations will be numbered *6-1, 6-2,* and *6-3.*
2. All tables within the manuscript will be lettered for each chapter. For example, Chapter 6 tables will be numbered *6-01, 6-02,* and *6-03.*
3. All photographs within the manuscript will be numbered with roman numerals for each chapter. For example, Chapter 6 photographs will be numbered *6-01, 6-02,* and *6-03.*

5. Adhere to all publication standards and practices.

Reports and other documents may be published within the organization or by an outside publisher. Adhere to all publisher standards in the preparation of manuscripts and other materials.

Determine and agree on deadlines for submission. Does the publisher want the entire manuscript, or are you expected to submit chapters or sections as they are completed? Ask for detailed guidelines from the publisher. Read them thoroughly and follow all instructions. Establish a primary and secondary contact person within the organization for editing and for production (preparation and editing of the manuscript and actual publication).

Mathematical symbols

How mathematical symbols are styled in business correspondence and reports varies based on the topic, type of industry and company, and nature of the report. In highly technical applications, the individual preparing reports will be expected to conform to mathematical notation of an agreed-upon type, and based on an equation standard. For any other application, the guidelines that follow should be applied.

1. Determine placement of mathematical expressions.

Only very simple mathematical expressions should run in with the text. For longer, more complex expressions, space should be left both above and below the expression, and it should be indented.

Example of a poorly placed expression:

Correct application of the formula $[F + 1] + [Y3]^2 = C$ is to be confined to the primary tests.

Example of a clarified expression:

Primary testing is the only proper application of this formula:

$$[F + 1] + [Y3]^2 = C$$

It is preferable to italicize a formula to emphasize it and set it apart.

2. Be consistent in format.

The format selected for mathematical notation should be used consistently throughout the report or other document. The choices for methods vary widely, so selection of a clear and concise style for expression is an important step in communication and style.

Within scaled formula expressions, consistency of scale and system is essential. Do not, for example, alternate between meters and yards for length-related expressions. Do not alter expressions between numbering systems or use symbolic representation inconsistently. For reports containing a large number of mathematical expressions, help the reader by providing a legend of symbols used and their definitions, including mathematical value when applicable.

3. Be aware of conventional accounting and financial notation guidelines.

The most common form of mathematical notation in business involves finance: accounting reports as well as reports concerning financial results prepared by non-accounting departments. For reporting dollars and cents, the following guidelines should be observed:

1. Align all dollar amounts on the decimal point.

   Example:

   ```
   5,230.43
      13.99
     113.67
   ```

2. Use dollar signs only for the first value in a column and for the grand total. Do not use the cents symbol (¢) in financial reports. The dollar sign should always be aligned on the same location, and the totaling rule extends to under the dollar sign.

   Example:

   ```
   $5,230.43
       13.99
   ___113.67
   $5,358.09
   ```

   When financial values appear in text, (1) spell out round dollar amounts below $100, (2) use numerals for all amounts that contain both dollars and cents, and (3) use numerals for all values included in narratives of $100 or more.

   Examples:

   The unit price is seven dollars.
   The product price is below the ten-dollar level.
   The price is $7.03 per unit.
   The product costs $9.95 at the retail level.
   Each store nets about $200 per day.
   The average store nets $205.13 per day.
   The candy bar is forty-nine cents.

3. Dollar and cent values include commas and decimal points. Include decimal points for *all* dollar values, even when no cents are included. Always follow the decimal point with two digits for dollars and cents expressions, even if both are zero. Commas are inserted every three spaces to make the values easier to read.

Incorrect expressions:

$5230.

$42.6

Correct expressions:

$5,230.00

$42.60

4. **Financial values expressed in text should be limited to a discussion of significance.**

Do not merely repeat the information shown in a table.

Poor narrative repeating information shown in a table:

Salaries this period were $35,669.90. Office expenses were $47,800.42. Selling expenses were $37,593.20. The total of all expenses for the period was $121,063.52.

Preferred narrative style:

Table 1 demonstrates the relationship of the three major expense groupings. Overall expenses have not changed since the previous quarter. However, office expenses have declined, while selling expenses have risen because of improved internal budget controls and higher sales activity.

The second example is by far more informative, and more interesting too. It not only reports the outcomes but provides interpretation of their significance.

5. **Do not punctuate mathematical notation.**

Nonfinancial expressions provided in narrative are not punctuated. When an equation is referred to, no comma or colon is provided at the end of the narrative break.

Example:

The formula for this is $(x + y) + (x + z) = C$

6. **Break multi-line expressions at a sign of operation or at the equals sign.**

When expressions exceed one line, break the expression at a sign of operation or at the equals sign. (Signs of operation include instructions to add, subtract, multiply, or divide.) Do not break the line in the middle of a grouping enclosed by parentheses.

Incorrect break:

$(x + y) + (x$

$+ z) + [rate \div 12] = P$

Correct break:

(x + y) + (x + z) +
(rate ÷ 12) = P

When an expression exceeds one line, avoid expressing two segments on different pages. If an expression begins at the bottom of a page, skip extra spaces and place the entire expression on the following page.

7. Coordinate mathematical notation with explanations.

Some forms of mathematical expression are accompanied with narrative explanation. Two methods are recommended; the choice depends on the audience and the intent of the formula being explained.

Narrative with steps indented:

The steps to follow in computing monthly calculations of principal and interest are

(1) multiply the previous balance by the annual rate to arrive at the annual interest amount:

$37,950.20 * 10.00% = $3,795.02

(2) divide the answer by 12 (months) to arrive at this month's interest total:

$3,795.02 ÷ 12 = $316.25

(3) subtract the interest amount from this month's total payment to arrive at the principal amount:

$325.00 - $316.25 = $8.75

and (4) subtract the principal amount from the previous balance to arrive at the new balance forward:

$37,950.20 - $8.75 = $37,941.45

Narrative with steps to the side:

The steps to follow in computing monthly calculations of principal and interest are:

1. Multiply the previous balance by the annual rate to arrive at the annual interest amount. $37,950.20 * .10 = $3,795.02
2. Divide the answer by 12 (months) to arrive at this month's interest total. $3,795.02 ÷ 12 = $316.25
3. Subtract the interest amount from this month's total payment to arrive at the principal amount. $325.00 - $316.25 = $8.75
4. Subtract the principal amount from the previous balance to arrive at the new balance forward. $37,950.20 - $8.75 = $37,941.45

8. Use mathematical symbols consistently.

Use the same symbols throughout the document. For example, if the divide function is designated with / it should be used in all cases. If ÷ is preferred, it also should be used throughout and in every instance. The same rule applies for multiplication, using either * or x consistently.

Means testing

In expressing statistical outcomes, a *means test* (the difference between two means) may be a requirement for articulating results and assumptions. In some forms of research, the difference between means is of greater interest than the value of the means themselves. The test should be based on three assumptions: (1) The two or more populations are subject to the same or approximately the same levels of variance (homogeneity of variance); (2) they are normally distributed; and (3) the population samples were conducted independently of one another.

These criteria ensure that the analysis of outcomes, or a means test, is valid and that the independent tests are not influenced by each other. In expressing means tests, a report should clarify and explain that the three assumptions were in effect. A confidence interval is of great value in statistical studies based on the three assumptions. For example, a product marketing test may analyze consumer responses and produce different means. In reporting results, the three basic assumptions ensure that confidence levels are reasonable. A report may analyze the means test based on variables within the sample study (time of day, day of week, economic factors in the area) or among participants (gender, age, income). From these analyses, the analyst is able to articulate confidence levels which, in turn, should provide a reasonable assumption regarding results.

Measurement strategies

In writing about statistical studies, outcomes (expected and actual) may be subjected to measurement on some basis. The methodology for this measurement should be defined clearly in the report or article.

Measurement applies both to the attributes being measured (consumer preferences, management styles, or employee attitudes, for example) and to results (percentages of favorable or unfavorable opinions based on a question or attitude, for example). It is not enough to provide a conclusive statement without careful qualification.

Examples, lack of measurement definition:

Employee morale is low and is not likely to improve.

Product revenues have leveled off and stopped improving.

Examples, carefully defined testing and results:

Employee morale was tested with a series of questions concerning attitude toward management and working environment. Morale was low based on specific criteria tested: communication from management, working conditions, and attitudes toward the organization.

Product revenues have leveled off due to three factors: (1) increased competition in the sector, notably due to competitors producing their products overseas where labor is cheaper; (2) perceptions in the public that our products are outdated, based on packaging design; and (3) excessive internal duplication of research and development in creating new product lines.

The improved versions explained measurement strategies in testing and outcomes, and provide a clarified explanation of the underlying issues. The preferred system for explaining measurement on all levels requires well-developed standards for reliability, validity, and scale.

1. **Reliability**

The level of reliability is defined in terms of how thoroughly bias has been removed from measurement. This includes statistical procedures such as testing and retesting for accuracy or parallel-form reliability (when two or more measurements are conducted, such as consumer tests for two identical products with different names—Hellman's and Best Foods, or Hardee's and Carl's Junior).

2. **Validity**

The statistical measurement of validity is complex and extends beyond ensuring that data sets are consistent. Content validity measures whether samples are truly representative of a larger population; predictive validity measures responses between sample segments (male or female, income levels, time of day for testing, etc.); construct validity tests both convergent and discriminant validity levels based on interpretation and analysis of results.

3. **Scale**

A common correlation is expected among samples. This *reflective* scale enables statistical testing for relatively small samples of a much larger population. A common scale for this may include testing limitations (primary family shoppers in families with children, testing period limited by hour of the day, day of the week, or other limits). The assumption is that as long as the sample reflects the larger population, the scale will be reflective, meaning it has a higher degree of reliability.

A *formulative* scale is a combination of indicators among dissimilar samples within a population. In describing results of a study, when a formulative scale applies, the results should be interpreted with this distinction in mind. Without this distinction, interpretation of outcomes will be less reliable and cannot be interpreted or analyzed on the same basis as outcomes for a reflective scale.

Memos

The office memo is a popular way to communicate informally. The memo is a letter written to someone else in the same company. The longer title, "interoffice memorandum," is rarely used. Some memos are structured carefully, serving as internal reports. Others are less structured, taking the form of a letter or even a brief personal note. Memos can be written from one person or department to another, or issued for distribution to a wider audience, including every employee of the company in many cases. The historical written memo has been replaced by the easier and less formalized internal email.

The principles and guidelines for writing letters apply equally to memos. But because they are informal, internal documents, they do not need to conform as strictly to formatting rules. Good writing, whether in letters or memos, follows the same four guiding principles:

1. Place critical information first.
2. Avoid complex or technical language.
3. Refer to attachments or other reports for details.
4. Remember the audience for the memo.

A distinction is made between memos and internal reports. A memo is intended as correspondence and should be brief. You may want to write a cover memo for the longer attachment that serves as a report. The memo should highlight key conclusions, ask for a response, or draw the reader's attention to a section or page of particular interest.

1. Follow formatting guidelines.

The format for the internal memo is vastly different from that of the letter in several ways:

a. **Addresses are not provided.**
   Because the memo is written to an individual or department within an organization, the writer usually needs to indicate only the name.
b. **The sender's name is placed at the top of the first page in cases of hard copy memos.**
   The memo is not signed, although the sender may initial above his or her typed name. The entire document is usually typed without any written notation whatsoever. Use of formal titles *Mr., Mrs.,* or *Ms.* are not normally included on memos.
c. **The memo requires no closing statement, such as "sincerely" or "cordially," because there is no signature.**
d. **The headings of the memo are Date, To, From, and Subject or variations of these.**
   Each of these headings is followed by a colon. The information expressed in the heading *Subject* is often underlined for emphasis.
   Example, memo heading:
   Date: February 16, 2017
   To: Bob Robbins
   From: Sarah Thomas
   Subject: *Weekly staff meeting*

e. **There are no salutations.**
   After the heading classifications, the body of the memo begins at once.

2. **Include enclosures, copies, and postscripts according to proper guidelines.**

At the end of the memo, appropriate notations are made for any attachments. If copies are sent to anyone other than the person named at the top of the memo, the recipients should be listed at the end after the notation *cc:*. Postscripts are rarer in memos than they are in letters but can be included at the end. All enclosure, copy, and postscript rules should be followed.

3. **The guidelines for page headings and numbering are the same as for letters.**

Number pages beyond a single page using the same guidelines as those provided in the Letters section. The individual to whom the memo is sent, the date, and the page number should be listed on every page of the memo.

4. **Break up lengthy sections.**

In memos longer than one page, break up the discussion into separate paragraphs.

a. **Subheads:**
   The most appropriate way to break up a discussion is to use subheads. A topic exceeding one page probably can be broken down into several smaller topics. Subheadings make it easier for the reader to skim through the memo, grasp the scope of the discussion, and seek out points of greatest interest.

b. **Outline:**
   Memos can be broken down and organized in outline form. One method for explaining a complex topic is to design the overall outline headings and then fill in each one as the memo develops. This is an organizational tool for the writer and also serves as a guide to the reader. Outlines are recommended for exceptionally long memos.

c. **Summary:**
   For long memos, summarize the major points or conclusions at the front of the memo. The first page then serves as an overview, with the remainder of the memo supporting those major points. The reader can thus see from the first page the extent and scope of the memo. Rather than needing to read through the entire document, the reader can go to the points of greatest interest. When using this technique for long memos, cross-reference the summary section to each section of the memo by numbering the major points and using the corresponding number for each subhead.

Metadata

Data offering information about other data is termed *metadata*. There are three broad types:

1. *Descriptive* metadata includes summarized information, such as names of authors, titles, abstracts and key words for a range of published papers.
2. *Structured* metadata describes relationships between the elements of a document or series of documents.
3. *Administrative* metadata includes organization of files and file types, management of resources, and technical specifics within files.

In describing or organizing metadata, these distinctions should be kept in mind. When organizing a file organization procedures description, addressing these three types provides useful overviews and coordination requirements based on types of data being developed within a metadata set. Documentation for a metadata system should include the methods for creating the overall system, the purpose, location on an automated network, standards for use and for adding or deleting data, security protocols and enforcement, and provision or limitation on access.

Organization of a metadata registry or repository also must be planned and managed, so writing procedures should also take into account how and where the metadata will reside within a network or system. Due to widespread applications for metadata, a fourth type has emerged: *Accessibility* metadata is intended to addresses a multitude of requirements for the user audience, organization, or industry. As this expansion of metadata takes place, the needs for thorough documentation also have expanded.

Metaphors

The *metaphor* is a rhetorical figure of speech associated with irony, which mentions one subject in relation to another, unrelated subject. The use of hyperbole is also a form of metaphor, but a greatly exaggerated one. A simile makes a comparison with the use of words connecting two ideas, such as "like" (it hit me like a brick) whereas a metaphor focuses on a relationship (as hard as a brick). The two are very closely related.

Examples of metaphors:

We are drowning in a sea of uncontrolled expenses.
This market is as stubborn as a mule.

The mixed metaphor combines two unrelated topicsand is not as smooth as a related metaphor (drowning in a sea or stubborn as a mule). The mixed metaphor often serves as parody, intentionally making a point with the lack of relationship between the sides of a statement. *Examples of mixed metaphors:*

He had a long horse's face as the arrow missed the bull's eye.
You could smell the fear among the rats abandoning the ship.

Money and currency

Style for expressing amounts of money or specifying one currency against another should be consistent through a document or report.

1. **Spell out the numeric value but specify the currency with abbreviation.**
   The currency is expressed in business writing with the currency symbol followed by the value.
   Examples:
   €100 (Euro)
   £400 (pound sterling)
   $4,316 (dollar)
   ¥16,400 (Chinese yuan)

When referring to countries that use the currency of another, specify with abbreviated country symbols before the currency symbol. For example, the Australian dollar is denoted as A$ or AU$.

2. **Abbreviating larger currency values.**
   Larger values of currencies may be spelled out in the first use in a narrative; or used with common abbreviations in charts and figures. The proper abbreviations for monetary units in larger scales are denoted in one of two ways, with single or double letters or abbreviations:
   Examples:

Thousands	K or (000): $10k
Millions	M or ($mil): €4mil
Billions	B or Bn: ¥17Bn
Trillions	T or Tn: £5Tn

These abbreviation formats should be used consistently within a single document. When the unit is spelled out a space is left between the value and the increment: €4 million. But no space is provided in the use of the abbreviated form: €4m.

Negative values are denoted with a dash before the currency value, or with parentheses around the entire monetary value expression:
Examples:
-$10,000
($10,000)

When describing a range of monetary values, use the *en* dash without spaces or spell out the entire wording with spaces.
Examples:
€4m–€7m
€4 million to €7 million

3. Exchange rates

An exchange rate between two currencies is expressed with spelled out values or with symbols. The style should be consistent and should conform to other uses of currency descriptions within the same document.

Examples:

dollar/yuan
$/¥

Abbreviations for currencies may also be used in placed of spelled out names or symbols. These are referred to as FX (foreign exchange) abbreviations.

Examples:

EUR (Euro)
USD (US dollar)
CAD (Canadian dollar)
CNY (Chinese yuan)

When using this style, the three-digit descriptor appears in front of the value and no currency symbol is applied:

EUR2,000
USD600
CAD550
CNY6,000

N

Nominative, objective, and possessive pronouns

Pronouns are classified in one of three *cases*, indicating their use and meaning within a sentence. In technical books, pronouns, while their reference is clear to the author, often is not to the editor or reader and is the source of mistakes in trying to edit text. It is better simply to avoid pronouns even if it means repetition. It is better to be clear than misleading.

1. Nominative pronouns

Nominative case identifies a pronoun as the subject of the sentence. A pronoun may also be a predictive nominative, often an awkward form of expression.

Examples, nominative pronouns:

She is the departmental manager.

They are applying for the open job.

The nominated candidate is he. (predictive nominative)

2. Objective pronouns

When pronouns serve as direct or indirect objects in a sentence, or as an object of a preposition, the word is an objective pronoun. Examples are me, him, her, you, it, us, and them.

Examples, objective pronouns:

Management is impressed by them.

The competition offered me a position.

Our department is under the new division. (Our—pronoun—is the object of under—preposition)

3. Possessive pronouns

A pronoun is in its possessive case when it *describes* a noun without direct *use* of a noun. The pronoun sets up the possessive case in place of the noun or, in some instances, follows an adjective and indicates possession.

Examples of possessive pronouns:

That range of responsibilities is mine.

Responsibility for competing the report was theirs.

Success in this new geographic region is naturally ours. (pronoun follows the adjective “naturally”)

DOI 10.1515/9781547400218-013

Numerals and numbering

Numerals are used extensively in reports, memos, and manuals. Outline formatting uses several different versions of numerals to mark topic levels (see also Lists).

1. Express numerals in text as effectively as possible.

Numerical expression is so common in business that it is hardly possible to write any business communication without reference to some form of count or value. The measurement of success in business is invariably shown in dollars and cents; the measure of performance is quantity. As a result, style guidelines for expressing numerals in text depend on the matter being discussed.

a. Percentages, decimals, and fractions:

1. Use numbers combined with the word *percent* spelled out to express a percentage in text, regardless of the numerical value.

   Incorrect expressions:

   Net profit this year was seven %.
   Approximately 85% of customers return.

   Correct expressions:

   Net profit this year was 7 percent.
   Approximately 85 percent of customers return.

2. Express decimal-based values in numerical form, regardless of size. Do not include zeros to the far right except when discussing dollars and cents. For values below 1, include a single zero to the left of the decimal point.

   Incorrect expressions:

   The failure rate was 1.530 per 1,000 units.
   Variance of .45 in. is within acceptable range.

   Correct expressions:

   The failure rate was 1.53 per 1,000 units.
   Variance of 0.45 in. is within acceptable range.

3. Fractions should be expressed with numerals when they are large or complex; they may be spelled out if each side of the fraction contains a value of a single word rather than of a longer word.

   Incorrect expressions:

   Only twenty-one three-hundred sixty-fifths of those surveyed responded.
   About 4/5ths of our employees attended some college.

Correct expressions:

Only 21/365ths of those surveyed responded.

About four-fifths of our employees attended some college.

b. Combining whole numbers and fractions:

Whenever a value includes both whole numbers and fractions, the entire value is expressed numerically, regardless of the size of the value.

Incorrect expressions:

The size is thirteen and 3/5 for that project.

We worked only three and 1/2 days last week.

Correct expressions:

The size is 13 3/5 for that project.

We worked only 3 1/2 days last week.

c. Plural numbers:

When values are expressed in numerals, a plural is formed by adding an *s* without punctuation.

Examples:

the 1990s

temperatures in the 80s

Plurals for spelled-out values are made by adding *s* to the word, with the following exception: numerals divisible by 10 are made plural by deleting the *y* and adding *-ies*.

Singular	Plural
twenty	twenties
thirty	thirties
forty	forties
fifty	fifties
sixty	sixties
seventy	seventies
eighty	eighties
ninety	nineties

d. Use of commas:

Commas are used when numerical values exceed one thousand. Use commas to separate values in groups of three.

Examples:

1,000

13,533

426,385

e. Dates:

Dates in text are always combinations of fully spelled-out months or days of the week, with numerical values to express dates and years.

Incorrect expressions:

Mon, Jun. 13

February fourteenth, 2017

the first Mon. in 8.

Correct expressions:

Monday, June 13

February 14, 2017

the first Monday in August

In memos and other informal correspondence and in accounting and financial reports, dates are referred to in abbreviated form.

Acceptable date formats:

6/26/17

Aug. 27, 2016

f. Numerals or words:

As a general guideline, write out whole numbers of ten or lower; use numerals for whole numbers above ten.

When discussing exceptionally large values (millions, for example), use numerals even for amounts below ten; and spell out the value word rather than including a large number of zeros. When the large numbers are dollar amounts, include dollar signs rather than spelling out the word *dollars* (see also Money and currency).

Undesirable style:

more than seven million dollars

population growth of 14,000,000

Preferred style:

more than $7 million

population growth of 14 million

g. **Numbers beginning sentences:**
Always spell out numbers beginning sentences.
Incorrect expressions:
14 employees are in the department.
$20 is the balance of the fund.
Correct expressions:
Fourteen employees are in the department.
Twenty dollars is the balance of the fund.

Avoid beginning a sentence with the value if the number is especially large.
Large number at beginning of sentence:
Four thousand twenty-seven customers visited on opening day.
Preferred style:
On opening day, 4,027 customers visited.

h. **Consistency:**
When several numbers occur within the same sentence, be consistent. Do not change the form just to conform to the general rules of expression.
Incorrect expression:
The first shift reported three defects, the second shift 14, and the third shift only two.
Preferred expressions:
The first shift reported three defects, the second shift fourteen, and the third shift only two.
The first shift reported 3 defects, second shift 14, and third shift only 2.

Avoid statements mixing value expressions even for dissimilar values.
Mixed value expression:
The report showed that 14 stores reported seven incidents of theft, while the remaining six stores reported an average of 20 incidents.
Preferred style:
The report showed that 14 stores reported 7 incidents of theft, while the remaining 6 stores reported an average of 20 incidents.

2. Use numerical expressions to clarify a point.

The ratio is an effective tool for communication. Use this abbreviated expression to clarify what would otherwise be a difficult-to-explain series of numbers.

Unclear statement:

Although the company's profits were more than $70 million, direct costs accounted for $63 million in the same period.

Example of clarifying ratio statement:

After direct costs, the company retained only one dollar for of every ten dollars of sales.

3. Use numbering systems to clarify and distinguish.

Numbers alone or in combination with letters can be used in several ways, depending on the application. When several levels apply, combine the use of numbers of different systems with uppercase and lowercase letters. Levels can also be distinguished with the selection of a period following the number or letter or enclosing the number or letter in parentheses. If data becomes too complex in the presentation, seek ways to deliver the data more clearly (see also Lists).

Example of multiple levels:

I. Level one
   A. Level two

1. Level three
   a. Level four
(1) Level five
   (a) Level six

Such breakdowns are commonly used in outline form, where levels may be even more detailed.

A modified form of levels can be found in instruction and procedures manuals. Levels of headings are further divided by the use of levels broken up by decimal points. Headings in a book are structured in this way too. The author will use headings to break up chapters. In the following example, 1.1 is a section heading, 1.11 a subsection heading, and so on. In most books, the numbering is simply not shown. But it could be, for any book.

Decimal system numbering:

1 Major division
1.1 First detail level
1.1.1 Second detail level
1.1.1.1 Third detail level

Using this system, new information can be inserted in subsequent modifications or additions to a manual, without having to renumber the existing references. Some divisions can have a large volume of information and very large breakdowns within each section, while other divisions will not.

O

Obfuscation

Business writing in all formats should be plain and clear. Overly complex wording, called *obfuscation*, detracts from the message and frustrates the recipient. In many instances, obfuscation is used because the writer may not have a complete grasp on the subject matter, so the use of bigger or more complex words is a substitute for research.

Example, obfuscation:

> The cognizant management personnel are prompted to advise departmental personnel that Monday is a non-working day. Accordingly, they should refrain from appearing at the headquarters for work assignments.

Example, simplified message:

> Managers should remind employees that this Monday is a holiday.

Obfuscation also may be based on excessive use of jargon and cliché expressions that do not add value to the core message. The ambiguity resulting from such usage points to the importance of preferring the effectiveness of a straightforward expression. The author's overall purpose in any book is to teach, to make the book as clear and simple as possible, and at the same time to minimize the time required for the reader to learn the material.

Example, message based on jargon and cliché:

> The underlying intention of the forecasting and budgeting analysis is to generate a climate of bottom-line thinking and effective expenditure controls and pre-planning analyses to facilitate dynamic and positive outcomes rather than having to go adjust quarterly and going back to the drawing board.

Example, simplified message:

> The budgeting process adds to profitability through expense controls and forward planning, allowing us to avoid unending revisions.

Obfuscation may be intentional or unintentional, often occurring as a habit in business writing. Being direct and avoiding talking around the subject rather than addressing it directly, cures the problem.

A related but different meaning of obfuscation refers to a lack of clarification, although the preferred use of terminology avoids confusion.

DOI 10.1515/9781547400218-014

Example, reference to lack of clarification:

The problem of poor customer relations obfuscated the underlying problem of inadequate communication from the top.

Example, simplified message:

Poor customer relations was a symptom of poor top-down communication.

Objective and goal statements

The range of statements intended to define an organization, department, or individual has many names. Collectively referred to as *objective and goal statements*, these may also be termed value propositions, vision or mission statements, core values, strategic statements, and action plans.

To break down the terminology, the two primary areas—objectives and goals—are described below to capture all of the various terms used. Unfortunately, efforts to generate objective and goal statements often result in vague and lofty language so unspecific that the statements lose meaning. Simplicity improves the expression of objectives and goals.

1. Objectives

An *objective* should include a brief statement of the purpose for pursuing a course of action or appealing to a customer base. It is the "big picture" of operating philosophy, supported by goals and with actionable ideas backing up the brief statement.

a. Vision statement

The *vision statement* should briefly explain what the organization aims for in the products or services it offers.

Example:

Vision: to provide an affordable, high-quality range of products to a customer base expecting the best value for its money.

b. Core values

A statement of *core values* should be written to focus on the essential purpose of an organization and how it intended to accomplish this purpose.

Example:

Core values include the company's dedication to honest and ethical relationships with its market, above and beyond generation of profits.

c. **Mission statement**

The mission statement is very similar to the core values statement. It should identify the central purpose of the organization and its philosophy. Rather than being expressed in a complete sentence, the mission statement is an "action" expression.

Example:

To identify and provide the highest quality products.

2. **Goals**

Goals include many attributes, and the term often is overused. In writing a statement of goals, some clear standards should be followed.

a. **Value proposition**

Among goal-based statements is the *value proposition,* a description of values promised for delivery and aimed at a customer as part of a broad business strategy, customer service philosophy, and standards. In some definitions, a value proposition is an extensive listing of attributes, qualifications, and services. In a summarized value proposition, a very brief statement should focus on the value brought to a customer by the organization.

Example of a summarized value proposition:

The company applies its experience to ensure the highest quality of customer response, with products tailored to each customer's requirements.

b. **Strategies**

Descriptions of *strategies*, like any summarized statement, should be brief, to the point, and expressed with simplicity. Strategies should describe how goals will be achieved with specific programs, steps or approaches to the market.

Example:

The strategic approach includes three primary initiatives:

1. Close offices in locations that have not been profitable
2. Focus on the most profitable markets rather than pursuing geographic expansion for its own sake.
3. Create internal audit and oversight to ensure elimination of unnecessary expense and cost levels.

c. **Action plan**

The *action plan* briefly describes how strategies will be achieved.

Example:

The strategies will be accomplished by:

1. Identification of locations to be discontinued and deadlines to be set based on the interest of relocating employees to avoid market disruption.
2. Dedicated resources moved to identified profitable markets, including movement of managers and employees when possible.
3. Expansion of internal audit functions, including staff expansion, to create internal controls to reduce costs and expenses.

3. Problems with objective and goal statements

In an effort to create objective and goal statements there is the tendency to over-write, to use language that sounds lofty and important, but that expresses nothing of value. A second problem is in generation of statements with no meaningful action plan.

Example, ineffective objective and goal statement:

Objective: To ensure the highest-quality products to become the world's leader within our sector, and to create brand reputation superior to all competitors.

Goal: To strive for excellence through a series of appropriate and highly focused marketing plans based on studies by internal market and product committees.

Statements such as this do not describe specifically what the organization intends to accomplish through its core objective (marketing highest-quality products). It lacks action steps. Likewise, the goal is overly vague and appears to rely on committee studies aimed at "excellence" but without defining what that means.

Online etiquette

The concept of *style* in the modern business environment extends beyond how expressions in writing are made. For example, reports, articles, or books are subject to many basic requirements of grammar, punctuation, and voice. However, style also relates to how online expressions are made.

In describing *online etiquette*, many of the "rules" are obvious, but are offered as reminders for everyone (see also Electronic mail (email)). Online etiquette includes the following:

1. Avoid strong or inciteful language and hyperbole. This include the excessive use of exclamation points, all-caps ("shouting"), and other methods of emphasis. Never use obscenity or offensive language. Always assume that everyone you know will be able to see what you say online.
2. Remember that irony and sarcasm are easily lost in written communications. Take steps to ensure that the meaning of a statement is not misunderstood. It is very easy for an intended sarcastic or humorous statement to be interpreted as offensive or aggressive.
3. Always show respect in a live chat room or in anything that is posted on a site. It is easy to overlook the importance of first impressions in the impersonal medium of online messaging. A wise standard is to never say something online that you would not say in person.
4. Never post anything you would not want to come out in a job interview. With increasing regularity, employers are requiring applicants to provide their social media accounts so that their topics of discussion and methods of expression can be studied. Because of this, *never* post complaints or criticisms of a current employer or manager.
5. Review everything you write on a message board or social media site before posting. Look for misspelled words and, of equal importance, for unintended negative tone or voice. Read it out loud before you post.
6. Use full words and not abbreviations ("U" in place of "you") and follow all rules of grammar and punctuation. The tendency to ignore the basic grammar rules and to exclude punctuation make the intention of messages unclear. For example, consider the difference between two messages with the same words:

   No thank you
   No, thank *you*.

7. When posting facts or statistics, always cite your source and include a link so that others can see it for themselves. Never copy news and forward it without also checking its validity. For example, look for verification on sites set up to check on fake news, such as www.factcheck.org/hot-topics or www.snopes.com. Also be aware of *clickbait*, sites promising attractive or free items, but really set up to bring traffic to a site, often to promote other products or to build mailing lists.

8. Never repost or share questionable, offensive, or inappropriate images or stories, even to a limited range of trusted friends. Anything posted online is permanent and can harm you later if your name is identified with the item posted. Also avoid posting personal information about yourself and others, especially on a site representing your organization or your professional activities.
9. Be aware of your privacy settings and revise to ensure that you allow people to see your information based on your preferences, and not on universal access.
10. Never treat people as "disposable" online. By simply stopping a line of communication or blocking or "unfriending" someone, you create a negative impression of yourself and convey a belief that they are disposable.

Op. Cit.

Latin for "in the work cited" is *Op. Cit.* This term is used for citations in endnotes or footnotes when a previously cited reference occurs again. Rather than spell out the full reference, *Op. Cit.* it identifies by author name alone. When a different page number or other reference is used, it follows the abbreviation. The similar abbreviation *Loc. Cit.* means "in the place cited," and may be used in place of *Op. Cit.* (see also Ibid.)

When references are used more than once within a narrative, the common practice is to refer to the author's name and publication year. So the term (Anderson, 2018) leads a reader to a reference list or endnote where the full citation will be found. In the reference list, endnote, or footnote, the first reference would spell out the entire citation and subsequent notation would be identified either as *Ibid.* (when the second reference occurs immediately) or *Op. Cit.* (when the reference first appeared prior to the preceding entry.

Example, endnotes using both Ibid. and Op. Cit.:

(11) Anderson. J. (Spring, 2018). Analyses of financial trends. *Financial Journal,*
vol. 2, pp. 16–25
(12) *Ibid.*, p. 21
(13) Mackey, R. (2017). *Financial Trend Reporting Standards.* New York: Accounting Press, pp. 194–202
(14) Anderson, *Op. Cit.*, p. 23

In this set of entries, Anderson was cited twice. The second citation occurred immediately after the first, so *Ibid.* was the proper method for shorthand expression of the same source. The third reference did not follow immediately, so *Op. Cit.* was the proper method for abbreviating the source.

Some publishers may not want the use of *Ibid.* or *Op. Cit.*, but rather always have the full reference. This is because citations are important factors in the success of scholarly works and it is important that each is accurately accounted for in establishing the number of references attributed to a given article, book or journal. It is good form to be respectful of the authors and make sure they get credit for each citation. Instances of *Ibid.* or *Op. Cit.* may not register. Always inquire with a publisher whether this is an issue.

Organization charts

Organizations use graphic representations to demonstrate the chain of command in the company. The organization chart shows the reporting chain, usually with the highest rank on the top and the lowest on the bottom.

1. Exclude stockholders and directors.

The organization chart normally begins with the chief executive officer (CEO) or the president at the top. Although stockholders and a board of directors are actually higher in rank than this position, they are not usually included on the chart, at least not by name. If the board of directors is included, it normally is restricted to the title, "Board of Directors," and does not name each member. The organization chart is normally limited to the internal organization and should not include "Stockholders" as part of the chart.

2. Limit the amount of detail.

Because organizations have complex reporting systems, often over many different operating segments, the organization chart should be limited in scope. Except in relatively small companies, not everyone's position can or should be included. Cut off the detail at senior or middle management positions, depending on the number of posts included. Remember the purpose of the organization chart: to demonstrate the broad reporting perspective of the company, not to include every detail.

3. Connect with solid lines only.

As a general rule, each position should be connected to those above and below with a solid line. Arrows are not used, since the reporting chain is already obvious. Positions equal in rank should be on the same horizontal line.

A solid line should be used between all levels to indicate a clear path of the chain of command. Some organization charts connect boxes with a broken line, which often indicates that the chain of command is unclear at that point. When an executive hires a special assistant, for example, that individual reports exclusively and may not fit within the traditional chain of command. One business author, Robert Townsend, wrote in his book, *Further Up the Organization,* that "the traditional organization chart has one dead giveaway. Any dotted line indicates a troublemaker and/or a serious troubled relationship." This statement might seem humorous, but there is enough truth in it to merit attention. If the organization chart cannot be constructed with a clearly understood chain of command, there is probably a serious reporting problem. And that is the point of going through the effort to construct an organization chart. It forces definition.

4. Include titles but not names.

When organization charts are published in orientation manuals, displays, annual reports, and other documents going outside the company, the title of each position should be included but actual names should be left out. When organization charts are for internal distribution, names should be given along with each title, so that employees know not only the reporting chain but the people at each executive and management level.

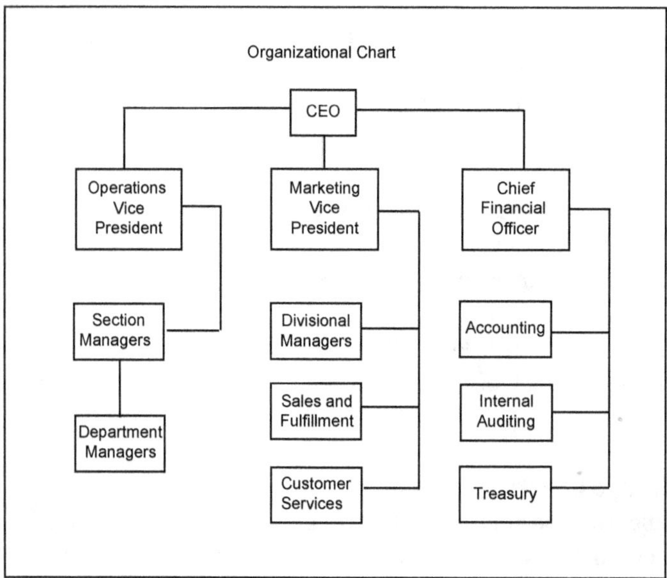

Figure O.1: Organizational Chart

Outlining

The outline is a useful device for organizing thoughts prior to writing reports, memos, letters, and other documents. Outlines should be compiled from notes or from a large body of information, so that the sequence of presentation can be decided prior to beginning the writing task. The sequence of information is one of the most important factors in style, since clarity of expression is determined by the way that information is presented.

1. Follow the guidelines for labeling outline levels.

Use numbers and/or letters consistently to identify the different levels of an outline. A *level* is a distinct topic or subtopic. For example, the first level may be one of six major points made in the outline. Within each of the six major categories, a number of secondary points are made; and within each of those, several third-level points are made.

Example:

I. Roman numerals distinguish level 1
  1. Align roman numerals on the decimal
  2. Indent second-level points

II. A limited number of major topics is presented
  1. Follow the same numbering system throughout
  2. Note the similarity of numbering at the second level
    (a) Numbering is the same
    (b) Indentation is the same
    (c) Each level has a distinct numbering designation

2. Limit the number of outline levels.

Outlines can become confusing if too many levels are used. Strive for a limited number of sublevels. Major points are the beginning for organizing your outline. Start by listing the major points; then identify two to five second-level topics. Within those, add detail as needed at a third level. Going beyond a third level might be unnecessary except in extremely lengthy and detailed outlines. Be aware that when you reach beyond fourth and fifth levels of detail, readers begin to lose their perspective about what the outline conveys. Avoid excessive detail at this phase. Always focus on what the outline is intended to achieve.

3. Use outlines for thought organization.

Outlining is an excellent way to break down and organize a complex topic. When preparing a report or even an especially long letter or memo, use outline form to prioritize your message. Outlines can help you to identify the proper sequence of teaching blocks. Without using the outline form, information might be disorganized, out of order, and ineffective.

4. **Use outlines for organizing presentations.**
   Outlines are effective tools for organizing a presentation in several formats.
   a. **Speeches:**
      When speaking on a topic you understand well, reading from exact notes or a PowerPoint slide is stilted and uninteresting. Outline form provides you with a train of thought, while still allowing an informal style. The outline allows you to interact with the audience without the thread of the topic in the middle of the speech. A PowerPoint slide should include outline points, and the speech itself should follow the format without repeating what the audience can already see.
   b. **Meetings:**
      Outlines for presentations made in meetings provide the same benefits as they do in speeches. You should be intimately familiar with the topic and with the material presented. Using outlines ensures that you will present material in the proper order, you will not overlook important points, and you will get through all of the material even if you are interrupted with questions or comments.
   c. **Reports:**
      When preparing reports for distribution, start with an outline to prioritize the presentation of data. The outline may later serve as a Table of Contents for cross-reference to each section, an idea of notable value in reports that exceed a few pages. The longer the report, the more important it is to provide the reader with an outline.

5. **Employ parallel structure in outlines.**

When presenting information in outline form, be sure that each statement at each level follows consistent parallel structure. If the outline contains action statements (a preferred and recommended format), all statements should be presented in that way.

Inconsistent structure:

I. Presentation of information.
   1. Identify needed data.
   2. Preliminary presentation.
   3. Review and modify.
   4. Make final presentation.

Action statements in parallel form:

I. Present information.
   1. Identify needed data.
   2. Present information (preliminary).
   3. Review and modify presentation.
   4. Present information (final).

The action orientation of the second example is effective, compared to the inconsistent and passive tone in the first example. Parallel structure is easier to read and gives others a clearer idea of the intention behind the outline.

P

Paradox

The use of *paradox* in business writing should be limited, but can sometimes serve a useful purpose in emphasizing a point or adding humor to a presentation.

The definition of paradox is an absurd, senseless, illogical, nonsensical, or contradictory statement. Because a paradox may be distracting, it is rarely appropriate in a presentation, where an audience expects a straightforward set of statements and may be confused, surprised, and distracted by a paradox.

Examples of absurd or distracting paradox:

> We have to abandon the market in order to dominate the market.
>
> His wisdom is based on his knowing that he knows nothing.

Such expressions are appropriate in business communication when limited, but also thought-provoking or used as a form of emphasis.

Examples of thought-provoking paradox:

> In this market, a sensible rule is to have no rules.
>
> We may open our eyes to the potential of our market. Remember, those who believe that the world is flat are found around the world.

Paragraphs

A *paragraph* is a group of sentences consistent in thought or theme. A break between paragraphs signals a new idea or thought, or expansion of previous material. The beginning sentence of the paragraph is transitional (from previous material) or forms the topic of the new paragraph. As the topic is introduced, the idea is developed in the remainder of the paragraph.

1. Provide a topic sentence.

The topic sentence usually appears at the beginning of the paragraph, although it may appear in the middle on occasion, especially when the paragraph begins with the transition. Ideally, the paragraph's topic and transition are merged together in one sentence, creating the most efficient and readable paragraph.

Example, topic sentence at the beginning (financial statement review):

> Financial statement review may be based on analysis of key balance sheet ratios. Among these are the current ratio, debt capitalization, and inventory turnover.

DOI 10.1515/9781547400218-015

Example, transition followed by topic sentence (transition to first ratio):

> Financial statement review may be based on analysis of key balance sheet ratios. Among these are the current ratio, debt capitalization and inventory turnover.
>
> These three key ratios are a starting point. The first one, current ratio, reveals a relationship between assets in liquid form and debts payable in one year or less.

2. Use transitions between paragraphs to ensure continuity of thought.

A paragraph is dedicated to a single idea or series of ideas; the break between paragraphs represents a move from one idea to another or an expansion of the thought. Transitions are bridges between paragraphs and are usually the first sentence in a new paragraph. The transition should also serve as the new topic sentence whenever possible.

Paragraphs with transitions:

> We are announcing our new product this week. After more than two years of research and testing, we believe that this improved product will be less expensive, more efficient, and safer than any other product for similar use on the market today.
>
> The attached test results dramatically illustrate the point. Never before has a product offering these combined benefits been offered at a lower price than the range of products it is replacing. We are confident that our customers will agree with our conclusions once they have tried the product.

In the first paragraph, the lead sentence establishes the subject and is the topic sentence. In the second paragraph, the first sentence serves two purposes: it is the topic sentence and serves as a transition from the material introduced in the previous paragraph, and the discussion that follows.

3. Vary paragraph length.

Although length should be dictated by the subject matter, a series of exceptionally long paragraphs is difficult to digest, and a series of paragraphs too short in length is distracting and disjointed. Paragraph length should be varied between two and seven sentences, as a general rule. A single topic will rarely require more length than this. However, when paragraphs exceed this length, they can be broken up with lists or, if quotations are included, indented sections for specialized text. The narrative of reports, memos, letters, and other documents should be visually varied—meaning paragraphs of different lengths—to keep reader interest at a maximum.

By definition, a paragraph contains more than one sentence. However, a one-sentence paragraph can be a dramatic form of emphasis if used very selectively. Such a device may be obvious or very subtle.

A dramatic one-sentence paragraph:

> This week's seminar includes an exceptionally busy program and more than the usual number of speakers. Accordingly, scheduling is going to be more difficult than possible, especially if the audience has a large number of questions.
>
> Do not go over your allotted time.
>
> There are no exceptions to this rule. If you do not stop on time, you will be interrupted and the next speaker brought forward. So keep an eye on the clock.

The one-sentence paragraph in this example, "Do not go over your allotted time," adds emphasis to the message. It conveys the idea clearly that the point is crucial.

A subtle one-sentence paragraph:

> Changes in last year's budgetary process were criticized at first as being too cumbersome for staff. However, once the process began, we discovered that the new procedures took no more time than before.
>
> The most dramatic result was fewer unexplained variances.

The transitions between these two paragraphs work because the original idea is introduced and explained (paragraph 1); and the major benefit is summarized in the one-sentence paragraph (paragraph 2). Because of the smoothness in the transition, the single-sentence paragraph works well and adds subtle emphasis.

4. **Use a consistent point of view to achieve unity in the paragraph (and throughout the rest of the narrative).**

Point of view refers to *who* is expressing the message. Most business writing employs various voices, depending on the nature of the document.

Inconsistent voice:

> We intend to continue monitoring the procedures in this department. I will be involved in this directly, as it is my responsibility to ensure successful completion and submission of the report each week. We will keep you informed.

Improved voice:

> I intend to continue monitoring the procedures directly, as I am responsible for ensuring successful completion and submission of the report each week. I will keep you informed.

5. **Organize paragraphs logically.**

Assume that a reader is unfamiliar with your material, so any explanatory matter should precede concluding remarks or suggestions. If background data are especially long, refer to them in the main body of the report, and include background discussions as an attachment.

If the narrative is exceptionally long, organize the writing and arrangement of paragraphs by first constructing an outline. Arrange important points in logical sequence, remembering to build the discussion on a solid foundation, establishing a case as you proceed.

As a method of emphasis or dramatic expression, a particularly interesting point can be placed at the beginning of a lengthy narrative, followed by background and supporting information. This makes an otherwise dreary discussion more interesting than the sequential discussion of a complicated issue. This technique, referred to as a *hook,* is used in some styles of writing, particularly in trade magazines and for book sales. For instance, on Amazon book descriptions usually contain three lines before it says "more" to get to the next page. The book must be sold in those three lines because if not, the reader does not click "more," and the sale is lost.

There are applications in business writing as well.

A hook in paragraph arrangement:

> We can reduce our budget by 20 percent this year. This is accomplished by adding a single step in the existing procedures, an idea that will cost nothing but will yield returns over many, many years.

This paragraph is meant to entice the reader into wanting to learn more. Of course, it should be followed with supportable proof of the claim. A decision maker reading this paragraph would expect to see data and to be convinced that nothing will be lost by following the suggestion.

6. **Indenting should depend on the nature of the document and the style of expression.**

In the traditional style, the first line of each paragraph is indented five spaces. No extra space is left between paragraphs. An alternative method is not to indent the first line of each paragraph but to leave one full space between each paragraph.

Indented paragraphs:

> Speakers at orientation seminars usually give long, boring speeches that put their audience to sleep. I intend to give a short, boring speech that will not put you to sleep.

I have a lot of material to get through, so let's get right to it. If anyone has questions as we proceed, raise your hand and ask as we go along.

Unindented paragraphs:

The market has not actually changed over the past 50 years, although our product line has changed dramatically. What does this mean? Is there a limit to the very idea of product development and improvement, and how do we recognize when we're there?

Our marketing department argues that there is no such limit. They would like to continue devoting a portion of their budget to product research and development, and their arguments are convincing.

The choice of style depends on the rules imposed by the organization, if any. Some companies prefer all letters to conform to one style, typically the unindented block style. If reports and other documents are doubled-spaced as a matter of practice, unindented style is a preferred formatting decision. The style selected for a specific type of document should be used consistently for each version and application.

Parallelism

Clarity and power of expression are improved by being aware of the need for *parallelism* in style. When you express a series of ideas in a list, in outline form, or in a table, use parallel construction. This is a method for making similar statements similar in format.

1. Use parallelism for list and outline organization.

Outline form is popular as a method for organizing thoughts, preparing presentations and speeches, and presenting reports or action plans. Use parallel structure on all outlines for clarity and consistency of style.

Unparallel structure:

A. Building parallel thoughts
   1. Identify the list
   2. Listing in sequence
   3. Write out the list
   4. Making the presentation

Parallel structure:

A. Building parallel thoughts
   1. Identify the list

2. List in sequence
3. Write out the list
4. Make the presentation

The second example contains a consistent listing of action statements; the list in the first example is a combination of action ideas and passive statements.

2. Use parallel forms of parts of speech.

When listing items, write so that parts of speech are set up in parallel form. This guideline applies to verbs, nouns, and phrases.

Unparallel verbs:

1. Following up
2. Communicate
3. Making changes

Parallel verbs:

1. Following up
2. Communicating
3. Making changes

Unparallel nouns:

1. Accounting department coordination
2. Manager of sales should prepare budget
3. Bob Smith to approve process

Parallel alternative:

1. Accounting manager coordinates
2. Sales manager prepares budget
3. Vice president approves

Unparallel phrases:

1. Problems:
    a. Communicating
    b. Of improving methods
    c. Executive level

Parallel alternative:

1. Problems:
    a. In communication
    b. Of improving methods
    c. At executive level

Parentheses and brackets

Enclosing a group of words in parentheses or brackets within text is one form of emphasis. It also serves other purposes.

1. Use parentheses for asides within text.

The use of parentheses can help add a conversational tone to narrative. The aside is a thought off the subject by way of added information, a side thought, or necessary explanation that adds to the discussion at hand.

Asides:

The director of sales (who has had over 20 years' experience in the field) expressed his opinion without hesitation.

Our sales volume last year (which was below projected levels but exceeded previous records) cannot be used as an indication of the future, due to substantial changes in markets.

Mr. Martin (who is approachable and open to suggestions from subordinates) could be asked to consider this recommendation.

In each example, the information enclosed in parentheses is not essential to the meaning of the sentence, but it does have an effect on how the reader will interpret the information. Parentheses can be used effectively without distraction, as long as their use is essential. Like any other style device, excessive use also destroys the impact and intention.

The aside can also be expressed with a dash, one each before and after the aside. This may be a preferred style because it draws less attention and may be less distracting.

2. Enclose citations and examples in parentheses.

Parentheses are used to provide documentation of source material and to provide examples within narrative. The intent is to avoid interrupting the reader's train of thought while providing essential secondary information.

Citations within text:

According to Dr. Hamilton (*Budgets on Computer*, 2015, p. 246), zero-base models were three times more likely to be attainable.

Research in this field (*Business Facts*, Oct. 2017) shows that only a small percentage of such programs are even minimally effective.

In-text examples:

The primary causes of defects (fatigue, monotony, low morale) are also the most difficult to eliminate.

> There is little we can do to cut further those overhead expenses established by contract (payroll, rents, leases, and interest).

3. Use parentheses to set aside definitions, abbreviations, and acronyms.

Use parentheses to clarify narrative explanations for definitions and acronyms used in the text. Within a single document, it is necessary to provide this type of clarity only the first time that the definition or acronym arises.

Definitions:

> The contingent liability (a liability that might or might not become an actual liability) is included as a footnote by standard practice.

Abbreviation:

> Our CFO (chief financial officer) has issued the report and is currently distributing it.

Acronym:

> The guidelines issued last month by HUD (Department of Housing and Urban Development) define how we must comply with those regulations.

4. Use parentheses for list distinctions.

Parentheses are used in enclosed lists.

Example:

> Our priorities are to (1) select deadlines, (2) assign work, and (3) complete the report.

5. Use parentheses and brackets for emphasis.

Parentheses and brackets can be used for emphasis; however, overuse may destroy the intended effect.

Parentheses for emphasis:

> Net profits ($45,769) exceeded the forecast by a significant margin.

Parentheses used excessively:

> Net (after-income taxes) profits ($45,759) exceeded the forecast ($38,000) by a significant margin (20.4%).

6. In contracts, use parentheses for numbers.

In contracts, dollar amounts and other numbers are often both spelled out and expressed numerically. This is meant to ensure fewer mistakes.

Example:

> The consideration of $10,000 (ten thousand dollars) will be paid in full within 20 (twenty) days.

7. Use parentheses and brackets appropriately in mathematical expressions.

Mathematical expressions are dependent on the use of parentheses, brackets, or both. This should be applied consistently when expressing several formulas in one document.

Example:

(x + y) + (r [2 * P]) = J

8. Follow the rules of punctuation for parentheses and brackets.

A brief phrase or word enclosed in parentheses or brackets within a sentence is not usually closed with a period. However, a complete sentence within these asides should be ended with a period.

Examples:

The manager (of the division) stood up and objected to the criticism.

The division manager stood up and objected to the criticism. (He has done the same at each preceding meeting.)

If the enclosed material asks a question, the question mark belongs inside the closing parenthesis.

Example:

The division manager stood up and objected to the criticism (has he done this at previous meetings?).

Parentheses are used in some cases to indicate either a singular or plural. The *s* at the end of the word, when enclosed in brackets, indicates that there is a choice or that the correct value is not known or can be either one or more.

Example:

The employee(s) preparing the report overlooked several important details.

9. Use brackets for errors in original quotations being cited verbatim.

Brackets are used in quotations when an error is included in the original quotation in spelling or grammar or when the quotation is confusing as it stands. When within the quotation, such errors should not be corrected. They should be followed with the bracketed word *sic* (Lt. "thus"), advising the reader that the error was part of the quotation and not part of your transcription.

Example:

According to the report, "Without fail, all members of the staff was [*sic*] part of the volunteer effort."

Brackets used when within a direct quotation imply that the enclosed word or words are not directly part of the actual quotation. This technique is used when, due to the way in which the quotation is being used, it would be awkward to quote directly. For example, consider the following passage found in a quoted source:

Text example:

These brave young women were unwilling to allow employers to take advantage of them because of their sex.

If you want to use this quotation in a paragraph already discussing females and job relations, it might read as an adjusted form of citation.

Application example:

Women of the 1890s were noteworthy in this employment rights struggle. The author noted, "[They] were unwilling to allow employers to take advantage of them because of their sex."

Because the narrative has already established the subject of discussion, the actual quotation would be awkward. By using brackets, the context of the quotation remains, and the writer uses the material in its proper context.

10. Use brackets for secondary asides within parentheses.

Avoid using parentheses and brackets excessively. If you discover the need for an aside within an aside, chances are that the thought is too complex. Consider the alternatives of two or more sentences, a footnote, or a complete division between paragraphs. Always strive for clarity.

When a two-part aside is required, use parentheses as the first level and brackets as the second.

Example:

The agreed-upon amount (defined by the contract as $20,000 [twenty thousand dollars] and finalized last month) is now being disputed by the other side.

The example is grammatically correct and follows the style guidelines, but an alternative method of expression can be used to express the same ideas better.

Preferred form:

The agreed-upon amount of $20,000 (twenty thousand dollars) is now being disputed by the other side. However, the agreement is defined by the contract that was signed last month.

11. Select parentheses as a first choice.

If the application allows either parentheses or brackets, give preference to parentheses. Use brackets for second-level asides or for other applications to distinguish their use from the first level, in which parentheses were used.

Participles

Verb forms that modify a noun, noun phrase, verb, or verb phrase are termed *participles*. They are modifiers similar to adjectives and adverbs and also are expressed in different tenses.

Participles may be active or passive.

Examples, active versus passive participles:

Breaking an agreement ... (active)
A broken agreement ... (passive)
An agreement broken by the vendor ... (relative clause)
With the agreement broken, we spoke with an attorney. (adverbial clause)
We saw the vendor breaking the agreement. (active, present participle)
The agreement was broken. (active, past participle)
He discovered the agreement broken. (passive, past participle)

Parts of speech

Each word and phrase within a sentence is assigned an identifying label known as a part of speech, each part serving a specific function within the sentence. A study of the parts of speech as they relate to the remainder of the words in a sentence helps form a basic understanding of grammar, expression, and style.

Parts of speech may describe, assert, join, modify, question, and explain.

1. Adjectives

Adjectives are modifiers. They add to and enhance the significance of nouns and pronouns. When a quality is brought forward with an adjective, it is called a *descriptive* adjective. The alternative is the imposition of boundaries, and is defined as a *limiting* adjective.

Descriptive adjectives:

an *experienced* manager
the *quarterly* report

The adjective *experienced* describes the noun *manager* in the first example. Without the descriptive adjective, a reader would know only that the discussion involved a manager, without knowing what kind of manager. In the second example, the adjective *quarterly* describes the noun *report*. With the adjective, the reader knows what kind of report is being discussed.

Limiting adjectives:

a group of *three* managers
a *partial* report

In these examples, the adjectives limit rather than describe the noun. In the first example, the adjective *three* limits the number of managers under discussion. In the second example, the reader is advised that the report is *partial* rather than complete.

Descriptive and limiting adjectives can be combined and used together. When this occurs, the limiting adjective almost always appears first. This rule makes sense because the limitation applies not only to the noun but to the descriptive adjective as well.

Limited and descriptive adjectives:

three experienced managers
a *partial quarterly* report

a. **Use *-er* and *-est* for comparative and superlative forms.**
Adjectives can be expressed in degrees of comparison: positive, comparative, and superlative. One-syllable adjective comparisons are usually achieved by adding the suffix *-er* in the comparative form and *-est* in the superlative form.

Examples:

Positive	Comparative	Superlative
small	smaller	smallest
big	bigger	biggest
long	longer	longest
short	shorter	shortest

b. **Create the comparative and superlative forms of adjectives with more than three syllables by preceding with the words *more* and *most*; or when reduced in degree, with the words *less* and *least*.**

Examples:

Positive	Comparative	Superlative
interesting	more interesting	most interesting
optimistic	more optimistic	most optimistic
profitable	more profitable	most profitable
substantial	more substantial	most substantial
disturbing	less disturbing	least disturbing
pessimistic	less pessimistic	least pessimistic
boring	less boring	least boring
limited	less limited	least limited

c. **Avoid illogical comparisons.**
The rules for comparison help avoid redundant forms of expression. Some words cannot be logically compared.

Illogical comparison:

less unhappy (*happier* or *less sad* would be easier to understand and more to the point)

d. **Do not use absolute words in comparative form.**
Exact, *unique, always,* and *never*, for example, are absolute words; they cannot be expressed in comparative form, although examples of this occur regularly and frequently in business communications. Such expressions are oxymoronic or confusing.

Improper comparison:

This answer is more exact.
Our product is the most unique of its kind.

Correct comparison:

This answer is exact.
Our product is unique.

Authors will use absolute words for effect when in reality there may be exceptions or disagreement. The absolute statements may be easily disproved and as a result will affect the author's credibility.

e. **Adjectives are used after verbs denoting the five senses and after linking verbs.**
A common mistake is to use adverbs when adjectives should be used.

Incorrect form:

The food smelled strangely.
The first draft looks roughly.
That decision appears correctly.
The western division became profitably this year.

Correct form:

The food smelled strange.
The first draft looks rough.
That decision appears correct.
The western division became profitable this year.

2. Adverbs

Adverbs modify verbs, clauses, and other adverbs. Verbs without adjectives can be virtually useless without the use of adverbs. Adverbs identify place, time, manner, and degree of action.

Adverbs modifying verbs:

The staff worked *furiously* to meet its deadline.
These meetings *usually* end on time.

In the first example, the adverb *furiously* sets the tone for the sentence. Without the adverb, the sentence lacks flavor or degree. In the second example, the adverb *usually* qualifies the verb *end* by specifying that meetings do not always end on time, an important distinction in reporting facts.

Adverbs modifying clauses:

Undoubtedly, they will rise to the occasion.
Certainly, we may depend on you.

In both cases, the adverb modifies the action (*rise* in the first case, *depend* in the second case). However, the entire action of the phrase is modified when preceded by an adverb in this manner.

Adverbs modifying other adverbs:

The improved budget worked *much* better.
We remained in balance *far* longer.

In the first example, the word *much* modifies the adverb *better*. In the second example, the adverb *far* modifies the adverb *longer*. In many instances, style is clarified by removing excessive adverbs; however, at times they serve a useful purpose in subtly adding significance and degree to a statement.

Certain adverbs are classified according to the way they qualify a statement (or question). A *conjunctive* adverb joins or qualifies a thought. Typical adverbs in this class are *nevertheless, therefore, however, then, accordingly,* and *consequently.* Another special class are the *interrogative* adverbs: *how, what, where, why,* and *when.*

a. Use adverbs to show degrees of comparison.

Adverbs of comparison follow rules similar to those for adjectives of comparison. One-syllable adverbs are generally constructed by adding *-er* in comparative form or *-est* in superlative form.

Examples:

Positive	Comparative	Superlative
slow	slower	slowest
quick	quicker	quickest

Use *more* or *less* (comparative) and *most* and *least* (superlative) to show comparison with adverbs exceeding one syllable. Such adverbs usually end in *-ly.*

Examples:

Positive	Comparative	Superlative
slowly	less slowly	least slowly
quickly	more quickly	most quickly

Irregular adverbs have their own form of comparison. The best example is the comparative form for *well:* the comparative form is *better* and the superlative form is *best.*

b. Many adjectives can be formed into adverbs simply by adding *-ly* on the end.

Some adjectives are interchangeable with adverbs with only a slight modification at the end of the word.

Examples:

Adjective	Adverb
significant	significantly
careful	carefully
occasional	occasionally

c. **Place adverbs as close as possible to the word being modified.**
This rule is especially true for adverbs of degree, such as *only, also,* and *almost.*

Incorrect placement:

The store only sold items marked down.
Managers also were asked to track absenteeism.
Our division almost had met its budget.

Correct placement:

The store sold only items marked down.
Managers were asked to also track absenteeism.
Our division had almost met its budget.

3. Conjunctions

A *conjunction* is a joining or qualifying word. It joins two or more other words, phrases, or clauses in a sentence. The most easily recognized form is *coordinating conjunctions: and, or, but, for*, and *yet.*

Conjunctions joining nouns:

managers *and* employees
corporations *and* partnerships

Conjunctions joining phrases:

the functions of the company *and* of the individual
to identify *but* not to correct

Conjunctions joining clauses:

We intend to realize a profit, *but* that will require a change in competitive conditions.
The meeting will begin on time, *or* we will have to pay more for the hall.

a. **Use a *subordinating conjunction* to connect or qualify two different sections of the sentence, which are usually clauses.**
This type of conjunction includes words like *before, after, until, unless, although, that,* and *since.*

Subordinating conjunctions:

Balance the books *after* posting the entries.
Don't write the letter *unless* the information has arrived.

b. **Use *correlative conjunctions* together, although they do not necessarily appear together in the sentence.**

Examples of such pairs are *neither-nor, not only-but,* and *either-or.*

Correlative conjunctions:

Not only the division *but* the entire company suffered severe losses.

Either devise systems to capture errors, *or* eliminate them altogether.

4. Nouns

Nouns are the names of persons, places, and things. Collectively, nouns are classified in two primary groups. *Proper* nouns are specific and are capitalized; *common* nouns are general and are not capitalized unless they appear as the first word of a sentence.

Examples:

Proper	Common
Chicago	city
Robert	man
Canada	country

Nouns are also described by their attributes:

a. *Count nouns:* Describe persons, places, or things that can be specifically counted (e.g., *employees, dollars, typewriters, shelves*).
b. *Mass nouns:* The reference is to an inseparable whole (e.g., *money, air, water, sunlight*).
c. *Abstract nouns:* Ideas or concepts that are intangible and cannot be counted, seen, or touched (e.g., *patriotism, spirit, dedication, pride, ego*).
d. *Concrete nouns:* Can be seen, felt, heard, smelled, or touched (e.g., *dollars, rain, noise, picture*).
e. *Collective nouns:* Groups of things in singular form but with a plural identification (e.g., *people, audience, staff, committee*).

a. Avoid style and punctuation errors when distinguishing between a noun's possessive form and its plural form.

As a general rule, a possessive form requires the addition of an apostrophe at the end of the noun, followed by an *s*. The plural form normally requires the addition of an *s* without an apostrophe.

Examples:

Possessive	Plural
manager's	managers
employee's	employees
supervisor's	supervisors

b. **Create the possessive for nouns ending in s (including plural form) by adding an apostrophe at the end of the word.**

Example:

managers' [possessive for more than one manager]

Beware: the language has ample exceptions.

Many nouns in the plural form do not end in *s*. In those cases, the possessive is formed by adding an apostrophe and an *s*.

Examples:

women's

men's

children's

c. **When referring to multiple persons in one sentence, show the possessive for each.**

Examples:

The manager's and employee's responsibilities are invariably connected.

Maria's and Robert's departments are on the same floor.

This rule applies, however, only when the verb implies separation. In the examples above, the structure of the sentences reveals different possessives. The manager's responsibilities are not identical to the employee's responsibilities, and Maria's department is not the same place as Robert's department. Possessives are placed only on the last noun when the verb applies to both nouns.

Verb applying to both nouns:

The manager and employee's responsibilities cannot be logically separated.

Maria and Robert's department is on the second floor.

In both examples, the content of the sentence changed to indicate the sameness of the verbs. In the first example, the word *responsibilities* is shared by both indicated nouns; and Robert and Mary are in the same department in the second example.

d. **When referring to one individual by title, place the apostrophe and the *s* at the end of the last noun in the title.**

Possessives in titles:

The chief financial officer's report was delayed.

The certified public accountant's report approved all of the records as reported.

e. **Form the plural form of some nouns by adding *es*, in place of just an *s*.** Some exceptions to forming a plural include nouns ending in *s*, *z*, *x*, *ch*, and *sh*. These require the addition of -*es* to form a plural.

-es *plurals:*

We paid more in corporate income *taxes* last year.

The budget *slashes* were devastating.

f. **Form the plural for a noun that ends in the letter *o* and is preceded by a consonant by adding -*es;* however, when a noun ends in *o* and is preceded by a vowel, the plural is formed with an *s* alone.**

Examples:

The *echoes* of dissatisfaction were heard.

The *ratios* demonstrated the point quite well.

g. **Irregular nouns do not conform to any rules.**

The following list indicates the range of potential plural forms for nouns that cannot be subjected to any clear set of standard rules.

Examples:

Singular	Plural
addendum	addenda
axis	axes
basis	bases
crisis	crises
criterion	criteria
datum	data
man	men
matrix	matrices
medium	media
parenthesis	parentheses

Singular	Plural
radius	radii
symposium	symposia
synopsis	synopses
terminus	termini
thesis	theses
woman	women

h. Form the plural for compound nouns by adding *s* or *-es* to the primary descriptive word.

The plural word may appear as the first, middle, or last word in the compound term.

Examples:

assistant financial officers
assistants to the president
attorneys at law
deputy supervisors
powers that be

i. Form plurals for acronyms, abbreviations, and some slang expressions by adding *s*.

This exception is widespread in the business environment, where abbreviations and acronyms are in common use.

Examples:

ABCs
CEOs
regs

5. Prepositions

The preposition, a word linking other words or phrases in the sentence. It reflects direction, time, or location and is the first word of a prepositional phrase. This phrase consists of the preposition and the object (and, frequently, the object's modifiers).

Prepositional phrases:

The company is moving *toward* the ultimate goal.
We prepared the report *for* management.
Our profits this year are estimated to be *above* the previous year's results.

In the first sentence, the preposition *toward* links the preceding parts of the sentence to the object, *goal.* The adjective *ultimate* also modifies *goal.* The second sentence shows an example of a prepositional phrase with only a preposition, *for,* and an object, *management.* There are no modifiers. The preposition links information about the report to the object following. In the third example, the preposition *above* relates to the object *results.* The words *previous* and *year's* modify the object *results.*

a. **Use *among* when more than two things are at issue and *between* when only two things are at issue.**
   A common mistake is confusion for the prepositions *between* and *among.* Use *between* when two different things are at issue, and use *among* when more than two things are at issue. In some applications, the more-than-two situation is satisfied by using either word, notably when the precise number is not indicated; but apply this rule consistently to avoid problems.
   Examples:
   We had to choose between the two plans.
   Resources are divided among our seven divisions.
   Let's pick the best solution from among all ideas presented. (*Between* could be used, but *among* is preferable.)

b. **Avoid using prepositions if they are not essential to the meaning of the sentence.**
   Sentences can be made more forceful by the removal of unnecessary words. This is true when using prepositions.
   Preposition unnecessary in sentence:
   All *of* the employees attended.
   Preferred expression:
   All employees attended.

c. **Do not capitalize prepositions in titles if they contain fewer than four letters.**
   If the preposition is the first word in a title, it is capitalized. A preposition within a title with four or fewer letters is not capitalized.
   Examples:
   Of Human Bondage
   Applications of Budgeting
   Business Without Bosses

d. Avoid double prepositions and ending sentences with prepositions (often characterized by following a preposition with the additional *of*).

Both of these habits weaken style and tend to confuse the meaning of a message.

Misused prepositions:

We took the numbers *off of* the report.
The department is *inside of* the building.
We need to know the report this came *from*.
They want to know where headquarters is *at*.

Preferred expressions:

We took the numbers *from* the report.
The department is *in* the building.
We need to know *from* which report this information came.
They want to know the location *of* headquarters.

This rule often makes an expression awkward. With this in mind, some exceptions are practical. For example, at times a sentence ended with prepositions is less awkward than strict adherence to the general rule.

Prepositions at the end of sentences:

The market is worth going into.
This is the report I told you about.
The plan was objected to.

e. Prepositions can be coupled with verbs, adverbs, and adjectives. Prepositions are sometimes preceded by verbs, adverbs, or adjectives.

Prepositions in non-phrase form:

interested *in*
aware *of*
comply *with*
capable *of*
conform *with* (or *to*)
object *t*

Common simple prepositions:

at	by	in	of
on	to	up	for
off	out	down	from
with	through		

Common complex prepositions and phrases:

according to	against
beneath	by means of
in front of	on top of

6. Pronouns

A pronoun replaces a noun or a noun phrase. This enables expression without the monotony of repeating the noun several times in the course of a paragraph, letter, or essay.

a. **Use personal pronouns to replace nouns of people speaking (first person), people spoken to (second person), or persons spoken about (third person).**

The three "voices" of personal pronouns are important to ensure proper style. Consistency in the voice used, also known as *point of view,* determines the quality of writing focus.

Incorrect voice style:

I prepared the report from our database, knowing that they wanted to see all of the summaries and projections we had available. You have to study our report with the knowledge of how I proceeded.

Correct voice style in second person:

We prepared the report from our database, knowing that all summaries of available data and projections were of interest. The report should be studied with the knowledge of how we proceeded.

First person should be reserved for personal letters and memos directed to someone the writer knows. *We* and *us* may represent a department, a company, or a division. Second person is the most commonly used business style. You (or your department), for example, refers directly to a group of people. Third person is often mixed with second person when second person alone would be preferable; third person alone tends to become passive.

Second- and third-person combined use:

We addressed our correspondence to the correct agencies, and their responses were general in nature. When we inquired about the original request, they said they had never received them.

Preferred form, second person only:

We addressed our correspondence to the correct agencies, whose responses were general in nature. When we inquired about the original request, we were told it had not been received.

Personal pronouns are further divided into three cases:

Subjective case pronoun, the subject of the verb

Objective case pronoun, used when the pronoun is the object of the verb

Possessive case pronoun, used when the form indicates possession.

The table below summarizes personal pronouns in each voice and for each case.

Table P.1: Personal Pronouns by Voice

	Subjective	Objective	Possessive
First person singular	I	me	my
First person plural	we	us	our
Second person singular	you	you	your
Second person plural	you	you	your
Third person singular:			
Masculine	he	him	his
Feminine	she	her	hers
Neutral	it	it	its
Third person plural	they	them	their

b. Use demonstrative pronouns to point out or indicate.

Only four demonstrative pronouns are used, and they can be broken down into singular or plural, and distinguished by implied distance—close: *this* (singular) or *these* (plural); far: *that* (singular) or *those* (plural). These are the most subject to error as their antecedents may be in the eye of the writer and unclear to others. So for clarity, it is often better to use the noun rather than the pronoun. The rule should be: If there is a chance of ambiguity, do not use the pronoun.

The close-far distinction is similar to the distinction made in personal pronouns between first and second person. *This* is analogous to *I*, and *that* is analogous to *you*. It is not accurate, however, to assign the characteristic of voice to demonstrative pronouns.

c. **Use indefinite pronouns to identify a grouping or classification of people or things.**

The indefinite pronoun can be interpreted in many ways, as it does not specify the exact number.

Examples:

all	another
any	anybody
anyone	anything
anywhere	both
each	either
every	everybody
everyone	everything
few	many
more	most
much	neither
nobody	none
no one	nothing
nowhere	others
several	some
somebody	something
somewhere	such

Indefinite pronouns sometimes act as adjectives, depending on their use.

Examples:

Several employees are absent today.

Many customers prefer the more expensive model.

Excessive use of indefinite pronouns, especially as adjectives, tends to weaken style. More specific descriptions are invariably preferred.

Less specific descriptions:

A number of employees are absent today.

Many customers expressed a preference for the more expensive model.

More specific descriptions:

Twelve employees are absent today.

Fifteen percent of customers prefer the more expensive model.

d. **Interrogative pronouns ask a question.**
These include words such as *who, whom, what*, and *which*. Some interrogative pronouns are also relative pronouns; they take the place of a noun like other pronouns but also connect a relationship between a main clause and a dependent clause.

Relative pronouns:

The manager decided *which* report to prepare first.
We decided *who* to assign the job.

In the first example, the connecting pronoun *which* connects the clauses on either side. In the second example, the pronoun *who* serves the same function. Compared to relative pronouns, an interrogative pronoun, while the same word, serves a different function by merely asking a question without connecting two separate clauses. The use of *whom* is falling out of common usage, so using *who* in place of *whom* is becoming an acceptable grammatical choice.

Interrogative pronouns:

Which report should be prepared first?
Who should complete this job?

e. **Reflexive pronouns are distinguished by the ending *-self* (singular) or *-selves* (plural).**
The list of these pronouns is:

herself	himself
itself	myself
oneself	ourselves
themselves	yourself
yourselves	

One form of reflexive pronoun is the intensive pronoun, which also has the *-self* or *-selves* ending but serves the function of adding emphasis to a statement.

Intensive pronouns:

I *myself* interviewed the candidate.
They *themselves* are accountable.

f. **Reciprocal pronouns involve relationships between items.**
Because more than one person or thing must be involved, all reciprocal pronouns are plural. This list includes *each other*, which can mean two only, or *one another*, which means more than two.

Two only:

The managers of personnel and accounting work well with *each other*.

More than two:

All of the employees work well with *one another*.

7. Verbs

The verb describes action in the sentence. An action may be a feeling, a physical movement, a thought, an idea, or even the state of being. (*To be* is one of the most common verbs.)

A transitive verb has a direct object. The object and the action of the verb are linked directly.

Transitive verbs:

The employee *wrote* the report.
I *see* the street from my window.

In the first example, the report is the object of the verb. In the second example the verb appears earlier in the sentence; its object is *street*.

In comparison, *intransitive verbs* do not have direct objects. This verb can complete its meaning without needing to relate to another word.

Intransitive verbs:

The marketing plan *worked*.
Our employees *reported*.

In the first example, there is no object to finalize the action. The statement is simply made that the marketing plan worked; how, when, or why it worked is not specified. In the second example, there is also no object. The employees reported. It does not say when, to whom, or how they reported.

a. **Be aware of verb tenses.**
Every verb may be expressed in each tense, as basic, progressive, or passive.

Basic verb tenses:

present: *we speak*
past: *we spoke*
future: *we will speak*
present perfect: *we have spoken*

past perfect: *we had spoken*
future perfect: *we will have spoken*

Progressive verb tenses:

present: *we are speaking*
past: *we were speaking*
future: *we will be speaking*
present perfect: *we have been speaking*
past perfect: *we had been speaking*
future perfect: *we will have been speaking*

Passive verb tenses:

present: *it is spoken*
past: *it was spoken*
future: *it will be spoken*
present perfect: *it has been spoken*
past perfect: *it had been spoken*
future perfect: *it will have been spoken*

The selection of tense helps enliven writing style. Mixing tenses appropriately helps add variety. Consider the variations of tense in the following paragraph:

Variations in tense used correctly:

The problems with profitability in the western division had been brought to management's attention several months ago. We were particularly concerned with the apparent inability of the division to improve cost control procedures or to increase sales volume. We looked at the differences between that division and the more established eastern division, and we located what we thought to be the answer. We now apply to the western division the same control standards in successful practice in the eastern division. We hope that in the next quarter, we will see tangible improvements. We want to be able to say after this experiment that we had anticipated, planned, controlled, and then implemented the improved conditions.

This paragraph includes a range of tenses, appropriately used. Discussions involve the past, present, and future. Many business applications include this sort of discussion: the problems observed in the past, actions being taken today, and estimates of the effect in the future.

b. Every verb is conjugated.

Conjugation is the expression of a verb in every possible form, allowing for the tense, number, person, and voice. Following is a complete conjugation of the verb *to work:*

Table P.2: Verb Conjugation

Tense	Number	Person	Active voice	Passive voice
present	singular	first	I work	I am worked
		second	you work	you are worked
		third	he/she works	he/she is worked
present	plural	first	we work	we are worked
		second	you work	you are worked
		third	they work	they are worked
progressive present	singular	first	I am working	I am being worked
		second	you are working	you are being worked
		third	he/she is working	he/she is being worked
progressive present	plural	first	we are working	we are being worked
		second	you are working	you are being worked
		third	they are working	they are being worked
past	singular	first	I worked	I was worked
		second	you worked	you were worked
		third	he/she worked	he/she was worked
past	plural	first	we worked	we were worked
		second	you worked	you were worked
		third	they worked	they were worked
progressive past	singular	first	I was working	I was being worked
		second	you were working	you were being worked
		third	he/she was working	he/she was being worked
progressive past	plural	first	we were working	we were being worked
		second	you were working	you were being worked
		third	they were working	they were being worked
future	singular	first	I will work	I will be worked
		second	you will work	you will be worked
		third	he/she will work	he/she will be worked
future	plural	first	we will work	we will be worked
		second	you will work	you will be worked
		third	they will work	they will be worked
progressive future	singular	first	I will be working	I will have been working
		second	you will be working	you will have been working
		third	he/she will be working	he/she will have been working

Tense	Number	Person	Active voice	Passive voice
progressive	plural	first	we will be working	we will have been working
future		second	you will be working	you will have been working
		third	they will be working	they will have been working
present	singular	first	I have worked	I have been working
perfect		second	you have worked	you have been working
		third	he/she has worked	he/she has been working
present	plural	first	we have worked	we have been worked
perfect		second	you have worked	you have been worked
		third	they have worked	they have been worked
past	singular	first	I had worked	I had been worked
perfect		second	you had worked	you had been worked
		third	he/she had worked	he/she had been worked
past	plural	first	we had worked	we had been worked
perfect		second	you had worked	you had been worked
		third	they had worked	they had been worked
future	singular	first	I will have worked	I will have been worked
perfect		second	you will have worked	you will have been worked
		third	he/she will have worked	he/she will have been worked
future	plural	first	we will have worked	we will have been worked
perfect		second	you will have worked	you will have been worked
		third	they will have worked	they will have been worked

c. **Confusion about singular and plural leads to many problems in verb usage.**

The verb should be singular if its subject is singular and plural if its subject is plural. This rule is referred to as *agreement.* When subject and verb are separated within the sentence, you can easily fall into the trap of a subject and verb that do not agree.

Incorrect agreement:

The study of impacts for customers were revealing.

The manufacturer of our goods are visiting today.

Correct agreement:

The study of impacts for customers was revealing.

The manufacturer of our goods is visiting today.

d. **Look for opportunities to replace weak verbs with strong verbs.**

Although weak verbs—for example, *is, are, have, had, was, were, can, has, do,* and *did* – are essential in the language, they tend to lengthen sentences and obscure meaning.

Sentence with weak verb:

Our marketing report was presented today.

Sentence with strong verb:

We presented our marketing report today.

e. Use strong verbs to assert.

Strong verbs may be more difficult to fit into a sentence, but they should be used to assert and provide direct action rather than using passive voice.

Weak verb statements:

Budgets are put into action by staff.

The report preparation is the responsibility of my department.

Strong verb statements:

Staff acts on budgets.

My department prepares the report.

f. Improve weak verb phrases with stronger replacements.

The same distinction between weak and strong refers to verb phrases.

Weak verb phrases:

Employees who work hard . . .

Managers who are ambitious . . .

Strong replacements:

Hardworking employees . . .

Ambitious managers . . .

g. Avoid the use of the very specialized subjunctive verb form in most applications.

Use the subjunctive form in limited circumstances: when recommending a course of action; when speculating about unknown, uncertain, or untrue conditions; or when presenting a demand.

Subjunctive form:

Were our estimates correct, we would not be involved today with explaining variances.

If it were possible, we would increase every employee's pay by that rate.

We strongly recommend that this matter be settled.

I insist that we act at once.

Patents

Patents are exclusive rights granted to the inventor of a device or process that is unique and new. It is one of several forms of intellectual property. A copyright is granted for creative or artistic work, and a trademark is assigned for a unique image, phrase, or slogan (see also Copyright). A patent refers specifically to the invention and the rights granted acknowledging ownership of the device or process to the individual inventor.

In making a patent application, the services of an attorney may be required. The application must make the claim that meets the tests of novelty, utility, and originality. The purpose in applying for the patent is to prevent the manufacture, use, sale, importation, or distribution of the patented invention without permission from the inventor holding the patent.

Peer review

The *peer review* process may be applied to scholarly publication, professional standards, or government processes. It consists of evaluating the competence and work of others in a similar field and with similar backgrounds and experience (peers).

1. Scholarly peer review

Peer review is performed as part of the process of publishing an academic and scholarly paper, article, or book. Experts performing peer review are hired by a potential publisher to comment on the authority, research, organization, and conclusions in the draft document being considered for publication. The publisher will determine whether to publish or reject a work based on peer review, and may also ask the author to make revisions when appropriate. Most peer review is anonymous, but *open peer review* is gaining in popularity, when comments and identities of peers is available to the author.

In preparing a peer review of someone else's work, impartially comment on the tone, objectivity, and thoroughness of research and writing style; qualifications of the author; and documentation of citations, studies, and sources. Also comment on whether the material in a paper supports the conclusions the author has drawn. In book peer reviews, the same range of issues should be addressed in the review process, as well as added commentary for the level of authorship compared to the perceived level of a likely reader.

In a scholarly peer review, the reviewer should *never* provide a negative review along with the suggestion that a replacement work should or could be prepared by the person performing the peer review. To do so completely destroys perceptions of objectivity.

2. **Professional peer review**
   A professional peer review is evaluation of performance by others and is intended to note areas where improvement is indicated, whether standards are being met, and often as part of the process for granting (or denying) a form of certification. In academia, faculty peer review may be part of consideration for granting advancement or tenure.

   Ideally, the reviewer should be a peer, but not a competitor, for the same potential level of advancement or consideration for a position. Objectivity is an absolute requirement in peer review, and any potential conflicts should be disclosed as part of the review.

   Professional peer review is performed not only in academia, but in many other specialized fields—notably in medicine (clinical peer review), in law, in accounting, in engineering, and in aviation.

3. **Government peer review**
   In federal, state, and local government, peer review may be performed by individuals, co-workers, consulting experts, or committees of peers. The review may occur on many levels and, based on the role of the individual (or agency) under review, results may be published in open peer review and may also be available to the general public. In this case, the individuals writing the peer review need to be especially careful to understand that all opinions and conclusions are subject to review, criticism, or challenge.

Photographs

Photographs are used in many business publications: annual and interim corporate reports, brochures, promotional literature, and reports. They add interest and variety to the text and show readers the topic being discussed. When your report is intended to convince a decision maker, photographs can improve your chances for approval.

If you use photographs, you will probably work with a professional photography company or a corporate department, or use a public domain photograph available online.

1. **The subject of the photograph should be framed well.**
   This does not necessarily mean that the subject must be in the center of the photo; rather, a pleasing balance of light and dark areas is important. Many pictures can be cropped to achieve a more desirable effect.

2. **Photographs should be in focus.**
   Out-of-focus photos cannot be salvaged and should be rejected.

3. **Avoid overly dark photographs.**
   When photos are not well balanced in terms of light and dark, they are more distracting than helpful. When choosing from several different photographs, reject those with too many shadows or dark areas.

4. **Be aware that a print can be revised and improved in some situations.**
   You might find an especially good photograph that is too dark, for example. Consult with the photographer. By varying the exposure time during developing or by exposing different sections of the photo to varying degrees of light (called *ducking*), dark areas can be minimized or eliminated.

5. **Some photos can be flopped—printed in reverse of the true scene.**
   This should be applied only to non-landmark scenes, and never to photos with lettering, company buildings, work sites or individual faces. Flopping is appropriate when better page balance is achieved with it, and when producing the picture in reverse does not distort or misrepresent what is being shown.

6. **Be cautious when selecting photographs from color separations, slides, or negatives.**
   You don't always see accurately what a photograph will look like when viewing only a small, isolated version of it. Avoid making selections from negatives.

Planning documents

Organizations develop planning statements to serve as guidelines on several levels. First, a company objective statement serves as an overall guide to the organization's purpose. Second, a short-term statement of goals (usually one year or less) sets a course for the immediate future. And third, the same statement of immediate goals serves as a guideline for the development of forecasts and budgets.

1. Keep objective statements brief and direct.

The *objective* is a brief statement designed to identify the company's purpose. A good way to develop this statement is by identifying the sectors or elements of the organization, typically (1) management, (2) internal staff, (3) vendors or suppliers, and (4) customers.

The objective statement is more easily written once these groups are defined and understood. For example, an organization might identify a list of important objective elements.

Example of important objective elements:

1. Recruit the most capable management team.
2. Hire and train a spirited internal staff.
3. Find and work with the best vendors.
4. Work to earn customer loyalty.

These basic and simplified examples lend themselves to the development of an objective statement.

Objective statement:

> The Sample Corporation applies the skills of its management team with the purpose of hiring and training a professional internal staff. We recognize the importance of attracting and supporting a broad range of vendors and suppliers. Finally, we strive to retain and expand its base of loyal, satisfied customers.

2. Use goal setting for marketing expansion and for departmental programs.

Goals should contain a clear definition, a deadline, and a means for measuring the success of the goal. Goal setting is particularly effective in establishing goals for employees within a department. Establishing a goal, a deadline, and a measure of success enables the employee to operate with a clear definition of the manager's expectations. It also provides the means for performance review.

a. Definition:

A goal is defined with a brief statement, clearly spelling out what you want to achieve.

Examples:

Revise the filing system completely to conform to the company-wide filing procedure.

Develop a market tracking system that can be automated and put into effect in every branch office.

Reduce expenses by 15 percent or more without loss in efficiency.

b. **Deadline:**
   Every goal requires a deadline for completion. The deadline should be realistic, with enough time allowed to achieve the goal but within the near future—generally within one year or less—so that everyone involved has some sense of urgency.

c. **Means of measurement:**
   Goals should be defined in terms of how their success is measured, in order to know whether the goal is successful.

   Examples:

   The filing system will be completely in conformity with the company-wide system.

   The market tracking system will be in each office, working as designed, and personnel in each office will have been trained in its use.

   Expenses will be 15 percent or more below the current level, and work flow will continue at current levels without an increase in errors.

3. **Base forecasts and budgets on specific goals that can be measured.**

Goals are useful in the development of budgets and forecasts and can be used to establish the standard by which a forecast and budget are to be prepared. Goals should always be written down.

In forecasting and budgeting, the outcome is measured in dollars and cents—the easiest method for judging success or failure of a goal. However, the expected success of a forecasting or budgetary goal may also be given a range.

Goal with a range of outcome:

The outcome is either favorable (meaning actual expenses are lower than budget) or the unfavorable variance is lower than $500 or 5 percent of the budget amount.

Forecasts and budgets, like other forms of goals, are useful only if the outcome is measured as the period of time continues. A variation of the six-month or yearly forecast and budget is the longer-term budget document.

Important points about style of expression for forecasting:

1. The longer the period is that is being estimated, the less accurate it will be.

2. Without a clearly defined purpose, the work that goes into a long-range planning document is of no practical use. The purpose should be to make current decisions based on the best guess of long-range direction.
3. If an organization employs long-range planning techniques, the effort should be updated at least once per year. Even if the only benefit is to observe how long-range perceptions change with time, the effort may have a clear and specific purpose.

Possessives

A *possessive* denotes ownership, either literal or more figurative, on the part of the noun. The use of an apostrophe distinguishes a possessive noun from other forms (see also Nominative, objective, and possessive pronouns).

1. **Form the possessive of most singular nouns, proper and common, by adding an apostrophe and the letter *s*.**

   Examples:

   the employee's desk
   Sample Company's assets
   Hector's attitude
   the company's goodwill

2. **If a singular noun ends in *s* or *x*, form the possessive by adding an apostrophe and the letter *s*.**

   Examples:

   the boss's absence
   the fox's tail

Some conventions require that nouns ending in *s* or *x* should be made possessive with the apostrophe alone:

Alternative style:

the boss' memo
the fox' tail

This style does not match the way the phrase would be pronounced, so adding the *s* is preferable.

3. **If a plural noun ends in *s*, add an apostrophe to form the possessive; if a plural noun does not end in *s*, add an apostrophe and *s*, just as with singular nouns.**

The distinguishing mark of the possessive form is the apostrophe and the addition of an *s* to the word. This is usually the case for singular-noun possessives and for plural nouns that do not end in the letter *s*.

Examples:

the men's jobs
the children's parents
the employees' paychecks

When using titles or names of companies in possessive form, add the apostrophe and the *s* to the end of the last word.

Examples:

the chief financial officer's report
International Business Machines's stock price

4. **Possessive forms of personal pronouns.**

No apostrophe or *s* is required for possessive adjectives and pronouns, because these words are already expressions in possessive form. These words are:

my	mine
his	his
it	its
our	ours
your	yours
her	hers
their	theirs

Presentations

Presentations before groups may be formal or informal. Most business meetings involving two or more attendees take place in informal settings, within an office or meeting room. An individual presentation rarely represents the entire meeting, and is more likely to be part of it.

1. **Meeting preparation**

The better organized and prepared you are as the organizer of a meeting, the greater the efficiency and end result.

a. **Prepare and use an agenda.**
The agenda should define the purpose of the meeting through a title, invitees, and points to be covered in the agenda itself. Keep the agenda brief and when possible, assign timeframes.

Sample agenda:

Budget planning meeting
Chief accountant
Supervisor, general accounting
Accounting employees (2)

Time: 9:00 a.m. – 10:30 a.m., Tuesday, 10/31/17

9:00 – 9:15	Budgetary objectives and discussion
9:15 – 9:30	Schedule development
9:30 – 10:00	Presentation, Chief accountant
10:00 – 10:15	Questions and answers
10:15 – 10:30	Assignments and deadlines

b. **Respect starting and ending times.**
An efficient meeting begins on time and also ends on time. The use of specific timeframes within the meeting provides a means for ending a discussion of one item to move forward to the next.

c. **Generate action points and follow up.**
The generation of action points, assignment to attendees, deadline and follow-up processes are crucial if the meeting is to have any purpose. However, these all-important portions of meeting organization often are excluded.

2. **Invite appropriate people to attend, and avoid over-inviting.**

Invite only those who are essential and who will be likely to contribute to the meeting or receive assignments as a result. Too many meetings invite people who do not need to be there. This is either because they are not involved directly in the agenda items, or if they are involved, they can be briefed separately.

3. **Special situations.**

Some meetings are required due to regulatory disclosure, imposition of requirements by regulatory agencies, or as a result of internal procedures. In these cases, the meeting should be recorded and/or notes taken for later distribution to all attendees and to any oversight people, departments or agencies.

A stockholders' meeting is one example. Another is the meeting between financial executives and external auditors regarding audit findings and recommendations.

a. **Board of directors meetings**

   One special situation, especially in public agencies, NGOs, or publicly funded universities is the meeting of a board of directors. A presentation and report at this level requires special care because compliance and disclosure are an essential part of the process.

   The reason for a board of directors meeting is to provide information needed in order to execute the board's function. With this in mind, the style of presentation or report should focus on the essential requirements and how those requirements are documented.

   1. Ensure that all required board-specific information is available.
   2. Work to ensure full communication between the board and executives.
   3. Select the most appropriate method of communication with board members.
   4. Build and maintain a complete system for records retention.

Problem statement

A *problem statement* is used effectively in many reporting forms, especially one consisting of statistical analysis. It should define specifically what is addressed in the report. Rather than a broad or overly generalized problem statement, style should be narrowly focused.

Example, ambiguous problem statement:

This report analyzes various market attributes for the purpose of identifying specific shortcomings or oversights in the company's marketing and strategic initiatives.

Example, focused problem statement:

Product markets have not been effectively developed. This report summarizes three shortcomings in the marketing strategy and proposed short-term solutions.

The statement may be made more effective if expressed in the form of a question.

Example, interrogatory problem statement:

Have company products been effectively developed?
Is the marketing strategy adequate?
What three solutions are proposed for the short term?

The problem statement should accomplish several objectives, and these are expressed in the statement itself. First, it should clearly define the range and scope of a report or study. Second, the means for improvement should be indicated—a problem by itself is simply an expression; when a path to the solution is included, it provides true benefits.

Problem scope may include the following:

1. A problem is new and has not been addressed previously.
2. The problem is chronic and past initiatives have not resolved it.
3. Potential solutions have not been coordinated or centralized.
4. Decision-makers are not aware of the problem and need to be educated.

Procedures manuals

When writing and updating procedures manuals, employ a straightforward writing style. The manual documents work processes and should serve as a training guide. For the purpose of this section, the following definitions are used:

Job: A range of tasks performed by one or more people for the purpose of completing an identifiable result (report, summary, etc.).

Task: A step required in the completion of a job, usually performed by one person.

Routine: A simple task, often performed every day or on a recurring basis each week or month.

Department: The area of responsibility for a specific series of related jobs and tasks.

Desk: The location within a department where the job and its tasks are completed. The term *desk* is used in place of an individual name so that a description will not become obsolete when a person is transferred. Some individual employees also operate in more than one capacity, meaning they execute the jobs and tasks of more than one desk.

1. Select the best approach for preparing the manual.

Some organizations assign the task of developing procedures manuals to one department or person. Others assign the task to the personnel department or a specialized training department, or each individual department may be told to develop its own procedures. The potentially disjointed assignment of this task may create inconsistencies or incomplete results.

The advantage of centralized procedures is that a task will be performed consistently and has a better chance of being revised and updated regularly. The disadvantage is that a distant individual cannot know the job as well as the person who performs it. Centralized procedures often become obsolete because they are not updated as job performance methods change.

The advantage of having each person prepare their own documentation is knowledge: The person doing the job knows how it is done. The disadvantage is inconsistency. Some people perform the task of writing a manual well; others do not. Procedures will be updated only if employees are reminded to do so. Every manager and supervisor knows that employees exhibit a high level of resistance to the task of writing.

2. Use outline form.

Use outline form to create and write the sections of the procedures manual. Design the format of outlining so that all sections can be expanded without limitation. This might mean having to expand the outline references beyond two or three sublevels. As a general rule, outlines are clearer when the number of sublevels is limited; that is not always possible.

Procedures manuals should be organized so that the first outline level indicates the department, the second identifies the section or type of work, and subsequent levels are used for distinguishing specific desks, jobs, and detailed tasks.

3. Employ flowcharts as aids for narrative sections.

Relatively simple tasks, or *routines,* probably need little explanation. A routine performed daily can usually be described in a single paragraph. For example, a routine such as "opening the mail" or "telephoning the supervisor" does not need a visual aid. Routines often occur as part of a more complex task.

For tasks with numerous steps, flowcharts can be useful explanatory and training tools (refer to the Flowcharts section to examine different formatting choices). Even when using visual aids for a solitary task, indicate (1) points in the task when information or documents must come to the person performing the task, (2) when information or documents must be sent to someone else, (3) the exact point at which documents are to be generated, and (4) all deadlines for completion of the task.

4. Document report generation and deadlines.

Many tasks recur as part of a normal job and do not produce any tangible result; others are designed specifically to complete a form, prepare a report, or post a record. When any form of reporting or documentation is required, the procedures manual should include a line-by-line explanation of (1) the title of the document, (2) a blank sample, (3) a filled-in sample, (4) line-by-line instructions, (5) the desk responsible for completing the document, (6) the deadline and frequency of preparation, and (7) the distribution list.

5. Update references and guidelines.

Each page of the procedures manual and every document sample should include a date at the bottom. This is the origin date for the procedure, form, or document, or the latest date that it was revised. It advises anyone reading the procedures manual how recent (or out of date) the section is and may also indicate that there has been a replacement since that date. For example, an employee may know that the procedure for preparing a certain form was changed as of March 2016. All procedures pages in the manual indicate this. The blank form, however, shows a latest revised date of August 2017, and the line-by-line explanations don't make sense either. The employee will know from this information that the sample document is not the correct one for the task.

6. Identify the elements of each task.

A *task* is a series of steps required to complete a segment of a job. Each task, whether shown on a flowchart or explained in a narrative, is defined by a series of actions with clear starting and stopping points. The reason for identifying every task in a job is to describe what has to be done and advise the employee of the order in which tasks must be completed.

Some tasks, however, can be performed out of order. When working against a deadline, for example, it may be that a certain task has to be delayed; however, subsequent tasks may be performed so that time can be saved later. A properly constructed procedures manual will specify when out-of-sequence work can be performed.

Task breakdowns also help trainees digest information. An especially daunting task is more easily mastered when broken down into understandable, distinct tasks that can be memorized, comprehended, and executed without much difficulty.

7. Identify the elements of each job.

A job is a series of tasks with a clear beginning and end. The procedures manual should also explain the reason a job is performed. A job description should include an identification of the responsible desk, any deadlines, frequency of performance, documents to be produced as part of the job completion, distribution list, and all needed approvals.

8. **Label all parts of the manual clearly.**
All segments of the procedures manual should be marked clearly and separated by index tabs or other devices. Each heading and subheading within the manual should be readily distinguishable. Anyone opening the manual to a page should be able to identify (1) the department or division, (2) the title of the job and task, and (3) the placement within the overall outline.

9. **Strive for uniformity.**
Every department contributing to the procedures manual is expected to comply with the established format, not only for labeling and identification but also for the approach taken in providing documentation. The only way to ensure absolute consistency is to assign one individual to rewrite procedures documents so they all conform in format and style. The most effective procedures are those that conform with other departmental procedures, and can easily be revised and updated.

Ultimately, the success of a procedures manual is found when it can be used effectively as a training tool for new or transferred employees.

Proposals

A proposal is similar to some other types of reports in the sense that it presents information. Its distinguishing attribute, however, is that it offers a course of action that management might not have otherwise considered. When a consulting firm presents a proposal, it hopes to convince the company to hire it to perform a job or series of jobs; explains how it will accomplish those actions and offers a deadline; and provides a total of the cost. When a department or individual within the company presents a proposal, the purpose is to make a case for a course of action or executive decision, set a deadline, and describe the benefits of the course of action versus alternatives.

1. **Format the proposal for convenience.**
A proposal should be easy to read. Even someone who does not intend to read the entire document should be able to tell very quickly (1) the topic of the proposal, (2) the importance of or need for what is being offered, (3) the essence of

the proposal, which can usually be expressed in one or two sentences, and (4) the request itself.

All of this information can be summarized on the first full page that follows a title page. This format enables a reader to discern quickly who sent the proposal and what that person or department wants.

2. Arrange the content for ease of use.

Preface the proposal with the following pages:

1. *Cover page:* Include a title, identification of the person or department responsible for preparing the document, and the date.
2. *Table of contents*: Include if the proposal is longer than 6 to 10 pages.
3. *First full page:* Summarize the essential elements of the proposal.

Arrange information in the body of the proposal to make the best case. The following sections should be included:

1. *Explanation and background:* This section describes why this concept is a good idea and the important features that someone should know to make the decision.
2. *Financial impacts:* A proposal that can demonstrate a savings or recapture of investment has a better chance for approval. This section should not be exaggerated, however. Base pro forma estimates on conservative information.
3. *Examples of application,* especially if the proposal seeks changes in procedures, marketing, or utilization of equipment.
4. *Supporting information:* Statistical summaries, financial reports, productivity or work analyses, and any other useful information. These data should be included as attachments to the body of the report.

Cross-reference all sections of the report to important data. If statistical or financial summaries are included in appendices, label them and refer in the body of the document to the labeled material. Within the proposal itself, label all graphs, photographs, tables, charts, and other visual aids. Cross-reference between visuals and the narrative text for maximum effect. Explain the significance of each visual rather than taking up space to tell the reader what he or she can readily observe independently (see also Graphics; Photographs).

3. Document all facts and conclusions.

All facts cited in the proposal should be fully documented. If the proposal refers to other publications, websites, or outside sources, include proper citations using footnotes. For extensive citations, also include a bibliography at the end of the report.

Use facts sparingly. In the body of the document, make the case for the proposed change or new idea, and put the details in the appendix. Provide appropriate labels and refer text discussions to the more detailed section for ease of use, but avoid excessive repetition of numerical data within the body of the report.

If statistics are used, include a section documenting the statistical base. This section should contain an explanation of (1) the source for the statistical information, (2) how that information was applied, (3) any special changes made to the data, such as moving averages or selective use, (4) complete details concerning the assumptions used when statistical data were selected, and (5) the conclusions demonstrated by the statistical information. Numerical information is powerful and compelling in a proposal, especially as it relates to the viability of an idea. A proposal that demonstrates the likelihood for the financial success of a proposed idea has a high degree of acceptance and approval, unless the assumptions are successfully challenged.

4. Use graphics.

Visual aids— charts and graphs, tables, or photographs (when appropriate)— make a proposal interesting and easier to understand. Visuals also help the writer's style, since less narrative is required to prove the case. Visuals should be appropriate to the discussion and simplify the arguments being presented. Graphics are especially important for all numerical information, because the significance of such data is more easily comprehended visually than in the abstract.

The more numerical data there are, the more the proposal will benefit from visual aids. However, the scaling for related charts and graphs should be the same to the extent possible. Different scaling may be used for dissimilar information and may be beneficial as a means for distinguishing between two dissimilar sets of presented information.

Punctuation

All writing requires punctuation. Various marks indicate singular or plural, possessives, separate ideas, a series of related ideas, asides, quotations, emphasis, the end of a sentence, questions, and subtle variations of ideas.

2. **Apostrophe**
   a. **Use the apostrophe to indicate possessives.**
   The general rule for singular nouns is to add an apostrophe and the letter *s* to indicate a possessive (see also Possessives).
   Examples:
   manager's
   employee's

   b. **Indicate possessives for plural nouns ending in *s* by adding an apostrophe to the end of the word.**
   Examples:
   managers'
   employees'

   Personal pronouns (*my, your, his, its, our, their*) and personal adjectives (*mine, yours, hers, ours, theirs*) do not require an apostrophe; they are already in possessive form.
   c. **Use apostrophes in contractions to indicate the omitted letter.**
   Contractions are informal forms of expression. They should be used rarely in business letters or reports, and reserved for correspondence with peers or friends.
   Examples:

Full Form	Contraction
I am	I'm
you are	you're
he is	he's
they are	they're
they will	they'll

   d. **The apostrophe is used in descriptive terms, such as to denote time.**
   Examples:
   a month's time
   a day's work

   e. **Use apostrophes when numbers, symbols, and abbreviations are included in text.**
   Common use is moving away from this practice. Use the apostrophe when it clarifies a point; omit the apostrophe when it is not necessary.

Examples:

The #'s indicate numerical value.
When complete, write x's at the bottom.
The 35's are on the assembly line now.

3. Colon

The colon is used to change the rhythm and thought of the sentence and to signal a change to the reader.

a. **Set up displayed lists within narratives with colons.**

Example:

The three steps in this process are:

1. Speak directly with the customer.
2. Promise action by a specified date.
3. Follow up and ensure response.

Colons are not generally used in strict outline form. Indentation of subheadings replaces punctuation when not part of a narrative.

b. **Colons link connected ideas or expressions with emphasis on the last idea.**

Example:

The importance of service cannot be stressed too greatly: The customer has to come first.

In this example, the colon effectively draws attention to the material following, an affirming statement that follows the first part of the sentence. (A semicolon, in comparison, tends to give equal weight to both sides, and dashes set aside a thought within the sentence.)

c. **Use colons for emphasis.**

The preceding example, involving a colon to emphasize the second part of a sentence, is typical. Emphasis is even stronger when the same idea is isolated to one word or phrase at the end of a sentence.

Example:

We emphasize the need to provide for the single most important part of the marketing equation: the customer.

d. **Use a colon at the end of the salutation in business letters.**

In informal correspondence and personal notes, the colon is sometimes replaced with a comma or a dash.

Formal salutation:

Dear Mr. Anderson:

Informal salutations:

Dear Andy,

Andy–

e. **Use colons in a variety of other ways: as separation between hours and minutes in time notation, to separate volumes and pages when referring to publications, to distinguish between primary titles and subtitles, and to separate the two sides of mathematical ratios.**

Colon used in time notation:

12:45

Colon used in volume and page notation:

see *Business Journal* 11:35

Colon used between primary and subtitle:

Management Science: A Critical Analysis

Colon used to express ratios:

The current ratio should be 2:1 or better.

4. Comma

The comma has the greatest number of different purposes among types of punctuation. It can add emphasis, separate several ideas in one sentence, provide clarity, and avoid misunderstanding of the meaning of the sentence.

a. **Use the comma to clarify meaning.**

When a sentence or phrase can be interpreted in more than one way, use a comma to clarify the intended message

Unclear meaning:

The budget committee disagreed with increases and proposed revisions.

Clarified meaning:

The budget committee disagreed with increases, and proposed revisions.

In the first example, it is not clear whether the committee's disagreement included proposed revisions. With the inserted comma, the two thoughts are made clear: The committee disagreed with increases, and it proposed revisions.

b. **Commas signal the separation of two complex thoughts separated by a conjunction.**

Two relatively simple ideas do not require commas.

Complex thoughts with conjunctions:

The accounting review included discussions of numerous footnotes about contingent liabilities, and procedures in inventory valuation that increased net profits.

Simple thoughts not requiring a comma:

The review included discussions of contingent liabilities and inventory valuation.

The comma is also used when a sentence contains three or more ideas. An abbreviated style calls for use a comma following the conjunction. The "serial" style (also called "Oxford" style) includes commas after all items.

Example, abbreviated style:

The process includes initial review, preparation of the report and approval.

Example, serial (Oxford) style:

The process includes initial review, preparation of the report, and approval.

Do not attempt to join two clauses with a comma only. The conjunction or semicolon is required.

Two clauses without a conjunction:

Employees generally locate information, prepare the report.

Corrected sentence with conjunction:

Employees generally locate information and prepare the report.

c. Use commas for direct addresses within sentences and for short words or phrases that break the primary idea or expression.

Examples:

The report, Mary, is due tomorrow.
The budget, incidentally, was never completed.

d. Separate a parenthetical expression within a sentence by commas. Such expressions are often handled with dashes or parentheses; however, the comma will suffice without breaking up the flow of the sentence.

Example:

Mr. Mackay, according to the biographical data, is an experienced executive.

e. **Identify introductory elements at the beginning of sentences, whether single words or entire phrases, with commas.**

Exceptionally long prepositional phrases serve as qualifying or introductory statements and should also be followed by a comma. Introductory interjections should also be followed by commas.

Examples:

Incidentally, the meeting has been postponed.
In spite of all our efforts, we did not succeed.
Yes, the budget is complete.

f. **Use commas to divide numbers above 999 into groups of three.**

Whole numbers should be lined up on the far right; dollars and cents or decimals should be lined up on the decimal point.

Examples:

1,000
999
33.56
1,223,500.03
216,480

g. **Separate adjectives with commas when there are more than two; however, do not separate the final adjective from a noun that follows.**

Examples:

It was a brief, informative meeting.
We want to develop a program providing for sincere, responsive, and memorable service.

h. **Use commas to indicate omitted words in sentences.**

Example of repetitive expression:

Three divisions showed a profit and two showed a loss.

Example of comma used for omitted words:

Three divisions showed a profit; two, a loss.

Rather than repeating the term "showed a ..." the comma is used to set up contrast.

i. **Place a comma after the name of a city, followed by the country or state name.**

Examples:

Berlin, Germany
Duluth, MN
San Francisco, California

j. **Place commas in dates following the number of the day.**
Use a comma after the day when using the style of MDY.

Examples:

May 14, 1997
On January 3, 1996, the revised procedures manual was distributed.

k. **When material in a sentence is placed within parentheses or brackets and a comma follows the thought preceding, the comma belongs outside the parentheses.**

Incorrect placement:

The vice president (Ms. Green,) an expert on the topic, explained.

Correct placement:

The vice president (Ms. Green), an expert on the topic, explained.

l. **When stating a person's last name first, followed by first name, place a comma in between.**
Typical applications include file identification.

Examples:

Andrews, Mark
Combs, Dr. Andrea
Smith, Mark Jr.

m. **Place a comma between a person's name and title when the name comes first.**

Examples:

Dr. Combs, vice president of research, explained why the marketing idea would not work.

Mark Smith, manager of the accounting section, delivered the briefing at the finance meeting.

n. Use commas correctly with quotations.

When a quotation is part of a sentence, use a comma after the introductory text.

Example:

The speaker said, "No one can predict accurately what will occur more than two months out, even with the best data."

Do not use commas for indirect quotations.

Example:

The speaker said no one could predict beyond two months with any degree of accuracy, even with the best data.

When the quotation ends with a comma, place the comma before the closing quotation mark.

Example:

The speaker said, "No one can predict accurately what will occur more than two months out," and that the quality of data will not affect that problem.

5. Dash

Four distinct and different types of dashes are in use.

a. The em dash

The extended (longer) dash is called the em dash (equivalent in horizontal size to the letter "m"). It is used to set apart a sub-clause or aside. It is inserted before and after the sub-clause without spaces on either side.

Example:

The CEO—newly appointed last month—has a presentation to the board.

b. The en dash

The en dash (half the width of the letter "m') is used in description of ranges, numerically or for dates or page ranges.

Examples:

An estimated 4–5 employees took part.

The period February–March this year were studied.

pp. 307–308 (or 307–08)

c. The hyphen

The third dash style is the hyphen, used to join two words or to create line breaks for long words at the end of the line (see Hyphens, below, for more information).

Examples:

This was an example of make-work.

The purpose to this effort was to ensure that departmental supervisors were aware of the threat.

d. The minus sign

The mathematical symbol for minus is a hyphen or en dash. In using an equation editor online, it is appropriate to insert the minus sign, which is separate from the narrative hyphen.

Example:

$14{,}501 - 9{,}443 = 5{,}058$

e. Indicate emphasis with repetition using dashes.

Example:

We were pleased to note an increase in this quarter's profits—a significant increase.

f. **Use dashes with end-of-sentence matter to complete a thought or contradict a presumed conclusion.**

Examples:

It is fairly easy to budget expenses for a full year—according to the theory.

Some managers like to forecast five years ahead—although meaningful long-term forecasting is virtually impossible.

g. Set apart parenthetical material within the sentence with a dash, which provides the same distinction as a comma.

Dashes provide much greater emphasis than commas because they break up the thought and the appearance of the sentence. Parentheses can also be used in this situation, but that provides the least amount of emphasis.

Commas used for parenthetical material:

The reason for marketing strategy, profits, cannot be ignored in our planning.

Dashes used for greater emphasis:

The reason for marketing strategy—profits—cannot be ignored in our planning.

h. **Follow a quotation with a dash to identify the author.**

Example:

"The lion and the calf shall lie down together, but the calf won't get much sleep."—Woody Allen

6. Diacritical Marks

When including foreign words or phrases in a narrative report, the use of *diacritical marks* is indicated for certain words. These are marks above a letter within a word.

The acute accent is used for certain words as well, for example, in the word *cliché.*

An umlaut is used in many German words, such as the word for five, which is *fünf.*

In English, the umlaut appears infrequently but is used, for example, in the word *naïve.*

A cedilla is found in French and Portuguese, for example, in the name *François.*

The tilde appears often in Spanish, for example, in the word *Señor.*

Many additional diacritical marks are used in other languages.

7. Ellipses

Ellipses consist of a series of three periods (ellipsis points), each separated by a space, used to indicate an omission of material or a trailing thought.

a. **Use ellipses in quoted material to signal that some material has been excluded.**

Ellipses tell the reader that a direct quotation is not complete.

Original paragraph without exclusions:

The most significant finding by Dr. Harold and his crew of volunteer interns, none of whom wavered in their loyalty even once, was that employees develop opinions independent of the company's published, official statements.

Quotation with ellipses:

"The most significant finding . . . was that employees develop opinions independent of the company's . . . official statements."

b. **When a quotation begins and ends in the middle of a sentence, do not use ellipses at the beginning or end of the quotation.**

Original sentence:

Susan realized the flaw in her thinking after she reviewed the data.

Quotation:

Susan told me she "realized the flaw" finally.

c. **In mathematical notation, ellipses express an unknown or unspecified longer list.**

Example:

$(x1 + x2 + \ldots xn)$

8. **Exclamation Mark**

The exclamation mark expresses surprise, irony, or strong feelings. In certain advertising, it is used for emphasis.

Examples:

Sale! Three days only!
Hah! I doubt that very much.
Impossible!

a. **Use the exclamation mark rarely in business correspondence.**
Overuse of the exclamation mark should be avoided. It is appropriate in only rare circumstances.

Example, overuse:

The meeting began on time! Everyone was there! Input was exceptional and led to many creative alternatives and solutions!

Example, appropriate use:

The chairman admitted that the net loss came as a surprise. However, the latest quarter represented the fifth consecutive "surprise" the company experienced!

Even this example may not be appropriate, as it create an impression of sarcasm or intended humor in a situation that should be taken more seriously by the statement's readers.

b. **Place punctuation correctly.**
When an exclamation *and* question mark are used together, the question mark appears first, since the sentence is a question fundamentally. However, as a matter of style, avoid using both forms of punctuation in the same sentence.

When used within a quotation, the quotation marks should follow the exclamation mark if the punctuation applies to the quotation. Place the question mark after closing quotation mark when it applies to the entire sentence

Examples:

"Reform now!" was the title of the article.

The manager encouraged employees by advising, "Check your math"!

9. Hyphen

The hyphen serves as a connector in certain words or to show a range.

a. Use hyphens as connectors for some words.

Hyphens used as noun connectors:

follow-up
commander-in-chief
ex-employee

Hyphens used as adjective connectors:

year-round controls
month-to-date expense
error-prone shift

Hyphens used as verb connectors:

I will single-space the letter.
Be sure to spot-check the warehouse.
Let's double-time this task.

b. Use hyphens to separate words that are joined to form a new word.

This is common in technical writing, although some everyday usage and business style will also employ the technique.

Hyphens used to create new words:

accounting-style worksheets
marketing-intensive activities
employee-oriented programs

c. Hyphens indicate a range.

Examples:

0–100 [zero to one hundred]
5–10 minutes [five to ten minutes]
8%–10% [eight to ten percent]
4–6 employees [four to six employees]

d. Hyphens appear in numbers between 21 and 99 when those numbers are spelled out.

Examples:

twenty-seven
four hundred thirty-six

e. Use hyphens in two- or three-word modifiers expressing the same thought and preceding nouns.

As a general rule, if either modifier could work without the other, hyphens are not used. A hyphen is not used when the same modifiers follow the noun. No hyphen is used for adjective modifiers ending in *-ly*.

Examples:

A year-to-date report was prepared.
Do you have figures on our profits year to date?
A well-informed director is what this division needs.
The problem was easily resolved.

f. Hyphens are used for certain noun prefixes, such as *cross-*, *ex-*, *half-*, *quasi-*, and *self-*.

Many other common prefixes that should be closed up are often hyphenated incorrectly, such as anti-, mid-, pre-, sub-, and *un-*. Exception: To avoid a double vowel, sometimes even these prefixes are hyphenated.

Hyphenated noun prefixes:

Be sure to *cross*-reference your report thoroughly.
Most job applicants are *self*-conscious.
An *ex*-employee telephoned for a reference.
He has always been *anti*-intellectual. [to avoid double vowel]

Closed-up noun prefixes:

The entries arrived postclosing.
The prebudget expense was posted last year.
The survey revealed that many people in this company feel underemployed.
That group is antimarketing.

g. Hyphens indicate word breaks at the end of lines.

When text breaks at the end of the line occur in the middle of a word, the hyphen indicates the continuation on the following line. This break must occur at one of two places: (1) the end of a syllable or (2) the hyphenated point in a word.

Examples:

We met for lunch at twelve-thirty that day.
The timing of the report coincided with the meeting.

10. Period

Periods serve numerous functions in business communications. When narrative and numerical expressions are mixed, periods can appear in several forms within one paragraph.

a. **The period, also called a "full stop," is used at the end of all sentences that are not questions or exclamatory statements.**
Proper use of periods adds structure to a paragraph and should not be excluded except when replaced with other forms of stop. A sentence without the period is difficult to track.

b. **When a quotation ends with a period, the quotation mark follows the period.**
When unquoted material follows in the same sentence, the period is changed to a comma.
Examples:
The speaker said, "All in good time."
"All in good time," said the speaker.

c. **Periods are usually placed outside parentheses and brackets.**
The exception is when a full sentence is placed within the enclosed area.
Examples:
We prepared an annual report (last year).
The report was prepared on an annual basis. (It was finalized a month ago.)

d. **Periods follow titles and initials; they sometimes but not always follow abbreviations, and they do not follow acronyms.**
Examples:
Acct. dept. mngr.
Mr. Anderson
Dr. Smith
T. R. Jones
mktg.
AMA

e. **Periods are used in English style as decimal separators for numbers and to indicate a division between dollars and cents. In German style, the separator is a comma.**

Examples, English style:

The variation was 4.332 on the scale.
On average, 4.3 employees resign each year.
The total came to $1,336.32 last month.

f. **Periods are used as part of numbered or lettered sections and subsections in outline form or in lists.**

Examples:

1.
2.
3.
a.
b.
c.

g. **Avoid placing periods after incomplete sentences.**

Incomplete sentence:

The report, which was prepared yesterday. It was delivered to everyone on the list.

Corrected expression:

The report, which was prepared yesterday, was delivered to everyone on the list.

h. **Periods end sentences that serve as indirect questions.**

Examples:

The manager asked whether the budget was above or below actual expenses.
We wondered what was meant by the message.

11. Question Mark

The question mark (interrogatory point) is used to define a question versus other sentence forms.

a. **The question mark ends a direct interrogatory sentence.**

Examples:

Is this the correct department?
Where should the work be done?

In Spanish, a question mark is also used, but an inverted mark appears at the beginning of a sentence. For example, "Where is the boss?" appears in Spanish as: *¿Dónde está el jefe?*

b. **The question mark is used to end a declarative sentence that contains a question.**

This is an awkward style. A more assertive form should be used to avoid weakening the message.

A question within a sentence:

Each department is responsible, is it not, for completing its assigned tasks?

Improved style:

Each department is responsible for completing its assigned tasks. Isn't this the case?

c. **The question mark is used when a question is placed in the middle of a sentence.**

This method of expression should be avoided.

A question mark within a sentence:

How should be the product be marketed? is the important question.

Improved style:

The important question is: How should the product be marketed?

d. **Indicate that a declarative sentence is meant to serve as a question by inserting a question mark.**

Examples:

The books are balanced?

The shift is over?

e. **The sequence of question mark and exclamation mark is a matter of judgment; but since the sentence is a question fundamentally, it is preferable to place the question mark first.**

Such usage is rare in business.

Example:

How could Apex get its product to market faster than we did?!

f. **The question mark should remain inside parentheses or quotation marks when part of the expression.**

When the enclosed material is an aside to a larger interrogatory sentence, the question mark is placed outside the parentheses.

Question mark with quotations:

"Why this course?" asked the speaker.

Question mark with parentheses:

The shift's defects have increased (why has this occurred?) over the past three months.

Why have the shift's defects increased in the most recent study (three months)?

g. Use the question mark to indicate that some material is questionable or unclear.

Examples:

The report claimed a 450 percent increase in productivity(?).

He reported that 43 out of 50 cases were positive and exceeded expectations(?).

The events occurred over approximately 45 years (1456?–1501). This is an alternative to the more commonly used c. or ca.: (ca. 1456–1501).

12. Quotation Marks

When citing other material, quoting, or as a form of emphasis, quotation marks are used.

a. Enclose direct quotations within quotation marks.

Example:

Jerry said, "There is no time like the present."

b. Use quotation marks when citing material only for directly quoted sections.

Use ellipses or brackets to indicate any exceptions to this rule.

Complete passage:

Only a small number of all customers included in this survey were willing to participate in the study. This small response indicates that the request itself was perceived as too time-consuming or otherwise inconvenient.

Direct quotation:

The study failed because "only a small number of all customers" agreed to take part. The testing organization speculated that the test was perceived as "too time-consuming or otherwise inconvenient."

Ellipses and brackets used within quotations:

"Only a small number . . . were willing to participate . . . [indicating that the test would be] too time-consuming or otherwise inconvenient."

c. When a quotation appears within another quotation, use single quotation marks for the secondary quotation.

Example:

"We took the action based on the words of our mentor, who warned, 'Inaction is the worst action.' This guided us in all of our decisions and kept us moving forward."

d. Titles of articles in periodicals, chapters of books, songs, poems, and other short published material are enclosed in quotation marks.

Example:

Did you read this article, "Why I Love My Job So Much," in today's paper?

Titles of longer works (books, magazines) are italicized.

e. Draw attention to words or phrases that are odd or used in exceptional ways with quotation marks.

Example:

The applicant responded that he was "buzzed" by the possibility of being selected for the position.

Be sure not to overdo this style, however. It should be used only to make a specific point. In the example above, the use of an odd word, "buzzed," was highlighted as emphasis, which portrayed the individual in a particular way.

f. Place punctuation correctly.

Periods and commas belong inside quotation marks and colons and semicolons outside quotation marks. Question marks and exclamation marks should go inside quotation marks if they are part of the quotation itself; otherwise, they go outside.

Examples:

He said, "Send the report directly to me."

"Sure, I'd be glad to," I answered.

I don't know what they meant by "model employees"; Georgia and Kate were far from that in my opinion.

I wanted to meet "the big boss": the one Sally had told me so much about.

"Were they able to repair the computer system in time?" she asked uneasily. [Question mark goes inside quotation marks because it is part of the quoted sentence.]

What do you think he really meant by "corporate reorganization"? [Question mark is not part of quoted material, so it goes after quotation marks.]

"You'll never guess who I just saw!" exclaimed Julie.

But I was harried and wished she would stop distracting me with her "fascinating day"!

g. Quotation marks are sometimes used to indicate "same as material directly above."

This is to be confined only to strictly informal applications, such as worksheets, and not to be incorporated in reports or letters.

Examples:

Account 1234 is in balance.
" 1236 " " "
" 1242 " " "

13. Semicolon

The semicolon is an alternative to the period in some cases. It connects two thoughts that could serve as independent sentences but are related enough that a semicolon is justified. It aids in avoiding overly long and run-on sentences.

a. Semicolons may connect thoughts that, while related, need to be qualified by connecting words.

This is usually the case when the second part of the thought is contradictory.

Example:

Shift defects increased by 13 percent during the month, which alarmed management; however, the managers were not aware of the high volume of trainees assigned to the shift during the period studied.

b. Use semicolons in a narrative listing when some of the items in the list include commas.

When several items are listed but some segments of the lists include commas, the semicolon clarifies the meaning.

Example:

The marketing department has recommended that budgets include allowances for training seminars; orientation meetings for continuing education, product updates, and practice management; and production of a higher volume of sales literature.

14. Slash

The slash, also called a *solidus, virgule, slant line, bar,* or *shilling sign,* is used in a wide variety of applications. Be cautious in its use. When it is used carelessly, its intended meaning can be lost.

a. Use a slash to replace the word *per.*

Examples:

price/share [price per share]
cost/employee [cost per employee]

b. Use the slash in abbreviated forms of dates.

This is an informal style for personal notes and interoffice memos; it is also used on worksheets involving dates and values.

Examples:

3/16/97
4/10

c. Use the slash in mathematical expressions to signify division.

In business applications, this style may apply in equations as well as in ratios; both examples involve dividing the first number by the second.

Examples:

$B \div 12 * r = M$
2/1 ratio

d. Denote the division between lines of poetry with slashes.

Example:

Our recommendation not to proceed with this marketing plan is based on the belief that it will not be a profitable venture. As Shakespeare put it, “We go to gain a little patch of ground / That hath in it no profit but the name.”

e. **The double slash is used as part of a website's identification.**
The double slash distinguishes one portion of a web address from another.

Example:

https://www.google.com

f. **Use the backslash ("hack") for technical purposes.**
The backslash is used in programming languages and mathematical functions.

Q

Quotations

Quotations use another author's words in reports and other documents to bolster, support, or verify conclusions or important points.

1. **Place material in quotation marks when quoting exactly.**
   An indirect quotation should not be represented as anything else.
   Direct quotations:
   > The government report called attention to "exceptional levels of productivity" last quarter.
   > The report was extremely negative, highlighting the "blatant disregard for the comfort of the customer."

   Indirect quotations:
   > The government report emphasized that production levels were exceptional last quarter.
   > The extremely negative report highlighted what it considered a blatant disregard for customer comfort.

2. **Strive to use quotations only in context.**
   Facts can be misrepresented if they are presented out of context.
   Misrepresented facts:
   > The government report admitted that production levels were "exceptional," which is no guarantee that such outcomes should be expected in the future.

In this example, a positive report is used to represent inaccurately that the information was negative concerning the future. The quotations add an element of contradiction to the highlighted word.

Opinion added to factual quotes:
> Lower-than-expected production volume was blamed on "complete breakdown of machinery" during the shift. However, results in comparison with other shifts cannot be disputed.

This type of reporting should be avoided in business applications. Obviously, the complete breakdown of machinery is extraordinary and should not be overlooked in the interest of a purely numerical conclusion. In this situation, the phrase

DOI 10.1515/9781547400218-016

placed in quotation marks shows how the technique can be misused. The tone of the paragraph implies that the quoted material is inaccurate or distorted; in reality, the conclusion of the writer distorts the real problem.

3. **Cite the source of the quotation.**

Merely placing words within quotation marks is not enough. The source must be given as well.

Missing citation:

> An examination of the "productive business base" is the best means for locating likely future profits.

Proper citation:

> According to Dr. Mather's 1995 study, an examination of the "productive business base" is the best means for locating likely future profits.

4. **Place punctuation marks within the quotations if they are part of the quotation.**

Periods, question marks, and other punctuation should be included as long as the original wording included them as well.

5. **Quote only as much as needed.**

Use ellipses when omitting part of a larger quotation. Some quotations contain the relevant material needed to make a point but also other information that adds nothing. In such cases, exclude unnecessary sections, while taking care to preserve the original meaning.

Example text:

> The proper method for selecting sample data will depend on the purpose and use intended. Statistical bases have to be valid if the outcomes are to be of any value. Take great care that your selection does not create a false conclusion.

Improperly edited quotation:

> The report warns that even "the proper method for selecting sample data will . . . create a false conclusion."

Properly edited quotation:

> The report warns that the selection method "will depend on the purpose and use . . . if outcomes are to be of any value."

6. **When a misspelled word, an error in grammar, or a confusing expression is included in the quoted source, do not correct it.**

Follow a confusing section or word with [*sic*] enclosed in brackets, which means "thus" or "as it was said."

Grammatical error in original source:

> The report concluded that "the database of employees were [*sic*] considered to be broad enough to validate the study."

Confusing statements:

> The report concluded, "None of the data compiled, analyzed, studied, dependably indicated a definitive nor conclusive outcome which could be used [*sic*]."
>
> "We reported that we were advised of what decisions had been made in place of the correct procedure, taking place in the absence of the usual group [*sic.*]."

R

Redundancy and repetition

Efficient writing often translates to elimination of unneeded words and phrases. This is especially true in cases of redundancy and repetition.

1. Avoid using unnecessary words and phrases in business writing.

Business writing style (like all other writing) should be to the point. All writers must guard against bad habits in their writing, and redundancy is one of the most common.

Redundant wording:

> It is absolutely urgent to reach a final conclusion concerning the report enclosed herein. The proposed recommendations address the issues about basic fundamentals in our procedural methods.

Tightened wording:

> We urgently need to reach a conclusion concerning the enclosed report. The recommendations address the basics in our procedures.

The second example is clearer and more concise than the first. The redundant phrases add nothing to the message and, in fact, detract from it.

2. Examine all writing as part of a self-editing process, and look for words and phrases that can be eliminated.

This process helps to avoid the use of redundancies while improving your writing style. Apply these style guidelines:

1. Nothing can be *absolutely* essential, *attached* together, or *entirely* destroyed. The highlighted words are unnecessary.
2. Many sentences can have two or three words eliminated without any change in meaning.
3. Almost every communication can be expressed in a shorter, simpler way.
4. The tendency in business to obscure or to use more complex methods of explanation is misguided. Readers appreciate simple, well-written, well-communicated reports, letters, and memos.

DOI 10.1515/9781547400218-017

3. **Be aware of repetition.**

The selective use of repetition can be an effective way to add emphasis to writing, but it often denotes the writer's uncertainty that the essence of the message has been expressed.

Effective repetition:

Markets are the key. Markets are survival. Markets are the business of business.

This example employs two forms of repetition. Used in a speech, for example, the audience hears the speaker and realizes that markets are the message. In addition, the slogan "the business of business" is a useful and effective way of emphasizing the point.

Repetition used ineffectively:

We would like to see this change in procedure if management agrees with our premise. The procedure changes we are recommending will reduce costs. We really need to make a change in the procedure. Otherwise, we will still have budget variances if the procedure is not changed.

Rewritten statement:

This change in procedure is recommended as a method for reducing costs and saving money.

In the ineffective repetition example, a reader would believe that the writer lacks confidence that the message is coming through clearly. The resulting style is poor and unconvincing.

Relative clauses

When clauses begin with who, whom, whose, where, when, or which, they are classified as *relative clauses*.

1. **Relative clauses defining preceding nouns.**

In most examples where relative clauses appear, they expand or define a preceding noun.

Examples of defining relative clauses:

The CEO was the one who established a new policy.

That employee is a person whom can be trusted completely. (Note: It is considered archaic to use *whom* in written and spoken language.)

We attended a seminar whose sponsors work for a competitor.

This is an organization where employees are promoted rapidly.

First Monday of the month is when the meeting is held.

This report is a summary which describes a longer, expanded report.

2. Relative clauses providing additional information.

Some relative clauses do not define a preceding noun but provide added information about it. In this application, the clause is always separated by commas from the preceding and following sections of the sentence.

Examples of informative relative clauses:

The organization, which began operations in 1894, continues to thrive today.

This vendor, who provides nearly one-third of our products, is based in the U.S.

The program, which dramatically changed our culture, also led to higher profits.

3. Relative clauses not used when a pronoun is the object.

Relative clauses are not included in sentences when their object is a pronoun in place of a noun.

Examples of sentences with pronouns as objects:

We are aware of the person he's referring to. (excludes "who")
I have not yet reviewed the reports she prepared. (excludes "that")
She did not know about the promotion you received. (excludes "which")

Reports

A variety of specialized reporting formats is used in business, often depending on the nature of the business or the topic of the report itself. The essential style rule for reports is that the design, length, and detail of each one should be based on its purpose and the audience.

1. Recurring reports are most effective when they follow the same format.

Documents such as progress or monthly reports may use the same format each month, so that readers know where to find information. The format should be determined specifically by the contents and the requirements of the report.

2. Changing a report's format is not a decision to make in isolation or arbitrarily.

The entire readership of the report should be advised of proposed changes and their reasons, and given the opportunity to disagree or to provide ideas to improve a new format. Chances are that changing a report's format will require approval; be certain that the proposed change in format is done with complete documentation and through proper channels. Following are guidelines for suggesting changes in a report's format:

1. Explain the deficiencies in the current format.
2. Provide a cost analysis for the project. Consider existing supplies of blank forms, if applicable; changes in databases utilizing the report in its present format; and affected departments and how their needs are better addressed by the improved format.
3. Make a specific recommendation for the newly formatted report, including an example. When practical, present the most recently prepared version of the report in the new format, so that improvements are clear.

3. The proposal is a specialized report.

A proposal discusses a one-time idea and therefore has no set format to follow. However, since the proposal puts an idea in front of a decision maker, some important formatting rules should always be followed in the proposal (see also Proposals).

1. *A summary.* The first page should summarize what is being proposed, along with the major benefit for making the suggestion. A decision maker will then be able to judge quickly whether the overall idea appears to have merit.
2. *Problem presentation and the proposed solution.* Avoid merely presenting problems and expecting the decision maker to arrive at the solution. The report preparer's job is to present the answer as well as the question.
3. *The conclusion.* End with a brief summary of the key points made on the first page and answer these questions: What is the initial cost of the proposal? How are various departments affected? How long will the transition take? What are the long-term savings, in terms of both efficiency and time?
4. *Supplementary or supporting data.* Include this material in an appendix, clearly cross-referenced to the applicable section of the report.

4. Follow sensible rules for report organization.

1. *Number the pages of the report.* Unless the report is only two or three pages long, numbered pages are essential. For especially long reports, include a table of contents to show the reader at a glance what the report includes and to help him or her find the most important information quickly.

2. *Place summary conclusions at the front.* The summary page is the most important part of the report, and it should come first. It gives the reader an immediate, easy-to-find overview of the report's essential contents and recommendations.
3. *Minimize the overall size of the report.* Employ a professional, straightforward writing style to keep the report as short as possible but still communicate clearly.
4. *Provide details in an appendix.* The body of the report should contain as few pages as possible, with narratives devoted to interpretation of details, recommended actions, and critical information the reader needs. When reference is made to financial reports, statistical studies, and other material, include the details in the appendix.
1. *Use appropriate graphic aids.* Include a listing of all graphs, tables, and other visuals in the table of contents if there are more than two or three such examples.

5. If the report contains references to several other sources, include a bibliography.

The bibliography should follow the correct citation style. Bibliographic notes should be indicated by number or, if limited in scope, by way of footnotes on each page. If the report includes several detailed sections, reference notes should be summarized at the end of each section.

6. Provide cross-references to all graphics and all material in the appendix.

If the report contains more than one type of graphic, referencing should be distinct. If the report contains more than one section, the sections should be numbered separately, and graphic references should correspond. For example, the first table in section 3 should be numbered "Table 3-1." The fourth table in section 5 should be numbered "Table 5-4." Narrative references should be included within parentheses and may be capitalized for emphasis.

Examples:

The actual year-to-date results compared to forecast are shown in Figure 2-1.

A complete detailed listing of budget assumptions and content is included in the appendix (page 47, "Budget Assumptions and Worksheets").

Rhetorical questions

In some limited instances, *rhetorical questions* may be included in a business communication. These are questions that have obvious answers, or that cannot be answered.

Examples, rhetorical questions with obvious answers:

Does the company *want* to lose money this year?

They didn't think we would agree, did they?

Is this some kind of a joke?

Examples, rhetorical questions with no answers:

Why do we even try?

How many times are we going to publish useless reports?

Is there any chance of success?

Rhythm in sentences

Sentence rhythm that varies is more appealing than paragraphs containing sentences of the same length and rhythm. Self-editing enables you to adjust the rhythm to provide a more pleasing tone for the reader.

Example, sentences of the same length:

Expansion to new markets is a primary goal. Locating and identifying markets is a first step. Deciding on appropriate financing methods is next. Cash, stock, or combinations in acquiring smaller companies is always possible. No one method is suitable in every case.

Example, sentences of varying length:

Expansion to new markets is a primary goal. The first step in this process is locating and identifying markets, and deciding on appropriate financing methods is next. Acquisitions may consist of cash, stock, or combinations of both. No one method is suitable in every case.

1. Read your work out loud to spot instances requiring editing.

The lack of variety in rhythm is most obvious when paragraphs are read aloud. Once the problem has been identified, it is relative easy to fix.

2. Use rhythm to set a mood.

Business writing often is described as separate from creative writing. However, a business document can be made more interesting with variation in rhythm.

Example, plain paragraph lacking variation in rhythm:

Profits are essential, but customer relations has to accompany this profit-oriented mindset. Customers who are happy with service are far more likely to be repeat customers. They are also more likely to spread the word to other people about excellent service. However, poor service is even more likely to be spread from a customer to other people.

Example, plain paragraph with variation in rhythm:

Profits. This is essential, but customer relations has to accompany this profit-oriented mindset. Happy customers come back over and over. They will spread the word to others. Unhappy customers also spread the word ... perhaps even more so.

Roman numerals

Some documents will include *Roman numerals*, especially as second- or third-level outline breakdowns. For exceptionally large numbers, Roman numerals are impractical and difficult to interpret. For example, for the year 1997, the Roman numeral equivalent is MCMXCVII.

1. Calculating Roman numeral equivalents.

In the Roman system, there is no value for zero. The system involves both addition and subtraction. The following Roman symbols are applied:

1 = I
5 = V
10 = X
50 = L
100 = C

Values beyond the third count are subject to the following symbol and subtraction. For example, 3 is III but 4 is IV (the value of 1 subtracted from the value of 5). The value of 48 is XLVIII ("XL" represents the range of 40s and VIII is the value of 8. The value of 49 is XLIX; in this value, XL represents the range of values in the 40s and IX represents the value of 9.

2. Uses for Roman numerals.

The execution of mathematical functions using Roman numerals is difficult because the commonly used methods do not apply, and because there is no value for zero. However, Roman numerals are used for particular titles and names.

The names of heads of state and popes normally are further defined by Roman numerals. Examples include Elizabeth II, Henry VIII and Benedict XVI. They also are used to distinguish generations of people with the same name, such as John J. Astor IV. Certain sports events, including Olympic games and Super Bowls, are described with Roman numerals. (Exception: "Super Bowl 50" was used in place of "Super Bowl L" probably because many people are not familiar enough with Roman numerals to recognize that "L" is equal to 50. However, subsequent designation reverted to Roman style, such as "Super Bowl LI.")

In business, outline format with several levels is one application of Roman numerals. When a document (book or report, for example), includes front matter of several pages, those pages (in a preface or foreword, for example) may be expressed in lowercase Roman numerals (i, ii, iii, iv, etc.).

Run-in quotations

Run-in quotations are quotations within sentences or quotations within other quotations. The specific style format for these follows the same overall rule for the use of verbatim quotations.

1. Quotations within sentences

A run-in quotation may occur within a narrative section of a document. Whereas an extended quotation is set apart with indents, a single-sentence quotation is set apart with double quotations. This may be a single quotation or a split quotation.

Examples, run-in quotations within sentences:

The CFO explained the poor quarter as a "cyclical and unavoidable event."

She explained, "The deadline cannot be adjusted, but is fixed and firm."

"Our policy mandates how to respond," she wrote.

"No one is allowed to make that decision," the CEO declared, "without first gaining written approval from management.

2. A run-in quotation appearing within another quotation is set apart with single quotes.

When a quotation includes a separate run-in quotation, it should be set aside with single quotation marks.

Examples, run-in quotes within other quotes:

The document explained, "Marketing efforts are 'on-going and continuous' with few exceptions."

The visiting professor lectured that, "The free market economy has been defined within the context of 'the invisible hand' as explained by Adam Smith."

Run-on sentences and sentence fragments

One of the habits demanding editing in business style is the run-on sentence. This is found often in business documents. It is fairly easy to fix, however, simply by breaking up thoughts into more easily digestible sizes.

1. Look for separate thoughts combined into single sentences.

The basic flaw of the run-on sentence is in combining two or more thoughts into a single expression. This obscures the intended meaning and makes the document difficult to read.

Example, single sentence for separate thoughts:

Elements of management delegation are difficult for those managers interested in being perceived as a friend rather than as a leader, and this flaw is difficult to overcome, especially since it has been developed over many years, but those managers may also need to realize that the failure to lead makes for a poor form of management.

Example, separation of thoughts into several sentences:

Delegation is difficult for those managers interested in being perceived as a friend. Good leadership requires overcoming this flaw, and that is difficult. The habit has been developed over many years. The failure to lead makes for a poor form of management.

2. Look for misuse of conjunctive adverbs.

Two independent clauses are likely to be connected with a conjunctive adverb, such as *however*. This often points to the need to break up the sentence.

Example, run-on sentence with a conjunctive adverb:

The committee approved the quarterly budget adjustments, however the majority opinion was that a better job of documentation would lead to improved initial budgets.

Example, improved expression without conjunctive adverb use:

The committee approved the quarterly budget adjustments. The majority opinion was that a better job of documentation would lead to improved initial budgets.

3. Even short sentences can qualify as run-on sentences.

A run-on sentence often is lengthy. But this is not always the case, as any expression joining ideas that are properly kept separate creates a run-on sentence.

Example, short run-on sentence:

The quarter is ending next week, management is concerned about stockholder reaction to disappointing profits.

Example, improved expression with separate thoughts:

The quarter is ending next week. Management is concerned about stockholder reaction to disappointing profits.

4. Avoid the comma splice.

A comma splice is the use of a comma to join unrelated thoughts together, creating a run-on sentence. This can be repaired by either creating a separate sentence, editing the thought down to a more simplified expression, or using a semicolon.

Example, comma splice:

The meeting ran over the allotted time, as a result attendees were frustrated.

Examples, ways to eliminate the comma splice:

The meeting ran over the allotted time; attendees were frustrated.

Attendees were frustrated when the meeting ran over the allotted time.

5. Sentence fragments are rarely acceptable and need to be edited and corrected.

A sentence fragment is an incomplete sentence, and needs to be fixed.

Example, sentence fragment:

Management needs to enact new procedures to fix.

Example, improved expression:

Management need to fix the problem with new procedures.

Some use of sentence fragments is intentional and adds dramatic effect.

Example, intentional sentence fragment:

Growth. This is the primary objective for the next three years.

S

Salutations

Familiarity with a recipient determines whether an informal or formal salutation is appropriate. The format also affects this decision. Memos normally do not include a salutation, but recipients are identified in the heading. Email tends to be less formal in style.

1. Informal salutations

When writing to a peer or to someone known on a first-name basis, an informal style may be used. These include first names or nicknames. Avoid slang, obscenity, or inappropriate attempts at humor in all forms of business communication. For example, "Hey dude" is not an appropriate salutation for any message exchanged within a business setting.

2. Formal salutations

The most popular beginning to a salutation is use of the word "Dear." This is followed by the recipient's name or title. For example, "Dear Mr. Brown" or "Dear Professor Connors" would be applicable using the formal salutation. Avoid using a title along with first names: "Dear Mr. Andy Brown" or Dear Professor Sandra Connors" are not considered proper. An informal salutation for either would be restricted to first names: "Dear Andy" or "Dear Sandra," but combining titles and first names does not apply.

Follow the formal salutation with a comma in most countries. In the U.S., a colon often is used in place of the comma.

When the name of the recipient is not known, several qualifiers may be used in the formal salutation. Capitalize the title or other qualifier.

Examples, formal salutations lacking names:

Dear Sir,
Dear Madam,
Dear Sir or Madam,
Dear Committee Members,

Gender-specific titles are added in front of names. Mr. is popular for all male recipients. The use of Ms. encompasses either married or unmarried women. However, the use of Mrs. or Miss can also work as long as the status of the recipient is known. Although outdated, the use of "Miss" and "Master" are at times used to

DOI 10.1515/9781547400218-018

address young children. "Master" has been replaced by "Mr." as a more catch-all phrase for male recipients of all ages. Less commonly used for male recipients are the terms *Messieurs* for multiple male recipients, and even less often seen is the term *Mesdames* for multiple female recipients.

A formal use of "Sir" or "Madam" without names is considered exceedingly formal and is avoided in most business correspondence. It sets an unfriendly tone to the message.

3. Salutations in other languages

The rules for salutation usage vary by country and by culture. Two examples follow.

a. German salutations

In German business correspondence, formal salutations include gender distinction. The male salutation begins, *Sehr geehrter Herr* (Dear Sir) and for female, the term is *Sehr geehrte Frau* (Dear Miss). This is followed by title and family name. For example, *Sehr geehrte Frau Dr. Berg* combines the "Dear" with the title and last name.

Informal salutations in German may begin with *Hallo* (hello), a gender-neutral expression. Informal use of *Lieber* (dear, male) or *Liebe* (dear, female) are also used. However, it is reserved for someone well-acquainted. For correspondence with someone of higher or lower title within the organization, or of considerably different age, *Lieber* and *Liebe* should be avoided and may set a condescending or patronizing tone.

b. Spanish salutations

Informal salutations in Spanish begin with *Hola* (hello). When sent to a group of people, the salutation is expanded to *hola a todos* (hello everyone). This applies whether recipient names are known or not.

Less informal are salutations identifying time of day. *Buenos dias* (good day or good morning) is used when the correspondence is sent in the morning. *Buenas tardes* applies between noon and sunset. *Buenas noches* is used after sunset.

Formal written communication salutations are more structured. The word *Estimado* (for males) or *Estimada* (for females) means "Dear" and is followed by Sir (Señor) or Mrs. (Señora). After the initial greeting comes the first or last name, with last name more formal. When addressing more than one recipient, expand to add "es" [señores (gentlemen)] or "s" [señoras (ladies)]. A more familiar greeting for groups is Estimada amiga (Dear friends, male) or Estimadas amigas (Dear friends, female). For someone of unknown gender, the salutation begins with Querido amigo (Dear friend).

Exceptionally formal salutations begin Excelentísimo Señor (male) or Excelentísima Señora (female), meaning Your Excellency. The word Ilustrísimo (male) or Ilustrísima (female) may also be used (Illustrious). A formal message to an unknown recipient may begin A quien corresponda (To whom it may concern).

Sampling

In statistical reporting, *sampling* refers to the selection of a portion of a larger population. This should be representative of the characteristics or attributes of a population, but in too many statistical studies, the sample is not representative and is designed to produce a desired result. In business writing with integrity, the sample should be selected without bias.

1. **Detailed definitions of the population promote accurate sampling.**
   Before undertaking statistical studies, ensure an understanding of the population, and then determine how to select a sample that represents the population. Characteristics should be measurable.

2. **Be aware of potential distortions.**
   Not all members of a population are going to share the same characteristics. For example, there is probably not any "typical" sample of employees within a single organization. Differences between administrative, marketing, and assembly-line employees are likely to distort results of any test limited to only one of these groups. Customers also are dissimilar by age, gender, region, income, and other factors.

3. **Describe sampling methods carefully.**
   In developing a statistical report, devote enough time to describe sampling methods and why the methods are considered representative of the larger population. The population parameters need to be defined and when these are not identical throughout the population, a means for making a representative sample should be described.

4. **Sampling selection is the most critical segment of the statistical report.**
   In developing a sampling method, the selection of sampling units affects the outcome. Efforts to ensure the likelihood of a truly representative segment of the

population may include multiple sample tests, timing and location differences, and efforts to locate "typical" individuals. For example, in product testing, have steps been taken to identify the day and time when the primary family shopper is in the test location? If an inaccurate time or day is selected, the results are not reliable.

Sarcasm

The use of *sarcasm* should be limited in professional correspondence. It may be witty or clever, but often may be insulting or inappropriate.

1. Witty sarcasm

Many forms of sarcasm are witty and may be appreciated by a recipient, but this is a tenuous point. Someone well-known may appreciate sarcasm, but the same comment may insult someone else.

Examples of witty sarcasm:

I'll waste no time reading your article.
He is a legend in his own mind.

2. Banter versus sarcasm

Some forms of sarcasm may also play the role of *banter*, or a humorous remark intended to entertain. In business, banter may not be appropriate except with close peers.

Examples of sarcastic banter:

Honesty is the best policy, especially if money is involved.
I wish I were young enough to know everything.

3. Sarcasm and irony

Sarcasm and irony are closely related, and the distinction often is difficult to recognize. Irony is lost on many people, especially in written communication where the tendency is to take what is stated at face value.

Examples of irony:

The fire station burned to the ground.
The credit protection company suffered a massive data breach.

These examples point to the difference between sarcasm and irony. Only situations can be ironic, and only people can be sarcastic. Sarcasm may also be pointed out in subtle use of punctuation.

Examples of sarcastic punctuation:

The company reported its "profitable" quarterly results.
The outlook was reported as cautiously positive!
The success of the project remains to be seen ...

Scaling

The concept of *scaling* refers to several forms of style.

1. Scaling in surveys

Surveys and rating systems may ask participants to identify the scale of response. For example, a scale may be described for a presentation as one of five outcomes: Excellent, very good, good, poor, or very poor.

The problem of style in a scale is that poorly structured surveys may be self-serving or inaccurate. A scale for a product may be set for consumers to pick one of five choices:

Survey for a product:

What feature did you like the most?
Exceptional taste
Desirable nutritional value
Attractive labeling

In this survey, all of the possibilities are positive. No negative responses are provided. This is a self-determining "positive" survey, with one of the three choices dominating the results.

Follow-up actions should be indicated by what the survey reveals. If no opportunity for critique is included, then the style of the survey design is flawed.

2. Scaling in graphs

Graphs are based on intervals of the scale. These intervals should be sized consistently in order to provide accurate results. If the scale is adjusted, the outcome is distorted as well. Figure S.1 is an example of a chart with inconsistent scaling, resulting in distortion of reported data.

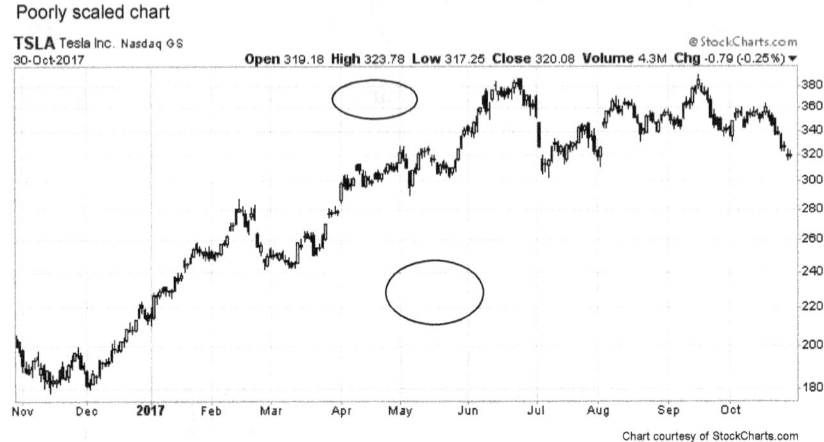

Figure S.1: Poorly scaled chart

The increments between prices are the same, but the scaling is reduced in the higher ranges. The purpose of this scaling is to fit all of the data on a fixed-size chart, but the problem it creates is inaccuracy in the chart's appearance.

In addition to consistency in scale, multiple illustrations in a single document should be scaled in the same way whenever possible. This avoids confusion or exaggeration.

Finally, axes should be labeled clearly to ensure that their meaning is clear.

3. Narrative rating scales

A third version of scaling is found in narrative sections of reports. Carelessly used ratings or scales, like undocumented statistics, often are exaggerations and are poor forms of expression.

Examples of undocumented scaling:

On a scale of 1 to 10, we are performing at 8.

Our potential for future growth in profits is 90 out of 100.

Improved narrative ratings examples:

Analysis of our growth trend places performance at a high level (see Appendix).

Future profits are expected to continue the previous trend, as shown below.

Both of these improved versions refer to verification of the scaling claims.

Scientific method

The *scientific method* is an approach to investigation and conclusion, based on unbiased examination of facts. Empirical or measurable principles are applied to a series of steps, which can be articulated and tested in order to reach a conclusion. As a matter of style, writing a document based on the scientific method does not need to be complex or lengthy, but should ensure that all steps, from hypothesis to conclusion, are fair and unbiased.

1. Characteristics

The beginning of the scientific method is documenting a series of observations, definitions and a means for measurement.

Example of characteristics:

> An examination of profits by branch office over a five-year period may demonstrate that profitability itself is influenced by the distance between the branch office and headquarters. "Profits" refers to net operating profits only within the branch, annualized to ensure consistent comparisons.

This statement includes an observation (profits vary geographically); definitions (the study was limited to annual operating profits in each branch); and measurement (comparisons were conducted among branch offices over five years).

2. Hypothesis

A hypothesis expresses an assumption that can be tested and either proven or disproven with further analysis. It interprets the characteristics of an initial analysis and states a possible conclusion.

Example of a hypothesis statement:

> This report tests the presumption that rates of return measured as operating profits may be expected to decline as the distance between headquarters and the branch office are increased.

3. Prediction

The next step in the method involves prediction, which consists of deductions and reasoning based on the hypothesis.

Example of prediction:

> The operating results over five years were conducted on sample branch offices located in comparison to headquarters, in four groups: within 0–100 miles; 101–350 miles; 351–500 miles; and 501–1,000 miles. The purpose is to compare sample outcomes for five offices within each of these

geographic regions, and to either prove or disprove the hypothesis concerning geography and net returns.

The prediction based on a sample of branch offices—limited to 20 offices divided among four arbitrary geographic areas—assumes several points. First, the selected branch offices are *typical* of the larger population of offices. Second, the hypothesis will be *supported* by the outcome. Third, the outcome will *indicate* the validity or lack of validity of the initial hypothesis.

4. Experimentation

The final step in the scientific method is testing. This may prove the hypothesis or disprove it based on true inconsistencies (or on flaws in the testing sample).

Example of experiment and result:

The hypothesis was tested based on geography and randomly selected branch offices. The initial outcome was disparate and failed to prove the hypothesis. A suggested revision to the predicted outcomes is to test company-wide outcomes as a secondary effort to prove or disprove the hypothesis.

If the initial hypothesis was based on a commonly-held but unproven belief (profits decline with distance), it requires analysis and testing. In this case, the sample disproved the hypothesis based on characteristics (geography). A solution was presented to expand the sample. Another solution may be to accept results as proof that the hypothesis was not true.

Screen shots

The *screen shot* (or, *screen capture* or *screen grab*) is a copy of a web page made for use in another document. Once a screen shot has been added to another document, it can be subjected to annotation or commentary in Word, PowerPoint, or Adobe Illustrator, among other programs.

The elements on the screen shot, including text, cannot be altered directly, as the entire page is interpreted as a digital image. Identifying the screen shot should include the name of the site, its URL, and date of the screen shot. Authors may strategically pick interesting screen shots to entice readers to purchase a book, or within organizations, to take greater interest in reports.

A copyrighted website may lead to controversy regarding use. Some companies claim that screen shots may not be incorporated into other documents without permission. However, the principle of *fair use* in most cases, allows the use of single screen shots regardless of copyright. If in doubt, a sensible policy is to request permission for use. However, whether permission is legally required or not, once a request has been made, a refusal places a ban on the use of the screen shot. Use of screen shots outside of the organization, especially in published work, may require a legal opinion.

Sentences

Written language consists of a series of sentences, strung together in paragraphs and conveying a consistency of thought. Each sentence expresses an idea that makes sense in the context of material before and after that sentence. A well-constructed essay, memo, letter, or report follows these guidelines, with sentences building upon one another so that the ideas are expressed clearly.

1. A simple sentence expresses one idea or complete thought.

Simple sentences should contain one subject and one verb only. The simple sentence is easily identified. It cannot be broken down into two or more other sentences without changing its meaning.

Examples:

The marketing analysis was late.
The employees are in the lunchroom.
Our seminar began today.

The designation *simple* means only that a single idea or thought is contained within the sentence. Some simple sentences meet this standard while being complex in the information conveyed. They may contain grammatical variations while remaining simple in construction.

Examples:

It was not a very long meeting. [the noun is a predicate nominative]
We provided them with a copy of the report and with some implementation ideas. [contains two direct objects and one indirect object]
The personnel department is located on the seventh floor, at the end of the hall. [contains two prepositional phrases]
Managers and supervisors need vacations, too. [contains compound subjects]
The efficiency expert lost his notebook and broke his stopwatch. [an ironic statement containing a compound predicate]

2. **A compound sentence combines more than one thought that, by themselves, would each constitute a complete sentence.**

The thoughts (also called *independent clauses,* because they can stand independently) are connected by a conjunction or a semicolon. Unless the two clauses are very short, a comma should precede the conjunction combining them.

Examples:

The report about staying on schedule was late, so the meeting ran over its allotted time.

Our seminar ended today, and we hope to stay in town for some sightseeing.

I report to George, and he reports to Cynthia.

The employees are in the lunchroom; they are discussing the recent announcement.

3. **A complex sentence contains a primary and a subordinate idea (also called *independent* and *dependent clause*).**

The independent clause is a complete sentence that can stand alone; the dependent clause does not meet that standard.

Examples:

The meeting was set up when the report was completed. (*The meeting was set up* is a full sentence on its own; *when the report was completed* is not.)

The employees are in the lunchroom, having ensured that the telephones are still being covered in their department.

Our seminar commenced today, even though a holiday weekend just began.

4. **A "minor sentence" is an afterthought or addition to the sentence preceding it.**

The "minor sentence" is not a complete sentence but a limited number of words added on.

Examples:

Was it important that the marketing analysis was late? How late?

The supervisor has suggested the radical approach of hiring outside services, arguing that we will spend less money than if we hire employees. Unlikely.

Whether or not a so-called minor sentence is grammatically allowable is debatable, especially in business writing. There are times and formats where incomplete sentences add emphasis. Some believe that these phrases are allowable in spoken English or in dialogue but inappropriate for business memos and letters. The opposite view is that the one- or two-word phrase, when used selectively, adds great emphasis and does have appropriate usage, even in business documents. The examples illustrate this point. Unless fragments are used excessively, they can be powerful writing tools.

In addition to adding emphasis, minor sentences break up narratives and help vary the rhythm of text. Everyone in business who has been exposed to long reports and analyses welcomes some variety in form. This is true for both analytical reports and reports designed to influence an executive to make a decision.

For example: You have an idea that management has resisted for some time, even though you have argued that it will save money. Now you're writing a report meant to convince the president that it's a good idea. You start your report with one of the following paragraphs:

Alternative first paragraphs:

> This report proposes a complete change in departmental procedures. While expensive to implement at first, we intend to show that the idea will ultimately save money, not just for the short term, but permanently.
>
> Saving money is a primary purpose of our budgetary and review procedures. Here's an idea that we believe achieves that objective. For an initial investment that is reasonable in perspective, we will be able to reduce costs permanently.
>
> Money. That's what the company will save by implementing this idea. This report proves that the investment we are suggesting will be recaptured within twelve months and create permanent savings from that point forward.

The third paragraph might be considered a hard sell, and placing the one-word sentence at the front is a gimmick—but an effective one. Be open to the possibility of using the minor sentence for emphasis or effect.

5. **Declarative sentences are statements of opinion or fact.**

A declarative statement expresses an idea without qualification.

Examples:

> The marketing analysis is late.
> The employees are in the lunchroom.
> Our seminar began today.

6. Interrogative sentences ask questions.

An interrogative sentence (a question) usually begin with words such as *who, what, when, why, where, how,* and *have.*

Examples:

Why is the marketing analysis late?
Where are the employees?
When does our seminar begin?

7. Exclamatory sentences express surprise and end with an exclamation mark.

Exclamatory sentences may appear hyperbolic or exaggerated, and are rarely used in business communications.

Examples:

Where is the marketing analysis? Late again!
To the lunchroom!
Let's go! The seminar is starting.

8. Imperative sentences are commands, even if politely phrased.

A request or command may be appropriately softened when used in business writing. These often begin with a verb.

Examples:

Get me that marketing analysis, please.
Go to the lunchroom as soon as possible.
Start the seminar on time.

9. Vary sentence rhythm so that the reader does not lose interest.

Reading a series of sentences of the same approximate length is boring; the reader may struggle to maintain a train of thought or to comprehend the intended message.

Sentences with identical rhythm

The marketing analysis is late again. This happens just about every month. I checked the marketing department to ask why. The employees weren't there just now. They are all in the lunchroom. We need an answer as soon as possible. The information is supposed to be presented at the seminar. It is starting today.

Sentences with varied rhythm:

The marketing analysis is late again, as it seems to be every month. I checked the marketing department, and found that all of the employees are in the lunchroom right now. We need an answer as soon as possible. The presentation is scheduled for today's seminar.

10. The run-on sentence does not stop at the end of one thought.

It is difficult to read a run-on sentence because it strings several thoughts together without pause. Consequently, the reader is unable to divide the thoughts into logical segments or to comprehend the message easily.

A run-on sentence:

The marketing analysis is late again, which happens just about every month and I checked the marketing department to ask why but the employees weren't there just now because they are all in the lunchroom and we need an answer as soon as possible as the information is supposed to be presented at the seminar, which is starting today.

Another type of run-on sentence is simply wrong in the grammatical sense, consisting of two or more thoughts connected without proper punctuation or attachment by way of conjunctions.

Example:

The store opened at the usual time there were no customers there that early we didn't expect any.

11. Avoid sentence fragments by recognizing phrases and clauses.

Phrases and clauses are not complete sentences, though they may contain the wording of complete sentences. In order for a sentence to be complete, the subject has to be accompanied by its own verb, and the thought has to be complete. In addition to being incorrect, an incomplete sentence requires readers to recreate it in their mind, no matter how simple the fragment. The meaning may not be clear and a partial sentence can be misread. It slows reading down and so wastes readers' time. If done consistently, the practice can become aggravating.

Sentence fragments:

Looking at the budget with a fresh point of view.

Heading for the seminar with the intention of learning many new management skills.

Our president, who hails from Minnesota.

The meeting scheduled for the third Thursday of each month.

Revisions to make complete sentences:

We are looking at the budget with a fresh point of view.

Heading for the seminar, I intend to learn many new management skills.

Our president hails from Minnesota.

The meeting is scheduled for the third Thursday of each month.

Each example reveals that fragments are corrected easily, often by addition or removal of a single word. In the first example, there is no subject for the verb *looking*. The same is true of the second example. In the third, the subject, *president,* has no verb; the problem is corrected by removing a word. The last example is yet another instance of the more common problem of subjects without related verbs. Adding the verb *is* fixes the problem.

12. Signal the beginning and end of sentences correctly.

The first word of every sentence begins with a capital letter, regardless of the word or its function. Every sentence ends with a period, question mark, or exclamation point. When faced with starting a sentence with something that has to be lowercase, (instance a URL or a programming function name like printf) adjust your sentence to accommodate this rule.

Example, awkward sentence:

www.samplesite.com is the website for proper sentence structure.

Example, adjusted sentence:

The website www.samplesite.com contains rules for proper sentence structure.

Sexist writing

Business style is best when gender specifics are avoided. The use of "he or she" is awkward and is easily corrected. In the distant past, the default writing style (in business as well as in literature) was to identify all unknown people in the masculine; today, the goal is to avoid gender distinctions.

1. Avoid using masculine nouns and pronouns when referring to both sexes or either sex.

Choose words that apply universally, such as *everyone, everybody, someone, somebody,* and *people.*

Sexist language:

We are counting on every man in the company.

One of the women in the department made a mistake.

You men need to attend this meeting.

Preferred language:

We are counting on everyone in the company.

Someone in the department made a mistake.
All of you need to attend this meeting.

2. **Avoid using words that clearly identify the gender of the individual (unless you are referring to a particular person).**

Select alternative words. An exception to this rule is when avoiding a sexist word makes a sentence awkward. The trend is toward applying sexually nonspecific terms to both genders.

Examples:

Sex-Specific Words	Alternatives
mankind	people, humanity
manpower	labor force
waitress	server
chairman	chair *or* chairperson

3. **Select letter salutations to be general when the sex of the receiver is not known or when the letter is addressed to more than one person.**

The use of gender identification in salutations is appropriate when using Mr. or Ms. Otherwise, salutations should be non-specific when titles are used.

Examples:

Sex-Specific Words	Alternatives
Gentlemen:	Gentlemen and Ladies:
	Gentlemen or Ladies:
Dear Sir:	Dear Sir or Madam:

Sometimes an individual's name does not indicate whether the person is male or female. In such cases, address the letter to the individual's full name. For example, if the receiver's name is Robin Smith, address the letter, Dear Robin Smith.

4. **Avoid hybrid forms of personal pronouns and possessive adjectives.**

These are distracting and unacceptable. The brief popularity of hybrids went out of favor and has not reemerged.

Examples:

s/he
his or her
he/she
(wo)man

5. Use plurals to avoid problems of agreement.

One of the problems that arises when trying to avoid sexist writing is that of agreement between singular and plural.

Incorrect agreement:

Each manager should pass the message to their departments and make sure their subordinates understand it completely.

Correct but awkward agreement:

Each manager should pass the message to his or her department and make sure subordinates understand it completely.

This problem often can be avoided by the consistent use of plural form. Considering the above example, plural is a preferable style of expression, as this type of statement often involves generalization.

Correct agreement:

Managers should pass the message to their departments and make sure their subordinates understand it completely.

6. Never use words like *girl* or *gal* when referring to women.

The preferred form of expression is to avoid identifying the sex of an individual.

Incorrect usage:

Give it to the girls in the word processing department.

Correct usage:

Give it to the people in the word processing department.

Signs and symbols

Each industry uses its own specialized language and glossary of specific words. Several industries also employ signs and symbols to abbreviate a larger and more complex meaning. The more an industry is involved in mathematical, electrical, chemical, and other technical sciences, the more likely it is that signs and symbols will appear in the communications of the organization.

1. Publish a glossary of commonly used signs and symbols.

If an organization's personnel consist of technical as well as nontechnical employees (virtually always the case), improve internal communication with a published glossary, and make it available to everyone in the organization.

2. **When unusual signs and symbols are used in narratives, explain them in parentheses or with a footnote.**

A sign or symbol may come up only in rare cases, so some readers might not understand its meaning. Explain such symbols in parentheses if the explanation is brief and with a footnote if longer.

3. **Use technical symbols in tables, charts, and graphs but not in narrative.**

In text, avoid using symbols—for example, use *54 percent*, not *54%*. As a general rule, spell out the meaning of the symbol in text. However, when a symbol is used frequently, spelling it out may not make sense. For example, in financial reporting, using % may be preferable, even in text.

Similar words

Many style problems grow from similarities in spelling among words or from the similar uses and meanings of phrases close in definition but not the same. Following are many common similar words and brief descriptions of proper use. (The explanation follows the order of the words.)

a/an: Use prior to a consonant, versus use prior to a vowel sound.

A better way is to research first.

An easier *method* should be found.

accept/except: The verb "to receive," versus the preposition meaning "excluding."

Will you accept and sign for this delivery?

All quarters were profitable except the second.

ad/add: An abbreviation for "advertisement," versus a mathematical function.

Place the ad in all daily papers.

Add the columns to find the total.

adapt/adept: To adjust, versus skillful.

Let's adapt our procedures so they will work.

They are adept at interpreting financial statements.

adverse/averse: Unfavorable, versus having a distaste.

The adverse comments led us to decline the offer.

We were averse to the expensive proposal.

advice/advise: A noun meaning "suggestion," versus a verb meaning "to recommend."

Our advice was to increase the budget.

I advise you to make a written report to personnel.

affect/effect: A verb meaning "to influence," versus a noun meaning "result, outcome, or consequence."

Customer attitude will affect buying habits.

The effect of the study has been to discourage risk.

agree to/agree with: To give consent, versus to have an understanding.

We will agree to a one-month extension.

I agree with you about the budget problems.

all ready/already: Reference to complete readiness or to plural readiness, versus past action.

The attendees were all ready and in the room.

We already balanced the accounts.

all right/alright: Correct form, versus informal, incorrect usage. Use *all right*, and avoid usage of *alright*.

all together/altogether: In unison, versus completely.

The inventory was finally placed all together.

It proved altogether too difficult to balance.

allusion/delusion/illusion: A reference to something, versus a false belief or idea, versus a mistaken impression.

We made an allusion to problems faced by employees.

The belief in creating profits by thinking about them is, in our opinion, a delusion.

He had the illusion there was no problem whatsoever.

alternate/alternative: Taking place in turns, versus a choice between two or more.

The job was made to alternate departments each month.

The alternative was equally unacceptable.

although/though: Used for the same references, with *although* having more emphasis.

We exceeded expectations, although that trend should not be expected to continue.

The company had begun operating in the black though the CEO had not made a formal announcement.

among/between: Several choices, versus usually only two (although *between* often is used for more than two).

The eleven employees decided among themselves.

It came down to a choice between Sue and David.

amount/number: Reference to uncountable quantities, versus reference to countable quantities.

We will require a large amount of sand to fill this hole.

What number of customers responded?

anyone/any one: Anybody or any person, versus any specific, singular person or thing.

Anyone who arrives early will get the best chair.

The job may be performed by any one of you.

anyway/any way: Even so or in any event, versus a reference to options for action.

We were not planning to attend anyway.

Any way it can be achieved will be appreciated.

appraise/apprise: An estimate of value, versus providing information.

The headquarters building will be appraised in anticipation of refinancing.

Please apprise us of the situation as it develops.

around/round: An approximation or loose reference to a location, versus a shape.

The total is around a half million.

The meeting room's table is round.

as/like: A subordinating conjunction, versus a preposition.

We stopped and talked as the meeting broke up.

We laughed like children.

ascent/assent: To rise, versus to agree.

Our average profit by division is on the ascent.

Will you assent to an audit?

assure/ensure/insure: All three words refer to promises or guarantees; however, *assure* refers to people while *ensure* tends to refer obliquely to less personal promises; *insure* is a financial term related to the idea of insurance.

I can assure you the task will be done on time.

The safeguards ensure compliance with all rules.

We have to insure our building against risk of loss.

bazaar/bizarre: A marketplace, versus odd or strange.

The ancient place for exchange was the bazaar.

His behavior was bizarre during the interview.

beside/besides: Next to, versus in addition to.

He sat beside me during the seminar.

We made a profit last year; besides, our future costs are anticipated to fall.

biannually/biennially: Twice per year, versus every two years.

The review is held biannually, in January and July.

We will meet biennially, in odd-numbered years.

bimonthly/semimonthly: Every other month, versus twice per month.
We meet bimonthly, in even-numbered months.
The review meeting is held semimonthly, on the second and fourth Tuesday.

bloc/block: A coalition, versus a solid mass or unit.
We joined with our competitors as a lobbying bloc.
The stock price is lower when transacted as a block.

board/bored: A body (or piece of wood), versus a tired or wearied state.
The board of directors meeting takes place next week.
A board is loose in our fence.
I am bored with the repetitive tasks of my job.

breath/breathe/breadth: A small amount of air, versus the act of respiration, versus width.
I need to go outside for a breath of air.
It's so stuffy I can't breathe in here.
The length isn't the problem; it's the breadth.

bring/take: Reference to something being brought or delivered, versus something being removed.
Bring me your notes.
Take these notes when you leave.

by/buy/bye: A preposition, versus the act of purchasing, versus a secondary reference or parting comment.
We go by the book here.
The company wants to buy out its competitor.
Good-bye.

can/may: Ability, versus permission (with some overlap).
We can complete the report on time.
You may take the afternoon off.

canvas/canvass: A durable cloth, versus conducting a survey or poll.
The tents were a bleached canvas.
We canvassed customers in the area.

capital/capitol: The central site (or investment, or upper-case lettering), versus a government building.
Washington D.C. is the capital of the United States.
Businesses have invested a large amount of capital.
The first word of the sentence begins with a capital letter.
The capitol is recognized by its large dome.

cash/cache: Money, versus a hiding place or safe place.
We do not accept cash by mail.

Think of the reserve account as a cache for corporate-level emergencies.

cast/caste: A collection of players or a verb, versus a societal class.

The marketing cast consists of a strong executive and aggressive, knowledgeable field managers.

They were prone to cast dispersions on others.

Our lower-level employees often think they are viewed as a lower caste.

casual/causal: Informal, versus a reason for an event.

We viewed the problem with casual unawareness.

The causal data were overlooked by the method of questioning.

cede/seed: To give to another, versus the beginning or source.

We will cede those accounts to the competing marketing group.

The seed of our troubles was the vague agreement itself.

censor/censure: To suppress material, versus to criticize.

Please censor your personal opinions from this report.

We were censured by the regulatory agency.

cite/sight/site: A quotation, versus reference to vision, versus a place or location.

Please cite your source for that information.

Profitability is not yet in sight for the division.

This corner is the site for our new offices.

coarse/course: Rough, versus a path or method.

The previous marketing methods were perceived as being too coarse.

We have selected our course carefully.

collision/collusion: A colliding or conflict, versus a conspiracy.

The two managers had a personality collision that needed immediate resolution.

The embezzlement was achieved in a way that required collusion.

compare to/compare with: Similarity, versus to check or observe similarities.

Let's compare last year's numbers to this year's.

Please don't compare our results with those of dissimilar industries.

complement/compliment: The act of finishing or adding to, versus praise or acknowledgment.

The revisions complement the budget process.

The letter was a compliment for the work we did.

comprehensible/comprehensive: So that it can be understood, versus extensive.

Finally, we have a version of the report that is comprehensible enough for non-technicians to read.

I particularly admired the comprehensive analysis of every option available.

comprise/compose: To include, versus to create.

The department comprises three sections.

We need to compose a cover letter for the report.

confidant/confident: One with whom sensitive information can be entrusted, versus a self-assured attitude.

I consider you a confidant, or I wouldn't tell you any of this.

I am confident my numbers are accurate.

conscience/conscious: A moral standard, versus being awake or aware.

Our conscience would bother us.

We are conscious of the way you feel.

continual/continuous: Repeating or occurring frequently, versus ongoing without interruption.

We suffer continual unfavorable variances in this account.

The budget review process is a continuous job.

controller/comptroller: A financial officer of a company, versus a public official.

The company's controller issued a balance sheet.

The comptroller of the currency issued a press release.

council/counsel/consul: An organized group of people, versus the verb to give advice or the noun meaning "attorney," versus a foreign government's spokesperson.

The council advised the company to abandon the plan.

Please counsel us as to the best course to take.

We asked our counsel for an opinion.

The British consul will visit our main office.

councilor/counselor: A member of an organized group, versus an attorney or other adviser.

The councilors met at the usual time.

Our corporate counselor is preparing a brief.

credible/creditable/credulous: Believable and trustworthy, versus admirable, versus gullible.

After the proposed changes, the budget was viewed as a credible document.

We were pleased that the report offered a creditable alternative to the problem.

We were credulous to hire that individual without verifying his claimed background.

credit/accredit: A noun for one side of an accounting entry or a verb to post benefit, versus certification or acknowledgment.

The debit was offset by an equal credit.

I will credit the payment to your account.

He is an accredited professional.

criteria/criterion: Plural, versus singular.

These criteria have to be observed.

Accuracy is the only criterion.

data/datum: Plural, versus singular (however, data often is used incorrectly used for both, while datum is rarely used).

Those data are correct.

The datum is only one piece of the story.

definite/definitive: Certain, versus conclusive.

There is a definite trend toward profitability.

This is the definitive procedure.

depositary/depository: A person entrusted with funds, versus the place where funds are left.

He is the depositary for cash on hand.

The corner bank serves as depository for us.

deprecate/depreciate: To disapprove, versus to decline in value.

The report deprecated the motives and reputation of the company and the industry.

The machinery is worthless due to functional depreciation.

descent/dissent: A downward movement, versus disagreement.

Our volume continues its quarterly descent.

Voices of dissent within the company are not always productive.

deserve/disserve: To be worthy, versus to serve poorly.

The department deserves recognition for its work.

We have been disserved by the unfair criticism.

detract/distract: To take away from, versus to draw attention away from.

The introduction of personal views detracts from the main argument.

Our employees were distracted by the noise outside.

device/devise: A tool or utility, versus a verb, to formulate.

The computer is an essential device for inventory control.

We need to devise a method for faster turnaround time.

differ from/differ with: To be dissimilar, versus to disagree.

We differ from other companies in that our product cannot be duplicated.

We differ with one another about how to proceed.

disassemble/dissemble: To undo or take apart, versus to mask.
The machine has to be disassembled and fixed.
The report dissembles the real problem.

disburse/disperse: To pay out, versus to scatter.
The payroll department disburses checks on Friday.
As the meeting broke up, attendees dispersed.

discreet/discrete: Reference to tact or caution, versus individual or unique.
She was discreet in checking references.
The manufacturing process ensures that every product is discrete.

disinterested/uninterested: Without bias, versus lacking in concern or interest.
The arbitrator must be a disinterested party.
Because the decision will not affect us, we are completely uninterested.

egoism/egotism: Thought of one's self, versus speaking of one's self.
His egoism prevented his understanding of others.
The speech was characterized by egotism.

elicit/illicit: To draw out, versus improper or illegal.
We intend to elicit opinions on the issue.
This action was illicit and should not be repeated.

emigrate/immigrate: To go to another place, versus to come into this place.
Our product has emigrated to Europe.
The CEO immigrated from England.

eminent/imminent: With prestige, versus pending.
The keynote speaker was an eminent lecturer.
The collapse of this stock price, in our opinion, is imminent.

envelop/envelope: To enclose, versus a wrapper.
Our market strategy is to envelop the entire region.
Please place the report in a sealed envelope.

erasable/irascible: Able to be erased, versus hot-tempered.
They used erasable ink, which was a mistake.
The manager is known for his irascible personality.

especial/special: Extraordinary and exceptional, versus an exception.
This was an especial task, and it was done well.
There is a special reason for my request.

estop/estoppel/stop: To bar under law, versus a bar due to a previous action, versus to cease.
The law may estop you from proceeding without first having a court challenge.

The standard of collateral estoppel prevents us from trying this case again.

We were ordered to stop at once.

exercise/exorcise: To take action, versus to force away.

We will exercise our legal rights.

The poor attitude must be exorcised from the ranks.

explicit/implicit: Defined without doubt, versus implied or alluded to.

I was quite explicit so there can be no doubt.

The lack of response was taken as implicit agreement.

extant/extent: Still in existence, versus a reference to degrees.

A small degree of competition is extant in virtually all regions.

To what extent will we commit to investigating even the smallest variance?

facetious/factious/factitious/fictitious: Humorous or witty, versus promoting of conflict, versus fake or disingenuous, versus false.

His facetious remarks were appreciated.

The factious attitude only isolated the department from the rest of the division.

The study, because it manipulated data, has to be viewed as factitious.

The claim is fictitious, and we have ample data showing that the opposite is true.

faint/feint: In a weakened state, versus a ploy or deception.

I became faint in the stuffy room.

The announcement was a feint designed to force our hand.

farther/further: References to distance, versus nongeographic descriptions such as more advanced or more developed.

New York is farther from here than Trenton.

Upon further consideration, the offer was rejected.

We are further along on the task than the others.

fewer/less: Things that can be counted, versus unknown quantities.

Fewer employees are required in that department.

That is less important at this point.

first/firstly: Proper form, versus jargon. With all listings by number, avoid -ly endings. Use first, second, and third as preferred form.

flare/flair: A flaming outward, versus ability.

The new product has flared in the market.

She demonstrated a particular flair for the job.

for/fore/four: A preposition, versus in the front, versus a numeral.

This report was prepared for you.

We are in the fore among our competitors.

We report four times per year.

forgo/forego: To do without, versus to precede.

We will have to forgo our company picnic this year.

The foregoing section of this report demonstrated our point.

former/latter: the first of two, versus the last.

Of beige or tan, I prefer the former.

The committee offered budgets of $2 million and $3.5 million; we prefer the latter.

forward/foreword: Near the front or moving toward the front, versus an introductory section.

Move forward to the front of the room.

I was asked to write the foreword to the report.

good/well: An adjective, versus an adverb or an adjective describing health.

I have a good feeling about this project.

It was a job well done.

He did not feel well and left the office early.

guarantee/guaranty: Noun to warrant or verb to provide warranty, versus a financial security or policy.

The guarantee was enforceable in court.

Can you guarantee the accuracy of these numbers?

The guaranty bond is with our attorney.

healthful/healthy: Beneficial to health, versus being in good health.

Customers prefer buying and using healthful products.

Our customers are healthy.

hypercritical/hypocritical: Overly critical, versus pretentious and smug.

We believe that management is hypercritical when it comes to our reports.

The board demonstrated a hypocritical belief that they did not need us.

if/whether: Statement of a condition, versus alternatives.

We will present the information only if we are allowed to attend the full meeting.

I don't know yet whether to ask.

imply/infer/insinuate: To refer to a conclusion or consequence, versus to derive as a conclusion, versus to either make an indirect assertion or force oneself into a group.

While offering no proof, the speaker seemed to imply that new systems never work.

I infer from your comments that you are not available to help with this project.

The report appears to insinuate that the project will fail.

The manager was able to insinuate himself into the meeting.

in/into: Location or status, versus change of condition or place.

We are in New York now.

Our company is in trouble financially.

We moved into new offices last month.

Let's get into the project.

incidence/incidents: An occurrence or rate of occurrence, versus a series of occurrences or events.

The incidence of complaint is on the decline.

There was a high incidence of absenteeism just before the holiday.

There have been fewer incidents this past year.

incredible/incredulous: Unbelievable, versus unbelieving.

The report was incredible.

We are incredulous at what the report claims.

ingenious/ingenuous: Clear or brilliant, versus simple or childlike.

The solution was ingenious in its simplicity.

We provided the most ingenuous arguments.

insight/incite: Vision or understanding, versus instigation.

The discussion gave me great insight into your concerns.

Do not attempt to incite our competitors.

insoluble/insolvable/insolvent: Unable to be dissolved, versus the inability to explain, versus the inability to pay debts.

The material is insoluble, making it appropriate for its intended use.

The problem appears insolvable at this level.

The company has been declared insolvent.

instance/instants: Example or event, versus moments.

In this instance, the tests all failed.

We were in agreement for a few instants.

intelligent/intelligible: Having cognitive ability, versus understandable.

Our leaders have demonstrated their intelligence.

The technical report, although complex, was completely intelligible.

interstate/intrastate: Between more than one state, versus within one state only.

We are subject to federal rules because our markets operate on an interstate basis.

We are restricted to only intrastate activity under terms of the charter.

irregardless/regardless: The proper word is always regardless, which means the same as nonetheless. Avoid use of the improper form, irregardless.

its/it's: A possessive form of the pronoun, versus a contraction for it is.

We read the entire report, except its supplementary attachments.

It's clear to us that changes are required.

lain and lay/lie: Forms of the verb lie (meaning "to recline horizontally"); lie by itself is a noun or verb meaning "to prevaricate."

Obsolete supplies had lain in the warehouse for over a year.

The store lay on the main traffic route.

The building lies at the corner of Main and Broadway.

A lie is never acceptable. [noun]

Do not lie to others. [verb]

last/latest: Final, versus most recent.

The last store closed this month.

This is only the latest in a series of reports.

later/latter: A comparative form of late, versus reference to the second of two possibilities,

The decision will be made later.

Of Detroit or Chicago as a convention site, we prefer the latter [Chicago].

learn/teach: Acquiring information, versus giving information to others.

We are trying to learn the new procedures.

Let me teach you how to use this equipment.

lend/loan: A verb only, versus a noun or a verb.

We hope the bank will lend capital to our company.

We want to finance our expansion with a bank loan.

Are you willing to loan us the money?

liable/libel/likely: Responsible, versus a complaint in law or a written statement defamatory to another, versus plausibly.

We are liable for statements made by employees.

A libel suit was filed against the author.

You are likely to be promoted for your work.

lightening/lightning: To reduce in weight or responsibility, versus a natural event.

We are lightening our departmental workload.

The building was struck by lightning.

literal/littoral: Exactly, versus reference to shoreline legal issues.

This is a literal interpretation of the rules.

Our contract for acquisition of land by the water included our littoral rights.

loose/lose: Unfastened or unsecured, versus to misplace or part with.

The handle on my door is loose.

That is a loose interpretation of the rule.

I always lose my glasses.

We will lose money this year.

maybe/may be: An adverb meaning "perhaps," versus a verb meaning "possibly."

Maybe we will break for an early lunch.

The outcome may be beyond our control.

media/medium: Plural, versus singular.

The media are interested in this story.

What is the best medium for our news release?

metal/mettle: A solid substance, versus courage or resolve.

I ordered a metal desk rather than one of wood.

It required mettle to confront your manager.

modal/model: Of a mode, versus a prototype or style.

What is the modal payment: monthly or quarterly?

This is a model cost control plan.

moral/morale: Ethical conduct, versus mood or state of mind.

Admitting the flaw is the only moral thing to do.

Due to poor communication, morale is very low.

motif/motive: A theme, versus a reason for something's pattern.

We market this product with the "tasty" motif.

What is the motive for that behavior?

needed/needful/needy: Required or wanted, versus necessary or essential, versus in need.

We needed the report last week.

The proper treatment of customers is needful to our long-term success.

The charitable fundraiser will help the needy.

observance/observation: Compliance, versus the act of watching and learning.

In observance of the law, the reports will be filed.

My observation was that the work was done correctly.

OK/O.K./Okay: All forms of the same expression meaning "all right." The full spelling is preferred in formal documents; the abbreviation, with or without periods, is acceptable in internal memos or notes.

oral/verbal: The act of speaking, versus of words or by word of mouth.
We entered into an oral contract.
The subtle meaning was lost in the verbal translation.

past/passed: Time gone by, versus gone beyond or successfully completed.
That's what we did in the past.
The practice has passed with the advent of computers.
I passed the test.

peak/peek/pique: The top, versus a glance, versus to provoke.
The chart shows that profits peaked last year.
Let me have an advance peek at the report.
Don't pique him into a confrontation.

percent/percentage: The number of segments out of 100, versus the less specific relationship between a value and 100.
Only 35 percent of all customers returned.
A relatively small percentage of customers returned.

perpetrate/perpetuate: To cause or be guilty of, versus to keep something going.
The offense was perpetrated by an unnamed person.
The problem is perpetuated by continued poor fiscal policies.

persecute/prosecute: To oppress or harass, versus to sue or complain under the law.
Do not persecute me for my opinions.
The attorney general said he would prosecute.

personal/personnel: Individually, versus the staff or department engaged in employment matters.
This is a personal problem between the employees.
Send a copy to the personnel department.

perspective/prospective: Views or belief in balance, versus anticipated status.
Our perspective changed with more information.
All prospective customers want to be asked.

phenomena/phenomenon: Plural, versus singular.
These phenomena are unpredictable.
The phenomenon was undoubtedly a one-time event.

portion/proportion: A part or to divide into parts, versus relationships or ratio segments.
We received only a portion of the market share.
The work will be portioned among the staff.
The greater proportion of funds is spent in marketing and related efforts.

practical/practicable: Proven and realistic, versus able to be achieved. The words are used interchangeably. The recommended style decision is to use the simpler form, practical, for both meanings.

precede/proceed: To come before, versus to go ahead.

On the balance sheet, assets precede liabilities.

Let's proceed with the inventory audit.

precedence/precedents: Singular noun meaning "priority," versus plural noun meaning a "case or example."

Cost controls take precedence over other actions.

We sought out precedents to establish the legality of our position.

predicate/predict: To base upon, versus to forecast.

Our assumptions are predicated on experience.

We predict a twofold increase in sales volume.

prescribe/proscribe: To suggest or order, versus to prohibit.

We prescribe tighter cost and expense controls.

Payments without proper authorization are proscribed by our internal controls.

pretend/portend: To make believe or base actions on role playing, versus to foreshadow or signal in advance.

Let's pretend we're in charge of making the final decisions.

This financial statement portends serious trouble.

principal/principle: Noun meaning "head person" or adjective meaning "primary" or "leading," versus a standard or belief.

The principal of the corporation gave a keynote speech.

The principal reasons are listed in the report.

The principles of good accounting must be applied.

provided/providing: Conditional, versus to furnish.

We will agree provided we are granted a concession.

Our department will be providing the information.

quiet/quit/quite: With less noise, versus to give up, versus considerably.

We need quiet in order to concentrate.

The manager quit yesterday.

This is quite an improvement.

quotation/quote: A noun referring to a verbatim use of words, versus the verb to repeat (also used informally as an abbreviated form of quotation).

The quotation was used to make the point.

Please don't quote me.

The quote came from an old book. [informal]

raise/rise: To uplift or increase, versus to go up.
We were all given a raise.
Don't raise our expectations.
The elevator began to rise.
I hope to rise in the organization.

real/really: Adjective, versus adverb.
The real reasons are unknown to us.
We are really going to get approval this time.

register/registrar/registry: A record, versus an officer in charge of keeping records, versus the place where the register is maintained.
This is the official register of daily receipts.
The registrar is responsible for recording payments coming through the mail.
The registry is also called the cashier's cage.

respectfully/respectively: In a courteous or considerate manner, versus in the indicated order.
We respectfully asked for a meeting.
Net profits during the first, second, and third quarters were 8, 6, and 7 percent, respectively.

Respective/irrespective: belonging or relating to, versus not regarding
We defined the respective limits of duties.
The department performed irrespective of timing conflicts.

right/rite/write/wright: Correctness or a legal protection, versus a ceremony, versus to set words to paper, versus a worker skilled in a task.
We had the right to speak out.
The rite involved sitting and kneeling for hours.
We will write our ideas in a report.
The playwright produced his new three-act play.

root/route: The source or a mathematical value, versus a roadway or course.
The root of our problem is poor internal control.
The square root of 64 is 8.
We selected the shortest driving route.

scrip/script: A form of promissory note, versus a scenario or (in law) an original document.
The emergency management team handed out scrip to their workers.
The meeting was obviously scripted in advance.

set/sit: To put, versus to be seated.
I want to set the record straight.
Please sit down.

shall/will: Obligatory action or part of a question (sometimes used interchangeably with should), versus a simple future verb (the word shall, when used in legal documents, indicates mandatory actions rather than optional).

The corporation shall provide written notice within three weeks of such changes.

Shall we meet on Tuesday?

We will meet on Tuesday.

some time/sometime/sometimes: A period of identified time, versus an indefinite time or occasional role, versus occasionally.

We stopped using that procedure some time ago.

We will get around to a file audit sometime.

Our sometime master of ceremonies is a clerk in the legal research department.

We sometimes meet for lunch.

stationary/stationery: Remaining in one spot, versus paper and related writing supplies.

Our profitability has been stationary for four years.

Our stationery supplies are running low.

statue/statute: A model or piece of art, versus a law.

The statue in the courtyard is of our founder.

We must operate under restrictions of the statute.

straight/strait: In a direct line or correctly, versus a narrow opening.

I used a ruler to draw a straight line.

We were cautioned to keep the files straight.

The bay narrowed into a strait.

summon/summons: A verb to call or order to appear, versus a noun representing an order.

I was summoned to the manager's office.

The summons was addressed to me.

sure and/sure to: Improper form, versus intended form.

Be sure and call. [improper]

Be sure to call. [proper]

sustenance/subsistence: The basic necessities for life, versus expenses or maintenance.

Everyone's budget priority is sustenance for self and for family.

I was provided a meager subsistence allowance while out of town.

than/then: A word of comparison, versus an adverb denoting time.

This year's budget turned out to be more accurate than last year's.

We met in the lobby and then went to lunch.

their/there/they're: A possessive adjective, versus an indication of a place, versus a contraction of they are.

Employees balanced their own accounts.

The records are filed over there.

They're attending a field survey today.

through/threw: From one end to the other or passing within or done with, versus past tense of throw.

We went through the report from start to finish.

The new freeway passed right through town.

I am through with these arguments.

We threw the whole thing out.

to/too/two: A preposition, versus a word meaning "also" or an adverb indicating excess, versus the numeral.

We went to the executive office.

My friend, too, works here.

It was too hot to work.

We had two additional staff members available.

toward/towards: The former is preferred, although both have the same meaning and usage.

track/tract: A path or course, versus a parcel of land.

The proper track is described in our procedures.

The company purchased a tract for its new building.

transmission/transmittal: Sending a message without physical substance, versus sending a message with additional material.

The transmission came in by fax today.

The letter was accompanied by a transmittal.

try and/try to: Improper, versus proper form.

Try and remember. [improper]

Try to remember. [proper]

until/till: Until is more formal than till, although both are acceptable.

urban/urbane: Of a city, versus polished.

Our urban stores tend to have higher profits.

His urbane tone indicated that he was well educated.

venerable/vulnerable: Respected due to age, versus easily hurt.

The venerable chairman approached the podium.

You seem vulnerable to even the slightest criticism.

vindicative/vindictive: Clearing suspicions, versus seeking revenge.

This information is vindicative for those we suspected.

Rather than hearing our ideas as constructive, they were vindictive and angry.

wait for/wait on: To remain ready, versus to serve.

We are waiting for the report.

The server should be here to wait on us.

waive/wave: To give up a right, versus a hand motion.

We hereby waive our right to a hearing.

Wave to the audience as you leave the stage.

weather/whether: Natural conditions, versus an alternative.

Let's hope the weather permits an outside event.

We have to decide whether to say yes or no.

which/who: Reference to objects, versus reference to people.

Which department do you work in?

Who is your supervisor?

who's/whose: A contraction of who is, versus the possessive form of who.

Who's attending this summer's retreat?

Whose desk is this?

wont/won't: Accustomed, versus a contraction for will not.

They are wont to repeat themselves.

We won't allow this to happen.

your/you're: The possessive of you, versus a contraction for you are.

Your report was well received.

You're expected to speak at the task force meeting.

Similes

A comparison between two things is called a *simile*. It often relies on a connecting word (like, so, as, an), whereas the metaphor states a comparison without a connector (see also Metaphors).

Example, simile

He is as sly as a fox.

Similes often are cliché or trite expressions.

Examples, cliché similes:

cute as a button
busy as a bee
light as a feather
hard as nails

Appropriate use of simile adds flavor to language, but should be used sparingly in professional correspondence.

Examples of similes that may be appropriate in business style:

The new marketing document is as clean as a whistle.

The division managers fought like cats and dogs.

He read what was shown on the screen, making the presentation as interesting as watching grass grow.

Singular and plural

The method for forming a plural depends on the noun or pronoun. Many nouns do not follow a regular pattern, and their plural forms have to be memorized or learned through familiarity. The greatest problem for those unfamiliar with the rules is that of inconsistency. For each rule, there may be a lengthy list of exceptions.

1. Form most plurals by adding *s* to the singular form.

The most common rule is to add *s* to the singular form of the noun—the word's spelling is not altered at all.

Examples:

Singular	Plural
employee	employees
manager	managers
budget	budgets

2. For nouns ending in a *y* preceded by a consonant, drop the *y* and replace it with *ies* to form a plural.

Examples:

Singular	Plural
company	companies
inventory	inventories

When nouns end in a *y* that is preceded by a vowel, plurals are formed by adding an *s*.

Examples:

Singular	Plural
Monday	Mondays
Friday	Fridays
day	days

play	plays
key	keys

3. **Add -*es* to form plurals for some nouns ending in consonants or ending with an o.**

Nouns ending in consonants or with an *o* often require an -*es* ending to form the plural.

Examples:

Singular	Plural
echo	echoes
veto	vetoes
brush	brushes

4. **Be aware of unusual plural formations.**

Some words ending in *s* are made into plurals by changing the preceding letter; such a change usually involves turning an *i* into an *e*.

Examples:

Singular	Plural
echo	echoes
analysis	analyses
thesis	theses
axis	axes

Technical terms ending in *a* often require the addition of the letter *e* to form a plural. Some Latin terms are made plural by dropping the singular ending and replacing it with an *a*.

Examples:

Singular	Plural
larva	larvae
seta	setae
addendum	addenda

Nouns often change in form to convert to plural. This is the most troublesome aspect of plurals because there are no consistent rules.

Examples:

Singular	Plural
matrix	matrices
nucleus	nuclei

radius	radii
child	children

5. **Be aware of the irregular plural forms for pronouns.**

Pronouns tend to be very irregular when converted to plural form, with no pattern or consistency.

Examples:

Singular	Plural
I	we
me	us
he, she, it	they
him, her, it	them
you	you

6. **Turn some compound terms into plural form by adding an *s* to the key word rather than to the final word.**

Examples:

Singular	Plural
attorney at law	attorneys at law
grant in aid	grants in aid
chief of staff	chiefs of staff

7. **Do not confuse plurals with possessive form.**

The possessive usually involves the addition of an *s* with an apostrophe. The apostrophe follows the existing *s* ending when the singular form ends in *s* or when the noun is already a plural.

Examples:

Noun	Plural	Possessive
man	men	man's, men's
woman	women	woman's, women's
employee	employees	employee's, employees'

8. **If it can be done without creating confusion, add an *s* without an apostrophe to form plurals for many abbreviations and acronyms.**

Examples:

Singular	Plural
COD	CODs
OK	OKs
SOP	SOPs

Ph.D.	Ph.D.'s
M.B.A.	M.B.A.'s

Spacing

Decisions concerning spacing in documents affect the ability of a reader to comprehend information, degrees of acceptance or resistance even to reading the material, and the opinion the reader will have of the individual writer and of the company. Readers need to have text broken up with "white space"—areas with nothing on them that emphasize or offset text, tables, and graphics. This should be balanced, however, and offered in moderation. A key to all issues of spacing is consistency in a document.

1. **Select spacing of margins depending on the nature of the document.**
   As a general rule, all letters, reports, proposals, and other formal documents should leave at least 1 inch on the left, right, top, and bottom of every page. Some formats use up to 1 1/2 inches. For letters written on company letterhead, the arrangement of preprinted material determines the spacing. If preprinted matter appears at the bottom of the page, measure the desired distance from the top of the printed matter rather than from the page edge.
   For reports and other documents exceeding one page, the margin decisions should be consistent throughout the entire document.

2. **Single- or double-space the text depending on the type of document.**
   Business letters are normally single-spaced; reports, proposals, procedures manuals, and training material tend to be double-spaced for ease of reading. More white space usually means that readers are more willing to read a greater amount of material. If a letter is single-spaced, leave a double space between paragraphs and extend all margins to allow greater white space.

3. **Allow space around tables and charts.**
   Graphics usually appear in reports or proposals, which should be double-spaced. If the chart or graph appears on a page by itself, it should be arranged with the previously determined margin size kept consistent. If the graphic or table appears above or below the text or in the middle of a page, leave three or four spaces between the text and the graphic. Do not break up a table between two pages unless it is more than one page long. That is why tables are most often numbered in books and referenced in the text. When more than one page, organize to present the table on facing pages.

4. Space generously on title pages and for heads and subheads.

Even with other forms of emphasis, the break in thought and section should be obvious. At the end of one section, leave at least four spaces (up to six if single-spaced) before listing the next subhead. Leave an extra space (or two if single-spaced) between the subhead and the beginning of the first paragraph in that section.

Run-in headings are often used for lists, but it is better to not use run-in text for normal headings. It is preferable to distinguish heading levels by size. Organize documents by heading levels: First by section, then subsection and sub-sub sections if needed. Applying a standard size for each helps readers to follow the organization of the list. In some technical documents, numbering in the format 1., 1.1, 1.1.1 may be appropriate, especially if a large volume of cross references are required.

5. Use spacing to plan the size of documents.

If you need to extend the size of a document, allowing more white space is an acceptable method, as long as such movement of text is not excessive.

6. Follow punctuation guidelines.

The following rules are general and refer to most business documents. However, if you are preparing a manuscript for publication, even within your own organization, be sure to obtain precise guidelines prior to adopting spacing and punctuation rules. (For the purpose of this section, a "space" refers to the space bar on the keyboard rather than an index space on the page.)

1. Any punctuation ending a sentence or colon should be followed by two spaces in a business document. However, in books, most publishers use a style of one space after periods and colon.
2. Semicolons mid-sentence should be placed after the previous word without a space and should be followed with a single space.
3. When printing dashes or hyphens, do not leave space on either side.
4. Commas are always placed at the end of a word without a space, and followed by a single space.
5. Leave a space on either side of ellipses and spaces between the three periods.
6. Leave a single space on the outside of parentheses and brackets in text. Include no spaces on the inside before beginning enclosed narratives or after ending them.

Spelling

Convenient access to spell-check features helps avoid common spelling problems in English. Because so many words represent exceptions to general rules, there are only a few useful rules worth remembering. A listing of frequently misspelled words will help avoid common problems; a comprehensive listing is included at the end of this section.

Even with spell-check available, some misspelled words may be transmitted.

1. Use automated features to find and fix spelling errors, including typographical errors.

Virtually all word processors include a button for spell-check and grammar check of documents. Most include a function to suggest alternatives and to correct misspelled words. This quick and convenient feature should be used for *all* documents. Overlooking or ignoring this feature is a mistake.

2. No automated program can find a correctly spelled typographical error.

If *am* is typed instead of *an*, a spell-checker will not find the error in every case; a grammar checker will find it, however. It is still necessary to read through a document carefully. The advantage of a spell-checker program is that it finds errors the writer might not realize have been made. This includes a commonly found instance of unintended extra spaces between words.

3. Improve spelling by avoiding common problems.

Even a poor speller can eliminate common problems by memorizing a list of commonly misspelled words and by avoiding unnecessarily complex word forms. Most people have chronic problems with a very limited list of words they do not spell correctly. Make a list of such words, and check the list each time you use these words.

A good vocabulary does not necessitate long or difficult-to-spell words. Avoid complex words when shorter, more direct words have the same meaning. A simplified common vocabulary often translates to a clearer, more concise style and better communication. If vocabulary is overly complex in a book, it is less likely to be translated into other languages.

4. Learn a few general spelling rules to improve overall spelling ability.

These rules include:

1. Put *i* before *e* except after *c* (e.g., *conceit, receive, deceive, perceive).*
2. When adding a suffix to a word ending in *y*, change the *y* to an *i*. When adding *-ing*, keep the *y* (e.g., *try, tries, trying*). However, when the *y* is

preceded by a vowel, the change to *i* does not always apply (e.g., *play, plays; betray, betrays*).

3. When a word ends in a consonant, the consonant is often doubled when adding *-ed* or *-ing* (e.g., *stop, stopped, stopping; occur, occurred, occurring*).

5. Use the dictionary.

Many business writers compile a list of their own personal spelling demons. However, with online access it is easy to look up words to ensure that the proper spelling and definition are being used. The reliance on a hard copy dictionary or thesaurus is a hold-over, and online free references are replacing old-style printed documents. The online dictionary and thesaurus is easier and faster to use.

6. Study and master this list of commonly misspelled words.

absence
absorb
absorption
academic
acceptable
accessible
accidentally
accommodate
accompanied
accumulate
accustomed
achievement
acknowledgment
acoustic
acquaintance
acquiesce
acquisition
acreage
adapter
adjacent
advantageous
aegis
affect
affidavit
aggravate
aggression
aisle
alignment
alleged
altogether
amateur
amortize
analogous
analysis
analyze
anomalous
anonymous
answer
appalled
apparatus
apparent
appearance
appraise
appreciable
apprise
appropriate
approximate
aquatic
architect
arising
around
arrangement
ascend
asinine
assistance
association
attendance
attorney
audience
autumn
auxiliary
awkward
bachelor
bankruptcy
basically
belief
believe
beneficial
benefited
biased
boundary
breakfast

breathe
brethren
brochure
buoyant
bureaucracy
cafeteria
caffeine
calendar
caliber
campaign
cancellation
candor
canvass
caret
carriage
cemetery
census
changeable
characteristic
chauffeur
choose
chosen
chronological
coarsely
coincidence
collateral
colossal
column
committee
competent
competition
complement
concede
conceited
conceive
condemn
conference
confidant
connoisseur
conqueror
conscience
conscientious
conscious
consensus
consistent
controlled
controversial
coolly
council
counselor
courteous
curiosity
cynical
dealt
debtor
deceive
deductible
defendant
deficit
definitely
dependent
descendant
describe
desert
desirable
despair
desperate
despicable
detrimental
dignitary
dilemma
disagree
disappear
disappoint
disapprove
disastrous
discipline
disease
dissatisfied
dissimilar
distill
distinct
doctrinaire
dossier
dying
ecstasy
effect
efficient
either
elaborately
elicit
eligible
eliminate
embarrass
eminent
emphasize
enroll
ensure
entrepreneur
enumerate
envelop
equipment
equivalent
escrow
especially
exaggerate
exceed
exercise
exhaust
exhibition
exhilarate
existence
exonerate
exorbitant
experience
explanation
extension

extraordinary
eyeing
facsimile
familiar
fantasy
fascinate
fiery
financially
flammable
fluorescent
forbade
foreign
foresee
forfeit
forthright
friend
fulfill
gauge
glamour
gnawing
government
grammar
grateful
gray
grievous
gruesome
guarantee
guardian
guerrilla
guidance
harass
height
hemorrhage
heroes
heterogeneous
hindrance
humorous
hurriedly
hygiene
hypocrisy
ideally
idiosyncrasy
ignorant
illicit
illiterate
illogical
imaginary
immediately
immensely
impasse
inasmuch
incalculable
incidentally
incredible
indefinitely
independent
indispensable
inequity
inevitable
infinite
influential
initiative
innocuous
innuendo
inoculate
insistence
insurance
integrate
intercede
interference
interim
interrupt
involvement
irrelevant
irresistible
irritated
itinerary
jealousy
jeopardy
jewelry
judgment
knowledge
labeled
laboratory
ledger
legitimate
leisure
lenient
liable
liaison
library
license
lien
lieutenant
lightning
likable
likelihood
liquefy
literature
logistics
loneliness
loose
luxury
lying
magnificent
maintenance
manageable
maneuver
mantle
marriage
material
mathematics
meant
medieval
mediocre
memento
mileage

milieu
millennium
millionaire
miniature
minor
minuscule
minutiae
misapprehension
miscellaneous
mischievous
missile
misspell
morale
mortgage
movable
mysterious
naturally
necessary
negotiate
neither
nevertheless
nickel
noticeable
nowadays
nuclear
nuisance
numerous
obsolescent
obstacle
occasion
occurrence
omission
omitted
oneself
opponent
opportunity
opposite
oppression
ordinance
ordinarily
originally
outrageous
pamphlet
panicky
parallel
partially
particularly
pastime
patience
peaceable
peculiar
penetrate
perceive
performance
permanent
permissible
perquisite
perseverance
persistent
personnel
perspective
perspiration
persuade
phase
phenomenon
phony
physical
plagiarism
plausible
pleasant
politician
possession
possibly
practically
prairie
precedence
precipice
predominantly
preferred
prejudice
preparation
prerequisite
prerogative
presumptuous
pretense
prevail
prevalent
preventive
primitive
principle
privilege
procedure
proceed
process
programmed
prohibition
prominent
promissory
pronunciation
propaganda
propeller
prophecy
prospective
psychiatric
psychological
publicly
pursue
quandary
quarrel
questionnaire
queue
quizzes
rarefy
rarity
receipt
receive
recession

recipe
recipient
recognize
reconnaissance
reconnoiter
recruit
recyclable
reference
regrettable
regular
rehearsal
reinforce
relevant
relief
relieve
religious
remembrance
reminisce
renaissance
renowned
repellant
repetition
rescind
resemblance
resistance
restaurant
retroactive
rhapsody
rhetorical
rhyme
rhythm
ridiculous
roommate
sacrifice
sacrilegious
salvage
satellite
scarcity
scenery
schedule
scissors
secede
seize
separate
sergeant
several
shepherd
shrubbery
siege
signaled
similar
simultaneous
sincerely
sizable
skeptic
skiing
skillful
soliloquy
sophomore
souvenir
spacious
specimen
specious
speech
sponsor
stationery
statistics
straight
stratagem
strength
strenuous
stretch
studying
subpoena
subtlety
suburban
succeed
succession
suggest
suing
summary
superintendent
supersede
suppress
surely
surgeon
surprise
surreptitious
surround
surveillance
susceptible
suspicious
synonymous
tariff
technique
temperament
temperature
tempt
theater
theoretical
theory
therefore
thorough
though
threshold
tobacco
totaled
tragedy
transferable
traveled
tremendous
typical
tyranny
unanimous
unconscious
unctuous
undoubtedly

unforgettable
unfortunately
unique
unmanageable
unnecessary
unwieldy
usage
usually
vacillate
vacuum
various
vegetable
vengeance
villain
violence
visible
warehouse
warrant
warring
weather
weird
whether
whichever
wholly
wield
woeful
yield

Statistical references

In business correspondence, *statistical references* should be precise and fully documented. Avoid incorporating statistics without a study or fact to back up the claimed reference.

Examples of inappropriate statistics:

Our chances of success are 50/50.

This is the outcome 99 percent of the time.

About two out of three employees probably steal office supplies.

In each of these examples, the citation is not supported and the statistical references are cliché in form. A reader of a document with references such as these will either accept the claim without question, or view the entire document as suspicious due to the undocumented statistic.

Also avoid misusing statistics to make a point, when the outcome reveals nothing of interest or becomes a non-statement.

Examples, non-statements with statistics:

About 50% of male employees completed the health questionnaire, but one-half of female employees complied.

Nearly nine out of 10 customers were satisfied in the Northern region, whereas most of our customers reported satisfaction in the Western region.

Style and tone

Writers are faced with many decisions in the way they express ideas. The result is the tone of a document. The nature of the document and the intended audience dictate the style; the style decisions create the tone. The two are impossible to distinguish and should be studied together.

1. **Select the style with the audience in mind.**

A formal letter, report, or proposal should have a completely different style and tone than a personal note, memo, or internal newsletter.

An informal note:

> Hey, Bob, did you hear that McGee was promoted to vice president? I'll always remember him as the guy who was in front of the losing team at the company picnic's tug-of-war—covered with mud!

Company newsletter:

> Mark McGee was promoted to vice president of operations this month. Congratulations, Mark. We'll always remember your leadership at the company picnic; now we'll see how you do with a window office.

Press release:

> ANCO Corporation announced this morning the promotion of Mark McGee to vice president of operations. McGee, an employee of 12 years, was formerly manager of the Operations Department.

All three styles are different, and all are appropriate for the audience to which they are addressed. Everyone alters style depending on the audience, and the resulting tone of a communication reflects those decisions.

2. **Edit for tone as well as mechanics.**

Editing is associated with sentence structure, spelling, punctuation, and arrangement of material. Those are important editing points, but they are only the basics of good writing. Editing may be expanded for tone as well. Subtle writing decisions affect tone dramatically.

Pre-edited formal message:

> We ask that you consider our proposal seriously. We can do the job and would appreciate the chance to work with you and prove it. This is just the kind of project we are capable of.

Postedited formal message:

> We hope you will consider our proposal. We are confident of our ability to provide the highest quality work, and we look forward to the opportunity of working with you.

The second version is stronger and more direct, and it avoids the use of uncertainty or a weak message. The first version weakly asks the reader to "consider our proposal seriously." The improved tone of the second version, in which the writer hopes "you will consider our proposal," is only slightly different; however, it conveys confidence, is more direct, and has a tone of professionalism.

3. Select words carefully to improve style.

Business writing demands extreme diplomacy in many cases, and the method selected to convey an idea can make a vast difference in the response. Three different methods follow.

Emotional:

> I am so angry about your actions that I could scream. Believe me, the day will come when you need a favor from this department, and I won't forget the way you have treated me.

Discreet:

> I am perplexed. We have worked together on many occasions, always with satisfactory results. No doubt, we will have to work together in the future. I would have preferred a constructive dialogue with you, so that we might feel free to provide assistance to you as we have done in the past.

Formal:

> We were deeply concerned at the recent misunderstanding. I remain convinced, however, that constructive dialogue is still possible, and I suggest a conciliatory meeting at your earliest convenience.

4. Vary sentence and paragraph length.

Sentence and paragraph length determine reader interest and comprehension. Paragraphs in lengthy documents make a visual impression on the reader. If they all look about the same in length (especially if all are long), the document will seem formidable and uninteresting, even before the reader attempts to read it. If sentences are varied in length, the visual impression is more pleasing. The same argument can be made for sentence length. If all sentences are about the same length, they are monotonous, like a steady drumbeat in the reader's ear. The monotony destroys reader interest almost as soon as the problem presents itself.

Sentences of similar length:

> We need to meet next week to review the preliminary budget. Several problems have been pointed out in the document. We will need to prepare a complete revision before submitting it. We have also failed to provide adequate supporting documentation. As it is, we cannot justify the expense levels we have projected. I suggest we meet at your office on Monday or Tuesday, if convenient.

Sentences of varied length:

We need to meet next week to review the preliminary budget. Several problems need fixing. For example, some expense levels appear unacceptable and have to be revised. We also overlooked documenting our assumptions. Let's take another look at the whole thing at your office on Monday or Tuesday.

5. Choose a format to make the best impression.

The style chosen for letters, reports, memos, newsletters, and proposals determines how they are received. The appearance of documents makes an important first impression, and the significance of style decisions should not be overlooked. The following standards should always be followed:

1. Every document leaving the company should look completely professional in every way.
2. Check all spelling in every document, and correct all errors before the final draft.
3. On all documents, provide enough white space on each page so that readers will not be overwhelmed by the text.
4. Apply decisions about punctuation, margins, indentations, and other mechanics consistently within a single document.
5. Be sure employees always edit their own work for tone, seeking the right words and phrases for the circumstances. Encourage employees to work with one another for constructive criticism of style and tone.
6. Ensure that department managers establish minimum standards for style and tone of communications leaving the department, and institute procedures to ensure that these guidelines are followed.

Suffixes

Suffixes are formed when a group of letters is added to the end of a word to make a new word.

The word formed with a suffix may expand the meaning or create a word with a completely different meaning. The spelling may also be adjusted as a result of converting a word into a different word with a suffix.

Examples, words and suffixes:

Forget, forgetful
Govern, government
Create, creation
Heavy, heaviness
Possible, possibility

Suffixes convert one part of speech to another (verb to adjective, or verb to noun, for example).

Summarizing

The ability to summarize critical information is essential in business. The readership for the array of reports, proposals, memos, letters, and other documents is able to devote only a limited amount of time to each piece of paper crossing the desk. A summary enables the reader to determine quickly what the document is all about, why it is important, and whether it is necessary to read further.

1. Decide exactly what has to be summarized.

Make a distinction between a summary and an abstract. An *abstract* briefly summarizes the topics included in a document; a *summary* concentrates on the primary conclusion or point. For example, an abstract of a research article includes a range of points, intended to advise the reader of the range of topics covered in the entire article. A summary of the same article would list primary conclusions or the main point of revelation.

2. Select an appropriate format for the summary.

The traditional method of placing summaries at the end of documents is ineffective. The crucial facts should be presented at the beginning. Summarize succinctly. If it is necessary to expand on a simple statement, introduce the point and then provide a short listing of critical conclusions.

The summary should always fit on one page (or it is not truly a summary), and preferably in a single paragraph or structured with bullet points. The purpose is to enable the reader to understand what is included in the entire document in as short a time as possible. The more briefly this can be said in the summary, the more successful the effort.

3. Consider sending a summary only as a first step.

Some documents might not be of interest to everyone on a distribution list. In this instance, a summary can represent a one-page invitation to request a copy of the longer document. This will save the distribution expense for hard-copy documents, as well as time, and will mean more efficient use of file space (manual or automated).

4. Begin lengthy reports with a summary page.

Virtually all reports will be more effective if they start with a one-page summary. The summary page should explain:

1. The purpose of the report.
2. The major conclusion or recommendation.
3. Financial considerations (cost and savings).
4. Deadlines or implementation points.

5. Start proposals with the bottom line.

Assuming a proposal is an offer to perform work or a recommendation for a change in procedures within the organization, the reader is virtually always interested in the conclusion. A summary achieves this. The proposal can be constructed in four sections: (1) a single-page summary, (2) an expanded introduction introducing the issues, (3) the body of the report and conclusions of any studies or other materials, and (4) a supplement including any statistical information.

6. In books, a summary at the beginning helps readers to understand the scope of a chapter's coverage.

If a summary is provided for any one chapter, it should be provided for all chapters.

7. Write letters beginning with a summary of the most important point.

The initial paragraph of the letter should get the reader's attention. Follow the opening with a detailed discussion, and end with another summary. Think of the business letter as an opening and closing summary, with the details sandwiched in between.

Superscript and subscript

When characters or symbols are set at a smaller size and placed above or below alignment for the rest of text, it creates a *superscript* (above) or *subscript* (below). There are several applications for each within text.

1. Superscripts

The ordinal superscript is used to distinguish numerical values. For example, 1st, 2nd, and 3rd display the "st," "nd," and "rd" as ordinals. The alternative is to write out the value portions without superscripts: 1st, 2nd, and 3rd.

Superscripts are also used to denote signs for copyright ©, trademark ™, and registered trademark ® in text. A similar superscripting style is used in some documents to describe monetary values, with symbols and/or cent values expressed in superscript format rather than using decimal points: $\$5^{00}$ or $15^{¢}$.

Expression of fractional values may be spelled out (three-fourths) or expressed with the use of scripts: ¾ when included in text.

In-text reference to footnotes or endnotes also is made via superscripts. When the notation is given in text, it is followed by the notation ^{5}, for example.

Superscripts are used in mathematical notation to represent powers of values. For example, 15^2 represents the square of 15, and 12^n is a representation of 12 to the nth power.

2. Subscripts

The subscript is used in chemical formulas, such as H_2O, the symbol for water. It is also used in many scientific or technical expressions.

In mathematical expressions, subscripts are used to distinguish differing segments of a variable. For example, in describing how to calculate the average of a field of values, the expression $(V_1 + V_2 + ... V_n) \div n$ describes a function of adding together all of the values in the field with "n" values, and dividing by "n" to find the average.

Symbolism

Symbolism is the use of a word or object to express an idea that is otherwise vague or an abstraction. Symbolism often is used in business writing to emphasize a point or to strengthen an argument. It may create a particular mood, or may hint at a thought without being specific. However, symbolism should not be used excessively in professional documents.

Symbolism is found in several forms: figures of speech, actions, metaphors, or allegories. Any of these devices may add flavor to communications.

Examples of symbolism:

The potential markets present a *dizzying array* of choices. (figure of speech)
The competitors *galloped* ahead of us. (actions)
The manager is as strong as a rock. (metaphor)
The market is a swamp full of alligators. (allegory)

Synonyms

The *synonym* is a word with the same meaning as another word. Use of synonyms enable a document to be given variety rather than repeating the same word several times. Refer to a free online thesaurus such as http://www.thesaurus.com to expand vocabulary and locate a wider choice of synonyms.

Example, repetitive statement:

We will begin the project with analysis of the problems. This will begin the definition phase. Once we begin, we will next begin the deadline structure for segments of the project. Finally, we will begin drafting a final report.

Example, revision with the use of synonyms:

We will begin the project with analysis of the problems. This will start the definition phase. Once we initiate this phase, we will next introduce the deadline structure for segments of the project. Finally, we will draft a final report.

Although specific meanings of synonyms have variation, they add color to a document. So, *begin, start, initiate, introduce,* and *draft* clearly have distinctions, but they convey the core message effectively through variety of use.

Synonyms may vary between separate parts of speech or be the same part of speech.

Examples, verbs:

begin, start, initiate
end, stop, finalize

Examples, adverbs:

immediately, quickly, urgently
slowly, gradually, methodically

Examples, nouns:

office, base, headquarters
activity, event, undertaking

Examples, adjectives:

small, little, tiny
big, large, substantial

Examples, preposition:

on, upon, over
in, within, out

Synonyms become complex in use when one word is synonymous with two or more different words with different meanings.

Examples, multiple synonymous relationships:

died, expired and died, deceased

intern, imprison *and* intern, trainee

T, U

Table of contents

A Table of Contents is necessary in any document longer than eight to ten pages. It gives the reader a frame of reference for finding major sections of the report and indicates the scope and coverage of the report. In a book, the Table of Contents is a key factor in the purchasing decision. Therefore, titles of sections should be descriptive and interesting.

1. **Use the table of contents as an outline to organize work and the sequence and contents of the report.**

   In organizing the document, convert an initial outline to a sequence guideline, and ultimately to a Table of Contents.

2. **Decide how much detail to include in the table based on the nature of the report.**

   If the report has only a few sections but they are long, include all major subsections with page numbers in the Table of Contents. Indent subheads so readers know where chapter or section breaks occur. Chapter titles may appear in the header of a book page along with section headings.

3. **Coordinate all references in the Table of Contents.**

   Chapter numbers should be the same as those used for each chapter, and numbering systems should be the same. Apply this rule to chapter numbers as well as to subheads. For example, numbers should consistently follow the sequence of 1, 2, 3; or be labeled as Sections A, B, C; or Roman numerals i, ii, iii.

4. **Place one-page summaries before the Table of Contents.**

   If the document begins with a one-page summary, place the summary after the title page but before the Table of Contents. Refer to the summary by a lowercase roman numeral, and number the Table of Contents with roman numerals as well. Begin Arabic lettering with the main body of the report.

5. **Use leader lines to connect section headings to page numbers.**

   Although the use of leader lines is optional, it draws the reader's attention to the fact that it is a Table of Contents.

DOI 10.1515/9781547400218-019

Sample Table of Contents:

Tables

The use of *tables* either within narrative or as part of an appendix, is used to clarify or summarize information and is organized into tabular form rather than attempting to explain the same information within narrative sections.

The table should bear a direct relationship to text appearing nearby. For example, a table of budget variances may appear during a discussion of key variances and their causes. Placing the table elsewhere in the document would be ineffective and distracting.

The table should only be used to summarize or clarify the topic. When a relatively simple point is made, it often is easier to explain it in narrative. For example, if a financial report compares two periods with contrasting gross profit, it may not be necessary to display a full list of costs with percentages. It may suffice to declare in the narrative that "gross profit declined in the current quarter from the previous level of 51 percent to the current level of 47 percent."

If the table is drawn from sources that are not obvious, a citation should be included below the table. Typically, this section identifies the website or document from which information was drawn. This clarifies the validity of the table. In addition, however, the information in the table and its headings should be self-evident without the need for explanation in text.

When several tables are used, they should be cross-referenced in narrative sections and numbered consistently. Format should also be consistent. Each table should be spaced in the same manner, and headings should briefly explain what each column includes. The numbering and caption for the table are generally at the top of the table to account for their variable size and that should be consistent through the document.

Technical writing

Organizations involved with technical matters face the challenge of internal communication and documentation of processes. This type of company invariably is divided into two broad groups: technicians and administrators. This becomes a problem whenever the technical side is required to communicate with the administrative, especially when dealing with matters of budgets, projects, commitments of capital, or marketing.

1. **Take all steps necessary to facilitate communication between technical and nontechnical employees.**

   Develop a glossary for nontechnical employees to use, so that essential terms can be understood by both sides.

2. **Use a nontechnical writer to work with the technical experts.**

   A common mistake is to use technical style and language for reports aimed at a nontechnical audience. Too many technical writers write only for fellow experts. When reports must go outside the technical arena, communication is always difficult. The problems should be addressed at the draft phase rather than during a presentation meeting. The use of a nontechnical writer makes sense in these situations.

3. **Label reports carefully and provide footnotes to explain important terminology.**

   Follow general guidelines for report preparation. Highly detailed information should be included as appendix material, while the body should concentrate on primary issues: the cost and benefit of an idea to the company, the need for changes in procedures, compliance with regulatory reporting requirements, or nontechnical recommendations for the technical department, for example.

4. **Follow universal guidelines for reports, letters, proposals, and other document production.**

   Even in the most technical application, readers will not always be technicians. The most effective report makes a clear case for an issue without isolating nontechnical readers.

5. **Avoid technical style within the report, especially if the primary audience is nontechnical.**

Know your audience. Reports that are passed around exclusively among technical employees can be written at a high level; however, the writing style for most reports should avoid unnecessarily complicated language.

Unedited statement:

The primary purpose of the study was to observe data concerning operation of the newly designed equipment and to test assumptions in a simulated environment, thus providing the means for recommended improvements in subsequent prototypes.

Edited statement:

We conducted the study to test the newly designed equipment in a simulated environment, so that we could recommend improvements in the design.

Tenses

Every verb has three *tenses*: past, present and future. The verb should be expressed properly in professional documents.

Examples, present tense:

We work every weekday. (simple present)
The department is working on the report. (present continuous)
We have prepared too many reports to keep track. (present perfect)
The department has been reporting in this area for many years. (present perfect continuous)

Examples, past tense:

We worked every weekday. (simple past)
The department was working on the report. (past continuous)
We had prepared too many reports to keep track. (past perfect)
The department had been reporting in this area for many years. (past perfect continuous)

Examples, future tense:

We will work every weekday. (simple future)
The department will be working on the report. (future continuous)
We will have prepared too many reports to keep track. (future perfect)
The department will have been reporting in this area for many years. (future perfect continuous)

The future tenses are distinguished in specific ways. The *simple future* refers to a later time and declares the certainty of an outcome. *Future continuous* combines two elements together, the simple future of the verb "to be" and a present participle (adding "ing" to the verb). In the *future perfect* tense, simple future ("to have") is combined with the past participle of the verb. And *future perfect continuous* is created by adding the future perfect of the verb "to be" with the present participle of the verb (adding "ing").

Titles

Business writing involves the use of many titles. Individuals, organizations, references to published material, and government agencies are found in most types of business correspondence.

1. **Follow the correct format for publication names and titles.**

The title of a book, newspaper, or magazine is italicized but not underlined. The title of an article or a book chapter is placed within quotation marks when using some styles of citation, and left without quotation marks in other styles. The placement of the reference affects this distinction. In an actual citation, for example, it may be appropriate to not use quotations; but in the body of a report, quotation marks set a title apart from other narrative.

Examples of varying forms of a title:

"Producing the Business Newsletter." *Business Times Magazine* 31 (April 1996).
Inventory Alternatives. *Spokane Word,* May 12, 1996, pp. 12–13.
Budgeting for the 21st Century. Buffalo, N.Y.: Business Press, 1996.

2. **Identify the proper method for referring to people by name and title.**

If an individual has a special title, use it in place of the usual *Mr.* or *Ms.* The first time a name is mentioned in a letter or report, use the title and full name; abbreviate subsequent references.

Examples:

Ms. Harmon and Dr. Green arrived today at our corporate headquarters office. Following lunch, Ms. Harmon gave a speech to the board of directors, and Dr. Green went into a private meeting with the CEO.
Chief Financial Officer Harold Carter advised the finance committee that current forecasts were inaccurate. Carter said that until being appointed CFO, he had never seen such an unwillingness by management to face reality.

3. **Use full titles upon first mention only.**
When a person is first mentioned, precede the name with the full title, with the first letter of major title words capitalized. Subsequently, only the last name needs to be given.
Example:
Chief Executive Officer Maria Polmar has released the latest quarter's results. Polmar pointed out that several extraordinary items have distorted the profit picture, and she predicted a healthy third quarter.

4. **Do not capitalize titles when they are referred to without a specific person's name attached to them.**
Example:
Virtually every chief financial officer in the survey responded that education was not the key factor. Several agreed that vice presidents and senior managers in organizations have more hands-on impact than the president, whose task is to provide overall guidance.

5. **Treat organization and agency names, schools, and association names as proper nouns.**
Capitalize the first letter of each key word.
Examples:
Eastman Kodak
Department of the Interior
Harvard University
Rotary Club

Trademarks

Trademarks are used for claiming ownership by an organization or individual of designs or expressions for brands, products and services. Trademarks are identified with the use of two symbols:

The letters "TM" follow the name or phrase in superscript form, revealing that the claim of ownership has not been registered. For example, a product called Uni-Codex would be marked as Uni-Codex™.

The letter R is also encircled and superscripted, indicating that the trademark has been registered. Example: Uni-Codex®

Trademarks are used for a distinctive, original symbol, phrase, or title. In referring to a trademark, a distinction should be made between this and the separate claim of copyright to original or artistic expressions, works of art, or documents (see also Copyright).

Transitions

A transition is a bridge between one thought and another that smooths the flow of a message. Just as a conversation moves from topic to topic without discernable changes, the written word requires transitions to lead the reader from one idea to the next.

1. **Restrict paragraphs to a single idea to make sentence-to-sentence transitions easy.**

Transitions from sentence to sentence within a paragraph are relatively easy, since the paragraph is restricted to one major idea. Even the beginning writer usually has little trouble with ordinary transitions, the natural connection between fragments of a primary thought represented by a series of related sentences. Most writers run into problems when they end a paragraph and move to the next.

2. **Work to achieve smooth transitions between paragraphs.**

Transitions between paragraphs require thought. Because paragraph endings signal the resting of one idea and the beginning of another, transition is not always natural or easy.

Paragraphs lacking transition:

> The organizational requirements for putting together a hard-copy company newsletter make all the difference between a highly effective, current report, and a mere collection of stories.
>
> When selecting a printer, be sure to ask critical questions. Not every printing company operates in the same manner, and cost as well as quality considerations matter greatly.
>
> Where will you find your stories? This is always the main question on the mind of the first-time newsletter editor. Do not worry. Finding stories worthy of your newsletter will be the least of your concerns.

Paragraphs with transition:

> The organizational requirements for putting together a hard-copy company newsletter make all the difference between a highly effective, current report and a mere collection of stories.

The first step in organizing your new venture is finding the right printer. Be sure to ask critical questions. Not every printing company operates in the same manner, and cost as well as quality considerations matter greatly.

Of course, even with the most economical printing source, you still need to locate and write interesting copy. Where will you find your stories? This is always the main question on the mind of the first-time newsletter editor. Do not worry. Finding stories worthy of your newsletter will be the least of your concerns.

With only minor changes, the paragraphs now flow smoothly from one thought to another. The transition is nothing more than a bridge between thoughts.

3. **Use comparisons and contrasting thoughts to keep writing lively and conversational.**

Readers like to have ideas introduced by way of comparison and contrast. With these devices, reading is not merely a lecture of ideas; it becomes a lively demonstration.

Paragraphs lacking comparison or contrast:

An effective budget depends on careful coordination between last year's actual experience and your expectations for the coming year. Learn from your mistakes.

Don't simply view mistakes as failures. They are learning devices and you can improve the budgeting process for each expense account by keeping track of what occurred in last year's budget. Improve based on what you learned.

There is nothing wrong with the style or message of these paragraphs. They are easily understood and the intended message comes through clearly. However, the style and transition are not particularly imaginative or illustrative.

Paragraphs with comparison or contrast:

An effective budget depends on careful coordination between last year's actual experience and your expectations for the coming year. Just as a new driver dents a few fenders, anyone who prepares a budget should be ready to learn from his or her mistakes.

If you backed into another car the first time you tried to park, you wouldn't give up and determine never to drive. Budgeting is the same. Don't view mistakes as failures. They are learning devices, and you can improve the budgeting process for each expense account by keeping track of what occurred in last year's budget. Improve based on what you learned; and watch out for other traffic along your budgeting highway.

The use of analogy is not always appropriate, but it is instructive in enabling a reader to visualize the challenges and appreciate the message. Comparison and contrast leads to a more lively and entertaining writing style.

4. Avoid easy tricks to achieve transition.

Don't try to get around creative transitions by using devices, such as obvious connecting words or repeating the previous paragraph's concluding idea. Readers see through these techniques and consider such writing to be ineffective.

Transition with connecting words:

The site inspection is essential as a first step in organizing a seminar. Be sure to invest the time in examining the hotel, meeting room, and catering facilities in advance, and meet with the sales manager to arrange for essential services.

However, when your guests arrive on the first day of the convention, a number of problems will arise, not all of them anticipated. Be sure you have arranged with the hotel for receiving shipments, in case attendees and speakers instruct their home offices to send material to their attention. Too often, essential materials are misplaced because a marketing manager forgot to speak with the front desk.

The transition between the two paragraphs is not a real one. These are two completely different topics, and the use of *however* does not make a real transition.

A better transition:

The site inspection is essential as a first step in organizing a seminar. Be sure to invest the time in examining the hotel, meeting room, and catering facilities in advance, and meet with the sales manager to arrange for essential services.

Advance preparation is the key. However, you cannot anticipate every possible problem that will arise, even with the most detailed advance inspection. When guests arrive on the first day of the convention, a number of problems will arise, not all of them anticipated. Be sure you arrange with the hotel for receiving shipments, in case attendees and speakers instruct their home offices to send material to their attention. Too often, essential materials are misplaced because a marketing manager forgot to speak with the front desk.

In this improved version, a single sentence creates a bridge between the two paragraphs.

Transitions are not difficult; they require just a little thought to make the flow of communication effective and enjoyable for the reader.

5. **Use consequence, generalization, diversion, and other conversational tools to achieve smooth transitions.**

These useful devices serve as methods and aids in the construction of the idea.

Consequence:

The business meeting should always begin on time.

This obvious but effective rule ensures structure and organization as well as serving as good time management.

Announce this as a policy and do all you can to enforce it, and attendees will soon realize that it is in everyone's interest to show up at the announced time.

Be cautious, though. The president of the company might not appreciate being cautioned for being two minutes late to *your* meeting. There are probably countless reasons why even the best-run meetings will start late now and then.

Generalization:

The difficult, confrontative employee presents a special challenge to every manager. Such situations take a lot of time and thought, while producing little in the way of productive result.

In the majority of such cases, the problems can be largely defused by recognizing that the employee may be bored with his or her work assignments. Look for ways to expand the range of tasks, and many of those problems will dissipate as a result.

Diversion:

Asking the boss for a raise is never a pleasant task. Think ahead and come up with solid business-related reasons to justify the request. Financial need is *not* a good reason. Point to examples of how you have saved money by reducing expenses or streamlining procedures as evidence of your value to the company.

By the way, an especially good time to make such a request is following several months of balancing your department's budget. Be prepared to show some hard and fast numbers demonstrating not only that you are valuable but that you know your worth.

6. Use illustrative transition.

Make your writing stronger by using practical illustrations. This is an especially effective tool for business writing, because it lends power to a point the writer is trying to make. Business readers expect to be presented with facts, and the illustrative transition is probably the best way to get your point across.

Illustrative transition:

> Our recommendation for the purchase of equipment will require an initial capital investment of $30,000. However, we expect to recapture the entire cost in less than one year. From that point forward, reduced labor costs will save the company more than $2,500 per month.
>
> This translates to an offset equal to budget increases in Salary and Wage expenses for the previous six quarters in this department. These estimates are based on utilization by one shift only. If the procedure were put into place for all three shifts, the division could increase its labor force by 15 percent and still operate at today's cost level.

In this example, the primary point is made in the first paragraph, and the illustration in the second paragraph. While providing a transition, it also provides a convincing argument.

Translations

When a work in one language is translated to another, care should be taken to accurately reflect the original context and intention of the work. This is affected by the style and tone selected in the translation. When several choices of expression are possible, picking the shortest and most basic version often leads to better translations.

When citing works translated from other languages, the authorship is credited as well as the name of the translator.

Example, citation in APA style:

> Sorenson, J. (2017). Managementstile im Vergleich (Management Styles Compared). (R. Heinz, Trans.) Berlin: Geschäftsverleger

Example, citation in MLA style:

> Sorenson, John. Management Styles Compared. Translated by Richard Heinz. Berlin: Geschäftsverleger, 2017.

Example, citation in Chicago style:

> John Sorenson, Management Styles Compared, trans. Richard Heinz (Berlin: Geschäftsverleger, 2017).

V

Variable measurements

Variables are unavoidable in statistical studies and reports. Among the messages required in reports, measuring and reporting on variables helps to frame the validity of outcomes and conclusions drawn. Variables define a range of possible outcomes as a means for measurement.

Once a range of possibilities for variables is defined, the next question is whether an upper limit can also be assumed, in order to define a finite range for the variable. The more complex the field of data being studied, the higher the potential level of variability. It may be necessary to assume an upper limit that represents a reasonable estimate. For example, in a study of 1,000 consumers regarding product preference, a carefully structured testing method might be assumed to contain a 15% variable potential. Thus, the measurement of the variable range might be:

$$V \geq 0 \text{ and } V \leq 150$$

The assumption of this range should be supportable in the data set, based on past testing and similar analyses. For example, previous product test outcomes are applicable for new product test studies. The identification of a range is difficult to pin down specifically, so the assumption used should be provided with a logical reason, such as a past, similar test.

Variable relationships

A statistical study involving two or more variables may need to quantify the relationship between those variables, to add order and predictability to the outcome. Some variables depend on one another. For example, a test of opinion among consumers may contain one set of variables for a given age range, and a second variable may be based on gender. Thus, the analysis of variables by age *and* gender establishes a reliable variable relationship.

This correlation between two variables improves the analysis of overall outcomes, notably when a particular sample is predictably related to a different sample based on the variances. For example, a product test may be favored by a younger population of single consumers, with particular favorability among fe-

DOI 10.1515/9781547400218-020

males. A sample of consumers a generation older and consisting of married consumers, may show a higher degree of favorability among female consumers. This relationship supports a conclusion that the product appeals to a particular population in a predictable manner, based on age, gender, and marital status.

In writing a descriptive statistical report, articulating the underlying assumptions and describing the variable relationships adds significance to the outcomes. It is not enough to merely state that a product test establishes a favorable opinion among married females in a specific age range. That conclusion should be supported by a methodical description of how the variable relationships were analyzed, and how testing was designed to compare responses among different demographic groups. If the descriptive analysis of these variable relationships is lengthy or technical, the conclusion may be reduced to a single sentence or paragraph, with supporting documentation in an appendix.

Video best practices

The use of video in business communications is gaining in popularity. In the recent past, the use of video was overly complex and expensive, and few organizations used video to communicate. The use of live webinars and recorded podcasts is one aspect of video usage. Less formal meetings combining voice and image are widely used through Skype, Facebook Messenger, and similar devices, many of which are free to use.

Some guidelines for video best practices for creation of recorded messages:
1. Shorter videos are more effective. The typical user is likely to watch a full video averaging between three and five minutes. Video presentations longer than this will have a reduced rate of interest. A business communications video exceeding 10 minutes is not productive.
2. For messages longer than 10 minutes, break the presentation up into five-minute (or less) segments that can be viewed over time.
3. Work from an outline or script to provide a well-organized video presentation. However, do not read a script that observers can see on the screen. This applies to PowerPoint videos as well as live feeds of the individual speaker. Adopt a conversational tone combining short sentences with a well-organized outline.
4. Use a friendly, professional tone. An overly formal presentation alienates the participant. At the same time, the tone should be professional and focused on the message. Read your presentation out loud in advance to ensure that

the desired tone is achieved. Rehearsal pays dividends by enabling a presenter to get the message to exactly the desired tone. Also check the lighting levels to ensure than both personal appearance and illustrative or narrative segments are well-lit and clear.

5. Combine narrative with images. As images are displayed, explain them and their significance to the core message. Do not assume that an image speaks for itself. Avoid saying the obvious, using words to explain what everyone can see. However, drawing comparisons from the image or explaining how the outcome affects other matters add value.
6. Be aware of how a presentation *sounds* rather than how it *looks*. Even though video is a visual medium, people listen to tone and message, and want to have clear explanations of what they are seeing.
7. Caption the video or offer a written transcript for any participants with special needs.
8. Keep your video message interactive by inviting questions. It is preferable to invite questions throughout the presentation. A recording may be made and provided later to those unable to attend, or to attendees wanting to review the video. Since questions from attendees are likely to be typed into the webcast screen, repeat the questions before answering them.

W

Webinar and conference call etiquette

With the increasing use of live webinars and conferences, business communications have become more interactive than ever before. For this reason, a number of etiquette issues should be addressed. These are the visual representations of style applicable to all formats of business communication.

1. Guidelines for presenters

At the beginning of a presentation, introduce yourself briefly and welcome your attendees. Maintain a positive tone to the message.

For preparation in advance, test the software to make certain that all aspects are working properly. This includes the use of microphones, visuals, live webcams, and split screens. Speak slowly, remembering that attendees may have difficulty following your message if it moves too quickly.

As you show slides, do not read what shows on the screen. Doing so takes an interesting topic and makes it boring and ineffective. Think of slides as talking points. Do not repeat what everyone can see, but talk about the significance of each bullet point. Keep slides to a minimum of written words. Slides filled with narrative distract the participant and discourage interest.

As an alternative to excessive visuals, use illustrations when possible. Focus on financial information presented by pie charts, histograms, and bar charts. This is much more effective at conveying information than a series of financial columns on a screen.

Invite questions and comments from participants during the presentation, not afterward. This allows participations to feel more engaged and to get answers to questions at the time a topic is being discussed.

2. Guidelines for attendees

Come into the presentation in a timely manner. Joining late is poor form.

In a live give-and-take setting, wait for the proper moment to ask a question. If you are able to participate vocally, wait until someone else has finished their point and the presenter has answered.

Questions should be concise and to the point. Overly wordy questions are uninteresting and distracting. Do not self-promote or editorialize. If you have comments or opinions not in the form of a question, make certain they are appropriate and relevant to the discussion underway.

DOI 10.1515/9781547400218-021

Webpage references and citation

The format for webpage references and citations varies by the style in use. The three most popular of these are APA, Chicago, and MLA.

1. **APA website citations**

The structure of citation is: Last name, first name initial, (year, month, date published or retrieved). *Title*. Retrieved from URL.

Example, website citation under APA:

> Smith, A. J. (2017, April 14). How to cite a website. Retrieved from https://www.websitecites.com

2. **Chicago style website citations**

The structure of citation is: Last name, First name. "Page title." Website title. Web Address (retrieved Date Accessed)

Example, website citation under Chicago style:

> Smith, Andrew J. "How to cite a website." Website Citations. Retrieved from https://www.websitecites.com (accessed April 14, 2017)

3. **MLA website citations**

The structure of citation is: Last Name, First Name. "Page Title." Sponsoring Institution or Publisher. Publication Date: Page Numbers, Medium, Retrieved Date.

Example, website citation under MLA:

> Smith, Andrew J. "How to Cite a Website." Website Citations. The Web Style Company. January 6, 2017. https://www.websitecites.com, retrieved April 14, 2017

Websites

The design of a business website should emphasize simplicity and ease of use. Trying to add too much information may lead to navigation problems for users, and most individuals prefer simple websites with simple linkage from one part of the site to another.

1. **Content**

When content is extensive, break it out into logical sections and links. On the home page, include the major sections and provide links to each. Also include a linked site map. Websites that are difficult to navigate do not encourage frequent use.

Update content regularly. When a user visits a site for the second or third time, if the information is identical with each visit, subsequent use is less likely.

2. Branding

The "brand" of a website, whether corporate, blog-specific, or based on a message theme, should be consistent throughout the site. Brand identification includes selection of colors, logos, type font and size, and tone.

3. Complexity and technical issues

The development of an effective and easy-to-use website may require the use of an expert. Many technical aspects apply even when basic websites are easy to construct. The ideal combination is to develop the format and content of the website professionally, while enabling non-technical updates periodically, preferably on a daily basis.

Word processing

The range of functions performed using automation is universal. Very few writers use written or typed formats, and word processing has become the default system for written communications. This presents great convenience and many flaws as well.

Word processing is aimed at creating, manipulating, storing, and printing text, in the form of email, letters, reports, articles, and books. In its original form, word processing systems were expensive, awkward, and limited. Today, the combination of text files with graphics, along with electronic transmission of all types of files, merges, and email, have made word processing an efficient and inexpensive device for managing virtually all forms of business communication.

1. Learn the system thoroughly.

Every word processing system has its own special features and quirks. More and more, however, systems are becoming standardized. Today, an inexpensive system provides the ability to alter fonts, type sizes, and spacing and to format documents in a variety of ways. The better a user understands the potential and limits of a system, the more valuable it becomes.

2. **Set up formats that can be used repeatedly for similar documents.**

Templates and forms are convenient and easy to set up. Even a document as simple as a letter or memo should follow some basic formatting rules. Set up a blank file with the margins, tabs, top and bottom spacing, headers (if applicable), and other needed features. Use that file repeatedly as a default to set up other files with the same formatting.

3. **Work from standard formats used universally by your organization.**

Before setting up a template file for letters or memos, find out whether your organization has published guidelines for such documents. If it has, be sure to coordinate your format file with the procedural requirements.

4. **Use the functions that are provided with the system.**

Functions such as proofing, grammar check, and thesaurus are valuable features and should be used to improve manuscript format as well as writing style. Proofing is a fast and efficient feature, available with a single mouse click. You usually have to place the cursor at the beginning of the document, because the system will probably begin proofing from the point the command is entered. Most proofing programs allow several choices when a word appears that is not in the computer dictionary.

You can indicate the word is okay, add the word to the dictionary, enter a correction, or ask for a list of suggested spellings of words close to the spelling in the file. Such programs also question repeated sequential words. Grammar checking is also valuable because it enables corrections within a file to conform to proper grammatical expressions. Be cautious in using this feature, however. In some cases, style should overrule strictly correct grammatical decisions. Use the grammar check feature to find obvious errors of grammar, but maintain the right to make style judgments as well.

5. **Save files often, and back up your files.**

Every computer manual gives this advice, and everyone training someone on a computer repeats it. Saving and making backup copies of files are easy routines, but they are too often overlooked or ignored as procedural matters. Hours of hard work can be lost in a split second, often for unexplained reasons. Files can and do vanish for no apparent reason. If they are not recoverable, the data could be lost forever. Set the autosave timing increment to a brief span, such as 10 minutes or less.

6. Label files so they can be found quickly and easily.

If you write letters to one person on a regular basis, it makes sense to label a folder with that person's name, within a path labeled "letters." If you have a large number of files, be especially careful to provide names that will make sense when look for them later. If your system provides a description box as part of the file name, use it. This convenient feature makes locating files easier later on.

7. Purge old files periodically.

If you are not sure whether you can get rid of a series of files, copy them to a backup file and erase them from the hard disk. Old files take up space and slow down the processing speed of the system. The more files in primary storage, the more tedious the task becomes of storing, retrieving, saving, and replacing files.

8. Make backup copies when working on revisions.

Always keep a backup copy of your work, especially when providing copies for other people to revise. If you work on projects with others, a draft copy of a document can be saved to a backup file and sent to someone else for additional changes.

9. Before your final draft, proofread.

Even when people are accustomed to working on screens, editing is not that easy. Proofread before finalizing the document, and when practical, ask someone else to proofread your work.

10. Avoid the use of abbreviations or unpunctuated sentences.

An easy habit to fall into is the use of abbreviations or shortened words. Avoid this. Use proper sentence structure, grammar, and punctuation.

Example, poor style:

I am certin u want the MBS sent to you ASAP please lemme no if this is not the case

Example, improved spelling, sentence structure, and punctuation:

I am certain you want the Monthly Budget Summary (MBS) sent to you as soon as possible. Please let me know if this is not the case.

X, Y

X and *y* axes

When constructing a graph as part of a business document, most often you use perpendicular lines referred to as the *x axis* and the *y axis*. The x axis is horizontal (left to right) and the y axis is vertical (top to bottom). The point where both axes intersect is called the origin and the two lines can be thought of as forming a grid.

When making reference to a specific point (place) on the graph, the x axis is always listed first, followed by the y axis. Each point can be described as an "ordered pair" with the origin considered (0,0). As an example, if you go out four units to the right on the x axis, from the origin and go up three units, you arrive at the point defined by the ordered pair (4,3). If you go left four units on the x axis from the origin, and down three units, the ordered pair for that point is (-4,-3). Typically, in applying graphs to real world problems, name the x and y axis. For instance, the x axis may show the year. So, the origin could be the closing price of gold on January 1, 2000 on the x axis, going out to perhaps 2018, and the y axis may be the price of gold on those dates. So, you can plot the price of gold each year on the graph to see the trend. You could plot the point for each day on the same chart and see the chart with a lot more detail. These distinctions need to be explained in the narrative accompanying the graph.

DOI 10.1515/9781547400218-022

Z

Zombie nouns

Zombie nouns (also called "nominalizations") are nouns, adjectives, or verbs converted to and used to create new nouns. This is accomplished by adding a suffix, such as -ity, -tion, or -ism.

Examples, Zombie nouns:

capital—capitalism (noun)
impossible—impossibility (adjective)
estimate—estimation (verb)

In business writing, excessive nominalization sets up expressions with jargon, often adding a pompous and self-important tone of abstraction, to what could be a plain, easily comprehended narrative.

DOI 10.1515/9781547400218-023

Index

DOI 10.1515/9781547400218-024

www.ingramcontent.com/pod-product-compliance
Lightning Source LLC
Chambersburg PA
CBHW061233220326
41599CB00028B/5408